SCENT
IN YOUR GARDEN

SCENT
IN YOUR GARDEN

STEPHEN LACEY

Photographs by Andrew Lawson

FRANCES LINCOLN

For Hannah and Rachel
Marielle, Helena, Lucy, Harriet and Laura

Frances Lincoln Limited
Apollo Works, 5 Charlton Kings Road
LONDON NW5 2SB

Scent in Your Garden
© Frances Lincoln Limited 1991
Text © Stephen Lacey 1991
All photographs © Frances Lincoln Limited 1991
except those on pages 2, 20, 25, 31, 32 left, 33, 34, 35, 36 top,
38 right, 41 right, 48 top left, 51 right, 57 left, 58 bottom left,
64 left and middle, 67 right, 69, 71, 75 left, 81 left and top
right, 84 right, 85 top left and top right, 86 bottom, 87, 88, 89,
91, 97 bottom left, 98, 99, 110 right, 119, 122 right, 123 right,
126, 128, 129 right, 132, 144, 145 top left, 147, 150 top, 152,
153, 155, 159 left, 160, 161 left, 162 top, 176 right, 178 left,
180 left, 183 right © Andrew Lawson 1991

British Library Cataloguing in Publication Data

Lacey, Stephen 1957–
Scent in your garden
1. Great Britain. Gardens. Planning
I. Title
712.60941
ISBN 0–7112–0638–4

Set in Palatino by Ace Filmsetting Ltd, Frome, Somerset
Printed and bound in Italy by New Interlitho S.p.A
First Frances Lincoln Edition: April 1991

1 3 5 7 9 8 6 4 2

Contents

Scent and the Gardener

Scent is the most potent and bewitching substance in the gardener's repertory and yet it is the most neglected and the least understood. The faintest waft is sometimes enough to induce feelings of hunger or anticipation, or to transport you back through time and space to a long-forgotten moment in your childhood. It can overwhelm you in an instant or simply tease you, creeping into your consciousness slowly and evaporating almost the moment it is detected. Each fragrance, whether sweet or spicy, light or heavy, comes upon you in its own way and evokes its own emotional response.

But although scent adds such a pleasurable layer to our enjoyment, few of us treat it at all seriously – it remains an optional extra in the composition of a garden, rather than an integral part to be managed and manipulated for maximum impact. We may have the odd scented plant here and there, but we rarely plan for specific effects or pursue deliberate themes. Often we do not even realize a plant is scented until we acquire it, for catalogues and reference books frequently make no mention of scent in their descriptions. And even if they do, it is generally as an aside which gives no clue of the precise flavour.

There are of course many good reasons why we fail to use scent effectively. First, although the nose can be highly sensitive, we seldom take the trouble to identify what we are smelling and to put our impressions into words. Consequently, we have not developed a means of comparing and classifying scents and our vocabulary for describing them is very primitive: the adjective 'sweet' encompasses everything from rose petals to five pound notes and dollar bills.

It has been suggested that this lazy attitude to scents has come about because the olfactory sense is no longer crucially important to us in our day-to-day life. For lower animals, scent is a means of navigating (salmon follow odour trails back to their spawning grounds), locating food (most mammals smell food before they see it), sensing danger (all hunters have to approach their prey downwind), establishing territory (many animals spray their surroundings with urine or rub their scent glands), deterring (skunk), communicating (deer produce an alarm scent; bees inform each other of the location of nectar sources; and many animals read tribal and social status from each other's scent) and advertising sexual ripeness.

Although we no longer rely on our sense of smell for survival, we do make use of it constantly: the flavour of our food and drink comes from our sense of smell. If you hold your nose while you eat and drink, you only receive general impressions of sweetness, sourness, bitterness and saltiness through the taste buds in the mouth. It is because of this close relationship between taste and smell, and because most of our smelling is done through our mouth, that when we do attempt to describe a scent, it is so often in terms of foods: lemon, honey, mint, blackcurrant, raspberry, pineapple, curry, chocolate, vanilla, coconut, clove and almond. To make description and comparison even more difficult, each of us has different levels of sensitivity to scents and each of us reacts to them in different ways. Some people catch the most elusive flavours, while others have a relatively weak sense of smell and appreciate only the sledgehammer scents. Dark-haired people are said to be more sensitive than fair-haired people (because the olfactory mucous membrane is slightly pigmented) and smoking also impairs your sensitivity. Most of us have favourite scents and scents we detest; sometimes our reactions are inexplicable, sometimes they are associated with places, people and events in our past.

Fragrances are themselves highly complex. They consist of a number of compounds that ebb and flow according to weather conditions and the life cycle of the plants. They can change and disappear from one moment to the next and can be quite different when savoured at close range than at a distance. So we can never exactly predict how they will taste or how we are going to react to them. But these uncertainties

Right *'Nathalie Nypels' roses and* Nepeta nervosa *line this path in the vegetable garden at Tintinhull, Somerset, but the strongest scent comes from Japanese honeysuckles (left). In the evening and early* *morning the fruity fragrance carries far. Honeysuckles on iron or wooden supports are also well worth introducing into the herbaceous border, where scent always tends to be in short supply.*

make the use of scent a more challenging and intriguing subject for the gardener. They should certainly not put us off trying to understand and manage it. As Gertrude Jekyll wrote, each step in gardening is a step into a 'delightful Unknown' and we should never be daunted by 'groping ignorance'.

By being more aware of scents, nosing them carefully whenever you encounter them, trying to identify their predominant qualities and seeing whether you can pick up the same notes in other scents, you can slowly educate your palate, exactly as a wine taster does. As well as helping you to build up your own internal library of scents, as it were, this will also increase the sensitivity of your nose – and, incidentally, make you more emotionally vulnerable.

To most gardeners, a capacity for memorizing things that they cannot see is, in any case, already a practised art. We invariably design and plant out of season, when plants are without flower and give no indication of their size and habit. And yet we manage to orchestrate colour schemes, to grade heights and to distribute shapes. The same artistry can surely be applied to the blending of scents.

Particular scents have been carefully selected by man for centuries: to be used as flavourings for food and drink, as religious offerings, to conceal body odours, to strew on floors to counter unpleasant smells, to keep laundry smelling fresh and to keep away bugs. More recently, there has been investigation into our emotional responses to different scents, with the result that fragrance is now used as a therapy to soothe patients; estate agents have been known to employ scents (usually fragrances of coffee and fresh bread) to influence potential purchasers into buying houses. The ultimate use of

Below *A sunny paved area is an obvious spot for the sub-shrubs of southern Europe, which give a subtle harmony of silver and grey-green colours as well as of pungent leaf aromas. The artemisias and cream-flowered cotton lavender must usually have their fragrances coaxed by hand, but the scent of the curry plant wafts freely in the air. Pinky dorycnium and carmine lychnis add colour.*

scents is, of course, perfumery, where fragrances are blended into sophisticated cocktails. It therefore seems extraordinary that gardeners, who are surrounded by and peculiarly vulnerable to fragrances, have not attempted to absorb scent into their art too, and harnessed its power for their own ends.

The danger of gardening books which focus on one subject is that the reader soon loses a sense of perspective. After reading two hundred pages on flowering cherries, for example, you see the world entirely through a veil of pink and white blossom; you forget that cherries are just one subsection of garden flora and one small highlight in the gardener's calendar. This is a book about the scented garden, but scent is not the most important consideration to the garden-maker. It is the visual impact of the composition, the interplay of colours, shapes, forms and textures, which is paramount. Gardens need an overall design, and planting schemes need structure, harmony and seasonal spectacle. If these are lacking, no amount of scented sorcery can compensate. I shall try to bear this in mind in this book and not allow myself to be so intoxicated by my theme that I forget the proper place of scent in the scheme of things; namely, as an undercurrent in the planting process, which can add another layer of pleasure to the composition and help to reinforce the chosen mood, but which must always be subservient to the visual impact.

Planning for Scent

When you are staring at a new plot and wondering how to tackle it, scent is likely to be far from your thoughts. You will be planning vistas, mapping out lawns and flowerbeds and determining the course of paths. You will be considering matters of style, and deciding whether the garden will have an emphatic design or whether it will follow nature in a casual tangle. Wherever your garden is, whatever type of garden you make and whatever features you install in it, you will have no difficulty in injecting scent later on. Period gardens can be filled with herbs and old-fashioned roses; orchards can be flooded with daffodils and the trees hung with honeysuckles; woodland can be planted with azaleas and carpeted with bluebells. Whether with dry or damp soil, sun or shade, there is no habitat for which a scented plant cannot be found.

If you really want to make the most of scents, however, there are some points which you might bear in mind at this early stage and some features for which you may want to make room. First, to enjoy scent to the full, the air must be fairly still. Gentle breezes may waft scent to you but strong winds quickly disperse it, so shelter is vital. Windbreaks of evergreen and deciduous trees and shrubs will be needed on exposed sites. Research has shown that windbreaks which are thirty to fifty per cent porous, and which thus filter the wind, are the most effective; solid evergreen hedges and walls cause great turbulence by buffeting the wind and creating wind tunnels. As a general rule, on level ground a windbreak is capable of sheltering an area of up to ten times its height.

In larger gardens, the ideal combination is a natural windbreak on the boundary, together with internal walls. For as well as seeking to contain the scent, we need to encourage its free production. Most plants need warmth to reveal their scent, and walls help to trap and reflect the sun's heat. In cool regions, there is nothing like a sheltered, walled garden for providing an unforgettable experience for the nose, as anyone who has made a June visit to the English gardens of Sissinghurst Castle in Kent or Mottisfont Abbey in Hampshire will know; both have great collections of old-fashioned roses and on a warm, still day the air is heavy with the heady aromas of fruit and spice.

Of course, few of us have walled gardens or the means with which to construct them, but it may well be possible to build a small walled sun trap somewhere in the garden. As the air cools, heat will continue to be radiated by the walls, ensuring prolonged warmth and fragrance in the late afternoon and evening. A paved surface large enough to accommodate a seat would be an essential part of the sun trap. Seats are invitations to linger and rest, and in a relaxed state you are more receptive to a fragrant siege. Certainly, wherever you install a seat in your garden, you might think how you can entertain the nose. The seat itself may even be made out of scented plants: a small raised bed or trough can be turned into a fragrant seat by being given back and arm rests and planted with apple-scented camomile, creeping mints or spicy prostrate thymes. Again using camomile, mint and thyme, you might be inspired to plan fragrant stairways, paths (you could either leave gaps for them between paving slabs or omit the paving slabs altogether), banks and miniature lawns. The camomile would make rivers and pools of fresh green; the flowering thymes would weave themselves into fine pink, purple and white oriental rugs. All these lowly aromatic plants need sunshine and good drainage so you will have to position your features accordingly.

Scented flowers should ideally be near nose height, so to enjoy to the full the fragrance of scented small bulbs like crocuses and *Iris reticulata*, dwarf shrubs like *Daphne cneorum*, and alpines like phloxes and primulas, you will have to raise them above the ground. This may involve some planning and construction. Rock gardens, picturesquely landscaped with boulders, are not always suitable additions to gardens in low-land settings, but raised beds or troughs, in geometric shapes, usually slip into any design quite comfortably. Window boxes are another means of lifting plants off the ground, and, of course, scent under windows is especially welcome. On warm days and evenings, the fragrance will drift through the open panes to engulf you in your armchair. Pots of fragrant plants beside doors (and beside garden seats) are similarly enter-taining. Arbours, pergolas, arches and tunnels give you the opportunity of hanging veils of fragrant plants at nose height. Climbing plants have more freedom to display their natural character when draped over such structures than when lashed back to walls. These plants can also be spun along trellises and picket fences to make flowering boundaries or internal divisions for the garden. I once saw a long herba-ceous border broken at intervals by a white-painted fence wrapped in honeysuckles and roses; this was a most effective means of introducing scent (the border perennials of high summer are not among the most fragrant groups of plants) and of providing architecture to counter the wispiness of the other ingredients. Climbing and rambling roses are also emi-nently suitable for stringing on ropes between upright posts.

Tunnels and arbours need not always consist of climbing plants tied to metal or wood but can be composed of free-standing plants. I remember seeing, in one garden in the South of England, a crossroads of grass paths in the middle of an open flower garden that had been turned into a bower of white blossom by the planting of a cherry tree on each corner. Standard wisterias and laburnums would create an equally memorable effect, and I rather fancy a bower of *Magnolia wilsonii* with its downturned creamy saucers scented of lemon.

Avenues of trees or shrubs, creating living walls of scent, are a luxury you may be able to afford. You would need a grand entrance drive to accommodate a procession of lime trees, and a broad walk for large shrubs like clove-scented viburnum or fruity philadelphus. But even very small gar-dens may have room for a stream of lavender or an edging of honey-scented winter box (*Sarcococca*). Such concentrations of one sort of plant enable you to submerge yourself in a single scent, at full strength and with no distractions, and is always exciting.

When you come to select hedges, evergreens and trees for the garden's framework, shape and form will usually be your primary concern; you are looking for features that will hold the design together throughout the year. Hedges must be dense and robust, screening trees fast-growing, and specimen trees and evergreens perhaps of emphatic outline or with a particular character. Yet before you look to yew and holly, Lombardy poplar and weeping birch, it is as well to know that you can usually find scented alternatives to all of these. And hedge-trimming is far more enjoyable when each snip treats the nostrils to a whiff of fruit; screening trees that waft balsam become a positive pleasure rather than merely a necessity; and a specimen evergreen that you can tweak and sniff as you pass is much more endearing than one which simply satisfies your desire for structure.

If you are a keen gardener, you will no doubt be allowing for a good number of flowerbeds as you design your garden. In the scented garden sunny beds are, on the whole, prefer-able to shady beds; this is partly because heat encourages the freer production of scent and partly because the largest pro-portion of scented plants are sun-lovers. But most of us end up with a mixture of sunny and shady beds, and I think it is help-ful at an early stage to decide how you are going to treat them.

If your garden is sheltered and mild enough and your soil sufficiently well-drained to accommodate aromatic shrubs like thymes, lavenders, rosemaries, cistuses, and their kin, then the sunniest bed might be reserved for these plants. They all love to be roasted and on hot, still days will fill the air with a Mediterranean bouquet garni. They will set a theme for the bed and you can then add to this, using scented and non-scented ingredients – euphorbias and irises for striking con-trasts in shape, perhaps; Spanish broom and tree lupin for yellow highlights.

Roses and a large cast of perennials, annuals, bulbs and shrubs which are, in the main, summer-flowering also require sunny positions. If you have only one sunny border, then I would be inclined to put them all in it together (including the aromatics just mentioned) and either organize a succession of entertaining incidents through the summer or stage one extravaganza, by favouring plants that come into bloom simultaneously. The larger shrubs and roses would furnish the back row of the border and create the promontories, while the lowly ingredients would fill the bays.

If you have several sunny areas, you can give each a different theme or season of interest, and break this cast of

Right *An awkward bank has been turned into a fragrant feature in this garden by being planted with an assortment of creeping thymes. Lavenders and sages take up the colour and scent theme in the foreground, with penstemons adding a splash of scarlet. The shrub in the top left hand corner is* Helichrysum ledifolium *whose flowers are honey-scented. Its sticky foliage smells of freshly baked fruit cake.*

thousands up into subgroups. You may, for example, plan a mid-summer medley of lilies, roses, philadelphus and pinks in one area, a rose garden or herb garden in another, and a late summer display of buddlejas, phloxes, tobacco flowers and sweet peas in another.

The main cast for shady areas consists of all those shrubs, perennials and bulbs from woodland habitats. It is fun to capture some of this woodland spirit in one area, but you will need somewhere away from brick walls and other evidence of human occupation. A single tree is often enough to establish the mood. If you are going to plant very close to it, or beneath it, choose something that forms only a light canopy such as laburnum, Japanese maple, amelanchier or halesia. If you have room, you can let your tree or trees stand alone, even in a grass clearing, and you can lead your drifts of shrubs between and around them. Here you have complete freedom in choosing trees, and you can opt for anything from pines and spruces to all but the densest of deciduous subjects.

Shrubs would be the mainstay of this woodland border, but under their skirts you would introduce bulbs like snowdrops and bluebells, and between them create pools of lilies, smaller shrubs, ferns and other perennials. Spring would be the season in which this border would reach its climax, with further flushes of colour in autumn and winter.

You can also plant a shady area in a more consciously structured way, exactly as you might plant a mixed border in the sun. This is usually the best way to tackle a shady bed by the house. The same plants would be used as in the woodland border but the shrub content will probably be reduced and the bays for perennials be made wider. The presence of walls, fences or paving will already betray this to be a man-made composition, and a more 'ornamental' planting scheme is quite in order, with more contrived contrasts of colour and shape. Annuals, climbers, shade-tolerant roses and even clipped evergreens can be admitted, and these will help maintain interest over a longer period.

Left *Shady areas planted with woodland shrubs and bulbs are usually at their most flowery in spring. Here a mixture of Spanish bluebells and the more fragrant English bluebells are naturalized in an informal setting. A carpet of bluebells gives off one of the most evocative and memorable perfumes of the season.*

Right *Azuleas are one of the few groups of scented plants which combine an intoxicating perfume with a range of hot, rich and gaudy colours. On warm, moist days their honeysuckle fragrance pervades the still, silent dells of woodland gardens. They give a second show of colour in the autumn, when their leaves ignite before falling.*

Colour and Scent

Whether I am working in sun or shade, my starting point when planting a border is to decide on a colour scheme; only after I have done this will I decide where the height is to be and where the evergreen bulk. Colour has almost as great an impact on the senses and emotions as scent and in plant-packed gardens it usually becomes the dominant visual force; the eye notices shapes before colours only when the range of colours is very limited. Each colour gives a different reading and, by using it in isolation or in combination with other colours, you have the means of establishing a wide range of different moods.

Various factors influence the choice of colours – existing features and background scenery, the quality of the light, personal preference and, most importantly, the availability of plants in each colour group. In temperate climates, yellow, white, pink and mauve flowers are fairly abundant all year; neither is there much of a shortage of purple or violet-blue. Orange is a little more scarce; our main supply comes from berries, hips and turning leaves in the autumn. Pure red is always rare, as is true blue, though we get a good quantity of it in the spring from bulbs and woodland perennials. Shade-loving plants also tend to come in quieter and cooler colours than those that are sun-lovers.

The desire for scent will also affect your choice. There is a vague relationship between colour and scent and, as a general rule, the less pigment there is in a flower, the more likely it is to be scented. White flowers are the most highly scented colour group, followed by pink, mauve and pale yellow flowers. Strong yellow and violet-blue flowers come next. The least scented colour groups are purple, true blue, orange and red flowers. If you are planning a single-colour border or garden, white, yellow or pink/mauve are the best colours to select; there are plenty of flowers to choose from, and plenty of different scents. If you have set your heart on the hottest reds and oranges and the inkiest purples and blues, but also want the garden to be full of scent, then you will have to be a little devious. First, you can make use of those plants whose flowers do manage to combine strong colour with scent: azaleas, wallflowers, sweet peas and roses, for example, have colourful, scented flowers; monarda, hyssop, lavender and salvias have colourful flowers and scented leaves; pieris has colourful bracts and skimmia colourful berries, and both have scented flowers.

You might also think of arranging marriages between two plants, one chosen for its scent and the other for its bright colour. Trees and shrubs can host climbing plants (try a scented rambling rose up a purple-leaved plum or an imperial purple clematis through a richly scented philadelphus); two climbing plants will happily interweave (spicy-scented akebia and ruby-red alpine clematis); perennials and bulbs will thrive around the skirts of shrubs (lily of the valley under an exotic tree peony or brilliant scarlet tulips in front of sweet-scented osmanthus); and bulbs will grow through rock plants (honey-scented *Crocus chrysanthus* through alpine phlox). A simultaneous display of riches for the eye and the nose is thus easily within our grasp.

There are scented plants for every season and no particular shortage at any one time. The many plants with scented leaves ensure there is never a dull moment for the nose, even if occasionally there is a lack of visual stimulation. So the goal should be to have a garden that entertains the nose at every turn on every day of the year.

The Nature of Scent

As garden-makers, we already wear many hats. We play the part of draughtsman, architect, painter, sculptor, plantsman and even poet in the course of transforming our virgin plot into an exciting design. Yet there is another hat waiting to be donned – that of perfumer. Like its colour, shape and texture, a plant's scent is a quality that deserves thoughtful treatment. Dropped into the composition at random, it is often submerged and lost; but sited with care and perhaps blended with complementary scents, it can deliver its flavour to maximum effect.

Success as a perfumer will always depend to some degree on chance. Who can say precisely how a scent will taste at a particular moment or how your friends will react to it? But if we can identify the types of scent we are using, and how and when they are released, we can at least try to anticipate their impact. There is no need to delve deeply into organic chemistry, but some understanding of the nature of scent and of the various scent groups will provide a useful basis from which to work. Not being a scientist, I have had to acquire botanical and chemical information on scents from various authoritative sources, in particular *The Scent of Flowers and Leaves; its Purpose and Relation to Man* by F. A. Hampton. Published in 1925 and alas long out of print, this is a delightfully accessible little book and an absorbing read, and it has been the lamp by which I have felt my way through the fragrant undergrowth.

Scent, I learned from Mr Hampton, derives from volatile 'essential oil' stored by plants, and is released when the oil is oxidized. In flowers, the essential oil is known as attar and is usually stored in epidermal cells in the petal or petal substitute; double-flowered forms of scented plants, which have more petals, are therefore often noticeably more fragrant than their single-flowered counterparts. Unusually, in the musk rose *R. moschata* and the Synstylae rambler roses such as *R. filipes*, *R. longicuspis* and 'Bobbie James', the scent is held in the stamens – double-flowered forms of these are therefore scentless. The scent is dispersed when the flowers open and varies greatly in strength and flavour from plant to plant; and even in an individual flower, it will appear, alter and vanish in response to temperature and the life cycle of the plant.

The flavour of a flower is usually complex as its essential oil is rarely pure; rather it consists of a number of different compounds that unite to present a scented bouquet. The different flavours are generally well integrated but often you can separate out the different notes when sniffing. *Lilium regale*, for instance, gives a piercingly sweet top note but at the same time you can detect something rather nasty lurking underneath. A flower may also give you its top note at a distance and its bass note at close range. I remember bringing my first potful of ginger lily, *Hedychium gardnerianum*, indoors and enjoying the delicious viburnum-like scent that filled the room; but when I went to smell it more deeply, I was repulsed by a powerful blast of mothballs. And again, many scents are pleasant in dilution and very nasty in concentration: while other scents have to be concentrated to be noticeable – a single bluebell gives off little perfume whereas a whole wood of them is ambrosial.

Flowers use their scents specifically to attract pollinators. Many insects are highly sensitive to scent, and so this is an effective lure. Scent is rarely the only attractant but together perhaps with colour, shape and even texture it is the extra ingredient that ensures seduction. Each scent is carefully blended to appeal to a particular pollinator. Indeed, flowers even mimic the scent of female insects in order to lure the males. Many species of butterfly and moth are receptive to scent and, although they also have colour preferences, they do use this to guide them to flowers. They prefer the heavy tropical scents of flowers like jasmine, the fruity scents of honeysuckle and the honeyed scents of buddleja. Butterflies are apparently particularly attracted to these scents because they themselves smell sweetly. Many garden flowers are adapted for pollination by butterflies and moths and they include scents that we find delicious. For night-flying moths,

Right *The white flowers of sweet rocket,* Hesperis matronalis, *glow especially brightly at dusk, when other colours are fading, and it is then that its cool scent is at its strongest. Although adapted for pollination by night-flying insects, during the daytime it is also popular with butterflies. It self-sows freely and is seen here filtering through the richly scented shrub rose 'Bourbon Queen'.*

scent is a particularly useful navigation medium, though the bright white petals, which many night-blooming flowers possess, also provide beacons.

Bees are guided to flowers more by colour than by scent, but scent often stimulates them to alight. Scent is an integral part of their mating behaviour and means of communication and they are very responsive to it. *Ophrys* orchids not only imitate the appearance and texture of female bees but apparently reproduce their scent as well. Researchers studying tropical orchids showed that each species had developed a different scent in order to appeal to different bees, and one species was even able to switch off its scent after it had been pollinated, to prevent re-entry and self-pollination! Bees seem to be easily intoxicated by scents, as anyone who has sat under a flowering lime tree and had drunken bees fall on them can confirm. But in spite of this sensitivity, scent is only a secondary consideration to a bee, and consequently few

bee-pollinated flowers are strongly scented, at least to the human nose. However, they often make up for this by having fragrant leaves instead.

Many beetles are attracted by scent, and they seem to prefer the spicier and fruitier flavours such as crab-apples, wintersweet, magnolias, roses and tree peonies. Many flies are also scent lovers, but their preference is for rotting matter, which certain plants such as stapelia, dracunculus and amorphophallus obligingly provide.

To select and blend flower scents effectively, we must know what flavours are available and which plants possess them. We also need an overview of the subject, so we can group related fragrances in our minds and contrast them with other scents. Because we all react slightly differently to scents, and because plant scents are often composed of a cocktail of ingredients that ebb and flow, there can be no universal system of classification that would prove meaningful to every

Left *Buddleja is such a favourite with butterflies that its common name is butterfly bush. Bees also love it, and on a warm summer's day the plumes of flowers tremble with activity. The white and golden yellow flowered buddlejas also possess the distinctive honey scent and attract almost as many insects as the common purple* B. davidii.

gardener. We must each follow our own nose. However, there are some generally accepted groupings that have been put forward by F. A. Hampton and other writers, and these can at least provide us with a framework. I have altered these groupings slightly to suit my own nose – and you may, of course, wish to alter my groupings to suit yours.

First of all, there are the unpleasant scents. There is no need to categorize these since we will not be wanting to include them deliberately in any scented scheme. But they do often find their way into the garden. The foul-smelling, fly-pollinated flowers are occasionally admitted because of their curious appearance: many practise visual deception on their pollinators and their blotched and bloody, flesh-like flowers do have a certain shock value.

Many gardeners grow members of the arum family. The most common is the bog arum, *Lysichiton americanus*, whose yellow spathes decorate many a pondside in early spring. Its scent is not as bad as other arums and if only a few plants are grown, it may not be noticed. But grown in quantity in a confined ditch garden, the sour scent is very unappealing. The dragon arum, *Dracunculus vulgaris*, is a different matter. When I first encountered it in a plantsman's garden I was nearly felled by nausea. Yet there is no denying that it is handsome, with its rich crimson spathe and maroon, rat's tail spadix.

Eupatorium micranthum (*F. ligustrinum*) also comes near the top of my personal list of unpleasant scents. A nurseryman's catalogue sang the praises of this bushy evergreen shrub with its heads of tiny, rose-tinted white flowers and I succumbed; but, unfortunately the description omitted any reference to its scent. The fragrance from some individual flowers can be beautifully sweet, but the overriding flavour is of urine, and on warm, late summer days the garden used to reek. Even its visual beauty did not save my plant from the bonfire.

Not all unpleasant scents are quite so evil. *Eucomis bicolor*, for example, is an extraordinary bulbous plant from southern Africa whose flowerheads look like greenish pineapples on sticks; they are not reliably hardy outside, except in warm regions, so I grow them in pots and overwinter them under cover. But I am careful not to site the pots near seats, for the meaty odour is nasty and is relished by flies. I have recently discovered that most other species of eucomis in cultivation have a more acceptable scent, similar to that of stale coconut.

The scents of shrubs like hawthorn, cotoneaster, mountain ash and privet come into my category of unpleasant odours, and they too are popular with flies. The scents are usually claustrophobic, sickly and lacking in sweetness, and many noses detect the flavour of fish in them. They do not always cause offence, and some people may even like them (especially hawthorn, for its nostalgic pastoral associations), but they are not for blending into scented schemes. You may also feel the same about flowers like those of common lilac and *Aesculus parviflora*, whose sweetness is sometimes overlaid with a rather stale smell; and candytuft (*Iberis sempervirens*) which to me smells of stale socks.

If you are going to grow flowers with very unpleasant scents, you have to try to find positions for them where they will give the least offence. If the scents carry, make sure they are far from house windows, main paths and sitting-out areas and that they are downwind.

Flower Fragrances

The pleasant fragrances are extremely diverse and warrant detailed subdivision. A group everyone should recognize is the 'exotic' scents – the heavy, tropically sweet perfumes possessed by such flowers as *Jasminum officinale*, nicotianas, clerodendrum, jonquils, tuberose and *Lilium regale*. The scent is not delicate and piercing but is thick and heady and often has a rather fetid bass note. This is most noticeable when you are smelling a plant at close range or when the flower is fading. The pot jasmine, *J. polyanthum*, is exquisite in thin wafts but can be overpowering in a warm sitting room or conservatory. One flower whose scent turns very quickly from sweetness to decay is *Hemerocallis lilio-asphodelus* (*H. flava*), that graceful yellow daylily; as soon as the blooms fade, they begin emitting the most foul stench; I once collected a vaseful for my desk, but never again. Many scents in this category have distinct flavours that are full of character. Trachelospermum, stephanotis, *Pittosporum tobira*, citrus flowers, *Jasminum sambac* and rhaphiolepis seem to me to have a definite taste of bubblegum; and most are free of any hint of decay. There is a whiff of mothballs, not only in hedychirium, but also in *Carissa grandiflora* and *Hosta plantaginea*. Philadelphus coronarius, the cottage-garden's mock orange, is deliciously fruity but its heady, cloying quality puts it squarely into this group. The group comprises many white and night-scented flowers.

Next, there are the spicy scents. At one end of the group are viburnums like *V. carlesii* and *V. juddii*; their scents verge on the exotic but their clove bass note nudges them into this group. I never find their scents unpleasant, even in quantity, and I think they are among the most exciting scented shrubs to use for a fragrant avenue. A similar sweet clove scent is

found in some stocks, phlox, sweet rocket, wallflowers, daphnes, *Lonicera × americana* and, of course, pinks and carnations. The scents vary from plant to plant in the degree of sweetness and spiciness, and in some flowers, like those of *Rhododendron trichostomum*, the fragrance is almost pure clove. White and pink are the predominant colours.

Aniseed can be detected in nearly all cowslip-scented flowers, such as corylopsis, *Clematis rehderiana* and, of course, many primulas, and I think of these as belonging to the spice group. Yellow is the main colour here. Different spicy scents, some with nutty and peppery seasoning and with different degrees of sweetness, come from rhododendrons like R. 'Fragrantissimum', *Magnolia stellata*, witch hazels, *Cestrum parqui*, *Hermodactylus tuberosus*, wintersweet and from many roses. There are a mixed bag of colours here.

Then there are the vanilla and almond scents. These are 'foody' and not too sweet, and are fortunately quite common in garden flowers, especially among woody plants. I include *Clematis armandii*, *C. flammula* and *C. montana*, abeliophyllum, heliotrope, fabiana, pieris (sometimes), *Polygonum polystachyum*, *Schizopetalon walkeri*, azara, *Choisya ternata*, androsace and cherries such as *Prunus × yedoensis*. White and pink are the principal colours.

Next come the pea scents. Many members of the pea family share a distinctive scent. This is worthy of note since scents within a family are usually so diverse; sometimes members of a genus have similar flavours but you have only to look at roses and scented-leaved salvias to see that it is safer to work plant by plant. Sometimes the pea scent is light and sweet, as in coronillas and wisteria; sometimes it is slightly heavy and musty, as in laburnum and some brooms and lupins, but it is always unmistakably pea. I place acacias, which are also members of the family, in this category; they can also veer towards sweetness or mustiness. Yellow is the main colour and there is much similarity in flower shape.

I call the next group 'French perfumes', though one or two are more like cheap suntan lotion. Included here are all those scents that are piercingly sweet but flowery, refined and without much spice or tropical heaviness: lily of the valley, *Mahonia japonica* and skimmias; sweet peas, cyclamen and mignonette; hyacinths (in spite of their fetid undertones) and

Left *The pea scent of laburnums can be pervasive, especially in the evenings when it fills the air with sweetness. But as the flowers age, the fragrance becomes unpleasantly* musty and claustrophobic. Few hardy trees give as colourful and elegant a flower display, and here it is shown picking up the warm tones of the stone and lichen.

Clematis heracleifolia; and the better scented lilacs. The violet scents also belong here; they are sharply sweet and very sophisticated. Apart from in sweet violets, the fragrance is found in *Iris reticulata*, *Leucojum vernum* and in some crab apples. A few of the French perfumes linger in the air but most require repeated sniffing; some, especially the violet scents, tire the senses quickly and you have to leave intervals between inhalations. There is a range of colours here, but white, pink and purple do perhaps dominate.

Rose scents are usually left in a category of their own, although they are varied and complex. Most roses have some hint of what we would recognize as a typical 'rose' perfume; it is also found, to my nose at least, in some crab apples and Japanese apricots. Perhaps the richest of the true rose scents is found among the old shrub roses, where the sweet French perfume is shaded with incense and spice, and among the modern shrub roses, climbers and Hybrid Teas, where it is blended with fruit and tea. The spicier scents seem to be the most pervasive in the air – the Rugosas, Hybrid Musks, Noisettes and Synstylae rambler roses; incense and fruit can also often be detected in these.

Often there is a dominant flavour in the rose scent and it is worth identifying this for use in scented schemes. Clove is clearly evident in the Rugosas, the climbing 'Blush Noisette' and the modern shrub 'Fritz Nobis'. The tea scent is found in 'Lady Hillingdon', 'Gloire de Dijon' and the new shrub rose 'Graham Thomas'. Fruity scents abound – raspberry in many Bourbon and Hybrid Perpetual roses, and in 'Cerise Bouquet'; apple in 'Max Graf', 'Nymphenburg' and the *R. wichuraiana* ramblers; lemon in *R. bracteata* and the shrub rose 'Agnes'; orange in 'The Garland'; banana in *R. longicuspis* and *R.* 'Dupontii'.

There is a strange scent, pleasant but lacking sweetness, apparent in some roses which the experts call 'myrrh'. It smells like cold cream or calamine lotion. It is found in 'Belle Isis', 'Félicité Perpétue', 'Constance Spry' and 'Little White Pet'. But beware of the unpleasant scent that lurks in *R. foetida*, *R. fedtschenkoana*, and some yellow- or orange-flowered bushes and shrub roses with *R. foetida* in their parentage.

The fruit scents encompass a range of delicious flavours. The fragrance is more often warm and full than sharp; sometimes the scent of a particular fruit dominates, but usually it is shaded by other flavours into a fruit cocktail. Lemon seems to be the main flavour in evening primroses, *Magnolia grandiflora* and *M. sinensis*, boronias, *Mirabilis jalapa*, *Primula florindae* and *P.* × *kewensis*, *Clematis forsteri*, and *Buddleja asiatica*; melon in *Magnolia hypoleuca*; banana in *Michelia figo* (*Magnolia fuscata*)

Above *The scent of* Mahonia aquifolium *and its hybrids is one of the strongest fragrances in the early spring garden, providing a background of honey for the bright displays of bulbs and blossom. Most other mahonias have a sharper perfume of lily of the valley, particularly intense in* M. japonica.

and *Muscari macrocarpum*; plum in freesias and *Iris graminea*; pineapple in *Cytisus battandieri*; raspberry in *Edgworthia chrysantha* and, some say, mignonette, though I cannot detect it; apricot in *Amaryllis bella-donna*, gardenia and the newly introduced shrub *Heptacodium jasminoides* (these last two should perhaps be among the 'exotic' scents). Other magnolias, honeysuckles and *Calycanthus floridus* deliver a well-balanced fruit cocktail. Appropriately, many of these flowers have colours in keeping with their scents – yellow for a lemon and banana scent, purple for a plum scent – but almost the whole spectrum is represented.

The honey scents are equally mouth-watering. The fragrance is rich and sticky-thick in *Crocus chrysanthus*, *Mahonia aquifolium*, crambes, alyssum, *Helichrysum ledifolium*, *Euphorbia mellifera* and sarcococcas; it is more flowery in buddlejas; and shades into 'musk' in sweet sultans and *Olearia moschata*.

Left *On a hot day, the air in a herb garden is infused with leaf scents. Here, sages, rue, cotton lavender, hyssop, chives and fennel provide an assortment of warm, pungent and aromatic flavours, while lemon balm and the flowers of pinks and old shrub roses add fruit, spice and layers of sweetness.*

Finally, I have a category for 'rogue' scents that do not seem to fit into any of the main groups. In this category, I put scents that I find pleasant but that are not particularly sweet – the milk of magnesia of *Drimys winteri*, the chocolate of *Cosmos atrosanguineus*, the mouse-and-sawdust of *Callistemon pallidus*, and the horse-and-elephant of *Rondeletia amoena*.

Scented Foliage

Some of the flower scents are also found in leaves, but here they are generally less sugary. This is because in leaves scent has a different function: its purpose is to repel not to attract. Scent is used as a protection against disease and many of the compounds found in leaf scents are strongly antiseptic – oil of eucalyptus, thyme and clove are examples – and play an important part in the composition of medicines. Scent is also used to discourage insects and browsing animals by presenting astringent tastes; some of the volatile oils act as natural herbicides.

Accordingly, leaf scents tend more towards the pungent, bitter and medicinal. How they are released depends on how they are stored. Where the essential oil is in capsules deep inside the leaf, it is released by rubbing or breaking. Where it is in cells close to the surface of the leaf, you need only to brush against it lightly. And where it is actually secreted on to the surface of the leaf, you can usually smell it without disturbing the leaf at all. Hot sunshine causes some scents to oxidize, while others seem to be most evident after rain.

Leaf scents are usually simpler in composition than flower scents, perhaps because subtleties of fragrance are not so important when you are producing a repellant rather than an attractant, but there are many more of them, and leaf scent groupings inevitably contain a diversity of flavours.

There are few really nasty odours among leaves but *Salvia sclarea turkestanica*, the tall biennial with white and pinkish mauve flowers that is such a part of grand herbaceous borders, and *Phuopsis stylosa*, a prostrate perennial with bright pink flowers, both have a nasty sweaty aroma. I also find the foxy scent of *Fritillaria imperialis* unappealing.

The meaty scent of clerodendrum foliage is awful and you notice it in the flowers sometimes too. The 'roast beef' in *Salvia gesneriiflora* is much too fatty for me but I do not mind it in *Iris foetidissima*. Actually, I have discovered that you can condition people to respond to these meat scents in a certain way by describing the scent in advance. If I tell people that *Salvia confertiflora* leaves smell of roast lamb and mint sauce (which they do), then they invariably sniff them and say 'How delicious'. But if I tell them to prepare for an unpleasant smell, they will sniff them and say 'How horrible'.

There are no leaves with a fragrance comparable to the exotic scents of flowers, but many have warm spice scents. They range from the culinary herbs like bay, thyme, basil, marjoram and rosemary to shrubs like sweet fern (comptonia), spice bush (lindera) and myrtle. Curry-scented *Helichrysum italicum* belongs here. Most of these scents are released into the air by heat. I do not think there is any cowslip scent in any leaves but there is aniseed. It comes in a purer form than in flowers, and the supreme examples are fennel, *Primula anisodora* and *Agastache foeniculum* (*A. anisata*); there is also a touch in *Magnolia salicifolia*. To my nose, the liquorice scent of *Myrrhis odorata* is quite close and I include it here. These leaves generally need to be rubbed for the scent to emerge.

I doubt if there are any leaves with vanilla, almond and pea scents or French perfumes. But rose scents are found in the leaves of members of the geranium family. Here the scent has few of the perfumed top notes of rose flowers, but is made aromatic with fruit, mint and spice. Among pelargoniums, *P.* 'Attar of Roses' is especially good; and among geraniums, *G. macrorrhizum* and *G. endressii*. The musky, honey scent is found in olearias.

Fruit scents abound, and in leaves the fragrances are generally sharper than in flowers. Lemon verbena and *Pelargonium* 'Citronella' are as bitter as sherbet; in lemon thyme and bergamot, the lemon is blended with spice; and in lemon balm and *Eucalyptus citriodora*, it smells more like lemon soap. Bitter zest of orange comes from *Houttuynia cordata*; a warmer, aromatic orange from *Pelargonium graveolens*. The best blackcurrant scent is found in salvias like *S. discolor* and *S. microphylla* and, on hot days, cedars waft blackcurrant into the air. The western red cedar (*Thuja plicata*) has a resinous peardrop scent, and the giant fir (*Abies grandis*) smells of grapefruit. *Salvia rutilans* has a delicious pineapple fragrance. And apple is found in *Rosa eglanteria* (*R. rubiginosa*), camomile and, mixed with mint, in applemint. The leaves of walnuts are remarkably fruity, and the scent often hangs in the air, as does

the fruit-cake fragrance of the sticky *Helichrysum ledifolium* foliage. The fruit of hypericum leaves I find rather unpleasant, the orange peel of rue is very pungent and in *Ledum groenlandicum* and *Nepeta* 'Souvenir d'André Chaudron' it is decidedly rotten; the blend of pineapple and rose in *Salvia dorisiana* should be nice but isn't.

Other leaf scents do not at all resemble the fragrances of flowers. First, there are the camphorous and pungent scents of plants like achilleas, most artemisias, tansy, and santolina. I am not fond of these scents but I know other people find them less objectionable; the group includes some of the best grey-leaved plants so they are always well represented in gardens, even in mine. Most of these have to be rubbed for the scent to be released.

Resinous scents are common among leaves. They range from the turpentine of pines and other conifers, through the cedarwood of *Hebe cupressoides*, the gummy resin of cistus, the incense of *Rosa primula*, the tobacco of *Calomeria amaranthoides* (*Humea elegans*), the fruity resin of thujas, abies and *Dictamnus albus*, and the pumpkin pie of *Nothofagus antarctica* to the cloyingly sweet resin of balsam poplar buds. Most of these infuse the air on warm days, especially in spring, and on a summer's evening the flower spikes of dictamnus are so covered with inflammable oil that you can set fire to them; the scent is sharply flavoured with lemon.

Mint and eucalyptus scents are very similar. They share a piercing top note and shade into each other in many leaves. Mint is also present in some species of eucalyptus, notably *E. coccifera*, which has a sharp peppermint fragrance. Most eucalyptus species have some sort of medicinal fragrance, and so do most lavenders, though sweetness and fruit often softens them. *E. glaucescens* is particularly fruity. Mint scents are also very often blended with some fruit or wintergreen, as in prostantheras, catmints, calaminthas and elsholtzia. They are at their coolest and most refreshing in the spearmints and peppermints of menthas and *Pelargonium tomentosum*.

Scents in the 'miscellaneous' category include the fresh, green scents of parsley and celery, the musty scent of ferns, the hay scent of *Dryopteris aemula* (syn. *Lastraea a.*) and the scent of wintergreen *Gaultheria procumbens*.

Scent can also be found in places less obvious than flowers and leaves. Many roots are fragrant. The best known are those of *Iris* 'Florentina', which are scented of violet; *Rhodiola rosea* (*Sedum rhodiola*), which are scented of rose; angelica; herb bennet, which are scented of clove; and magnolia. It is always a pleasant surprise to come across them, as you are digging in the border or taking root cuttings, but since they are not easily accessible, they can play little part in scented schemes. The same is usually true of the fragrant bark possessed by such plants as drimys, calycanthus and davidia. The best way to enjoy scented wood is actually through fire: the incense-laden bonfires of autumn and the log fires of winter.

Scented seeds can sometimes be enjoyed in passing. But, as with flowers and leaves, not all are pleasantly scented; the fleshy coat of ginkgo seeds smells disgusting. Fruits are better savoured in indoor warmth and most of the richest are, of course, tropical. The scents may carry freely when the fruits are assembled in quantity or are very ripe – pineapple, strawberry, apple, quince and chaenomeles (japonica) fruits, for example. Others have to be scratched or, when it is the flesh that is most fragrant, cut open to release their scent.

Apart from all the specific scents of flowers, leaves, roots,

bark and fruits, the garden as a whole always has a general blend of wholesome earthy and vegetable fragrances. There is the scent of damp soil and foliage, of sun-dried grasses, of freshly mown lawn and of surrounding countryside. These set the background harmony from which individual scented notes and melodies emerge.

Sites for Scented Plants

There are three points to bear in mind when choosing places for scented plants in the garden: how and when the scent is released and what sort of scent it is. All pleasantly scented flowers need to be within reach of the nose and most pleasantly scented leaves within reach of the fingers or the feet,

since they generally have to be rubbed for the scent to be released. This really means that scented plants ought never to be far from paths – certainly not at the back of wide borders or separated from you by water or prickly undergrowth. The exceptions are those scented-leaved plants that float scent on the air but never seem to have much scent close to (such as cistuses and *Rosa primula*).

Flowers that are free with their scent, such as jasmine, honeysuckle and Rugosa roses, do not have to be close to paths but I would never put them so far away to deny yourself the chance of drinking deeper draughts of their fragrance. At the Oxford Botanic Garden, the scents of mahonias and sarcococcas are used to guide the visitor to the secret winter garden, tucked behind the rockery. You might use osmanthus to guide you to a hidden garden of spring bulbs; philadelphus to guide you to an iris and peony garden; or Rugosa roses to a garden of summer annuals.

Very small scented plants, such as alpines and dwarf bulbs, have to be lifted above ground level with the aid of troughs, raised beds or window boxes. Pot plants can be stood on bricks or on steps. Another solution is to grow your lowly plants in the soil adjacent to a flight of steps, either on the top terrace, on the top of the bank or above the retaining wall, whichever you have; you can then stand below them and lean up to smell them, which is easier than bending down. A prostrate honeysuckle or climbing rose cascading down a bank can also be comfortably reached from steps; few people think of growing scented climbers like this.

Scents come and go in tune with the life cycle of the plants and atmospheric conditions and if we are to use them effectively, we must discover exactly when they appear. If a plant's fragrance comes from its flowers, we must also know its flowering season. This is important so that we can ensure continuity of interest through the year and build up schemes of different colours and scents. Its flowering season may also affect the placing of a scented plant. Plants which open in the coldest months ought perhaps to be grown near the house and beside the paths in regular use; unless you go out frequently to pick flowers for the house, their scents can easily be wasted if they are growing in far flung corners of the garden.

Leaf scents may also be seasonal. The majority of spice scents are at their best on a hot summer's day. Although the cistuses are evergreen, they also need the heat to reveal their gummy fragrance and it is their young leaves that are richest in flavour; accordingly, in the balmy days of early summer, their scent fills the air, while on a cold autumn, winter or

Left *An impressive specimen of* Euphorbia mellifera *adds a contrasting note of yellow to a pink and grey scheme that is founded on roses, Bowles' mauve wallflower and* Daphne × burkwoodii *'Somerset'. Both the euphorbia and the daphne are richly scented – the first of honey, the second of cloves.*

Above *Steps are a convenient means of raising fragrant pot plants nearer nose level. Here, at Barnsley House, Gloucestershire, highly scented daffodils provide welcome spring colour against the evergreen foliage of variegated euonymus and container-grown box.*

spring day, there is not a whiff. *Nothofagus antarctica* smells strongly only in spring. And the Katsura tree (*Cercidiphyllum japonicum*) produces its sweet caramel scent only when its leaves are falling in the autumn.

We cannot do anything to control the weather, but it is worth noting that many fragrances are best after rain. The scent from the foliage of roses like *RR. primula, serafinii* and *eglanteria* is unequalled at any other time. These might be grown near fountains where they would receive the occasional spray on a windy day, though they would not appreciate constant drenching.

Some flowers reveal their scent as the temperature cools in the evening. These night-scented bloomers include jasmine, tobacco flowers, honeysuckles, night-scented stock, phlox, sweet rocket, *Cestrum parqui*, daturas, evening primroses, abronia, verbena, *Mirabilis jalapa*, petunias and *Daphne laureola*. The scents are mainly exotic or spicy, though there is a touch of fruit from honeysuckle, evening primrose and mirabilis. Clearly, these must be assembled around windows, patios and wherever else you sit outside.

The 'flavour' of a plant's scent should also be taken into account. Just as, in a well planned garden, you are offered a succession of visual delights, each different and evoking its own mood, so you might be offered a succession of scented delights. As you move from one colour scheme to another, so you might move from one zone of fragrance to another.

I have already suggested massing individual plants like lime, viburnum, lavender and sarcococca to make fragrant streams and avenues in certain parts of the garden. Any plant that carries its fragrance on the air is suitable for massing. Because scents are so complex, they can never be monotonous, and it is always a pleasure to abandon yourself to the charms of a single fragrance; you are forever discovering nuances you had not noticed before.

The complexity of scents, and the fact that many have elements in common, also means that you never encounter serious clashes of flavour. Though I would say that moving from the very sweet to the very pungent and from the pleasant to the unpleasant are shocks for the nose that we would do well to avoid. The main worry is drowning one scent with another; if the air is full of jasmine, it is hard to catch the delicacy of mignonette. Nonetheless, when we are bringing scents together it is sometimes fun to make deliberate marriages, choosing those that you think might positively enhance each other. This involves dealing with them in terms of harmonies and contrasts, just as we do when matching colours. For close harmonies we will be selecting scents from the same group. We could choose a bowl of fruit scents perhaps – *Cytisus battandieri*, an apple-scented rose, a blackcurrant-scented sage and lemon verbena – or a clove pomander – pinks, sweet rocket and *Lonicera × americana.*

Instead of choosing plants that perform simultaneously, we can also arrange a single scent scheme that lasts for several months. If we planted one area, for example, with *Mahonia aquifolium*, crambe, alyssum and sarcococca we would give ourselves a perennial honeypot; this would contrast deliciously with another area given over to year-round vanilla and almond scents – azara, *Clematis montana*, heliotrope and *Polygonum polystachyum*.

Colour can point you towards an appropriate scent. If you decide on a yellow scheme somewhere, why not enhance it by injecting lemon fragrances; a bronze and white scheme could be flavoured with chocolate and peppermint. Many plants have exactly the scent that their appearance suggests – think of raspberry-scented, raspberry-ripple-coloured *Rosa* 'Ferdinand Pichard' or golden brown, honey-scented *Euphorbia mellifera*. It is exciting when the visual and olfactory impressions are as perfectly in tune as this.

Once we start mixing scents from different groups, we are really entering the realms of perfumery. I wish the great perfume houses could help us, but professional perfumers are concerned with extracted essential oils, which smell very different from scents as they occur in the garden. The makers of pot-pourri are not particularly satisfactory guides either, so it is a matter of feeling your own way. Certain scent groups seem naturally to harmonize – fruit and honey, almond and clove, for example. These are always fun to stir together: *Primula florindae* and sweet alyssum; heliotrope and stocks.

Other scents seem to make happy contrasts quite naturally. The combination of sweetness with spice or resin is the foundation for many a good scheme. We can generally look to flowers to provide the top note and leaves the bass note; and since most leaves have to be rubbed, we can control the release of the bass note to suit our mood. Thus the lemon scent of evening primroses might be enhanced by a drift of thyme; the apple scent of *Rosa wichuraiana* by a nearby pine. Roses teamed up with lavender is a well-loved association.

The combination of three compatible notes – rose, lavender, philadelphus – strikes an even more sophisticated chord. And walled rose gardens which are packed with every shade of scent, from fruit and spice to tea and myrrh, give you a complete sensual immersion and prove that the more layers of harmonious fragrances you add, the more delicious the result will be.

Scented Plants

Structural Planting with Trees and Shrubs

Trees offer a variety of exciting scents and it is a pity that we cannot employ more of them in the garden. Only those gardeners with acres at their disposal can indulge themselves to the full. The rest of us must be content with one or two and savour the others elsewhere.

Protection from wind, ugliness and prying eyes is essential to our fragrant idyll, and trees are as much a part of our defences as walls and hedges. Among the scented candidates for screens and windbreaks are balsam poplars, laburnums, limes and willows as well as a host of conifers; remember that a judicious mixture of evergreen and deciduous trees provides a better windbreak than a solid evergreen barrier. For strength of scent, balsam poplars and limes are hard to beat. The former are at their richest in the spring when the sticky buds are freely wafting their sugary, resinous fragrance; in summer, limes release their fruity scent through their flowers.

In mild areas, eucalyptus are potentially the fastest-growing garden trees and might be considered where an instant vertical feature is required. Hardier forms, from seed collected in the coldest regions of Australasia, are now in circulation. I have just planted six different species to break the outline of a housing development which has recently been built on the eastern boundary of my Welsh garden, and am hoping for growth in excess of 1m/3ft a year. The silvery blue foliage offers a variety of fruity, minty and medicinal fragrances and there is the bonus of honey-scented flowers.

Because of their size, trees have a major impact on the character of the garden. It would therefore be eccentric to choose one entirely because of its scent. Its height, spread, density, shape and personality all have to be taken into account. Fastigiate trees, for example, are dynamic. They make dramatic focal points when used singly, and, when marshalled into lines or symmetrically placed either side of a gateway or vista, are strong formalizing influences. Many of the conifers, notably the cypresses, junipers and grapefruit-scented *Abies grandis*, form columns and pyramids. A group of them, such as that famous phalanx of incense cedars (the fragrance, alas, is more like turpentine than incense) at Westonbirt Arboretum in Gloucestershire, England, can resemble a cluster of green rockets rising from a launch pad.

Equally sculptural are those trees that are emphatically horizontal, like the blue Atlas cedar and cedar of Lebanon, around which, on hot days, hangs the aroma of blackcurrant. But their shapes are less vigorous. In Britain, their presence usually betrays the whereabouts of a sizeable country house, and I think they have a rock-solid, conservative, unruffled air about them that is eminently suited to a park-like setting of close-cropped grass and sweeping drives. Scots pine, in a social class beneath the cedars, also has strong horizontal growth.

The weepers are more graceful, represented, among scented trees, by weeping silver lime and weeping cercidiphyllum as well as by a number of conifers, of which the most exciting is surely Brewer's weeping spruce. *Buddleja alternifolia* (listed under 'Shrubs'), with honey-scented flowers, is another candidate for the small garden. We tend to think of water as being the ideal backdrop for a weeping tree but they are striking anywhere, especially when contrasted with more conventional shapes.

Round-topped trees are generally less eyecatching as specimen plants, unless they are isolated against the horizon or display strong colour. Their informal, curvaceous outlines blur into the background. But they give the garden a relaxed

Right *There is no shortage of scented shrubs for shady borders and light woodland. On acid soil, the fragrant rhododendrons alone will provide a potent selection. The flowers of a number of the larger species and hybrids are fruitily lily-scented, shaded with spice and other flavourings.*

mood and many have great personality. The crabs and hawthorns lend a country air to the design, as do gnarled fruit trees (we must not forget the fragrance of pear and apple blossom); there are no better ways of bringing a 'cottage garden' character to a garden than by having a broken line of fruit trees down a path, or by positioning a crab on each corner of a small lawn. And how many centuries of garden history come with a quince?

Trees with striking leaves or bark are also worthy of prominent positions, since they entertain over such a long period. Large-leaved paulownia, exotically scented catalpa, vanilla scented yellow wood and resinous-leaved mockernut, and, in mild areas, glossy-leaved *Magnolia grandiflora* with lemon scented flowers, make fine lawn specimens; as do lace-bark pine, stewartia and, with their snow white and python-patterned trunks, many sorts of eucalyptus. Other round-topped trees, whose main contribution is a fleeting show of flowers or autumn colour, are, at least in the small garden, better kept as part of the garden's backdrop. They will step forward when their moment of glory comes but can remain unobtrusive afterwards. In this category come most magnolias, laburnums, limes, halesias and cherries, and cercidiphyllum, which, though having beautiful foliage, really only comes into its own in the autumn when its leaves are falling and it is infusing the air with the scent of burnt toffee. Try it with a *Nothofagus antarctica* which will start the year off for you in an equally mouthwatering cloud of pumpkin pie.

Where you have opted for a scentless tree, or where there is a scentless tree already in place, you can inject fragrance by letting it play host to a climbing plant. Honeysuckles and climbing roses are obvious contenders, and they combine particularly well with fruit trees. They can be chosen so that they perform simultaneously or provide two seasons of scent. A neighbour of mine has been very daring, encouraging a Chinese wisteria to ramble through a scarlet crab; the colour combination is startling but triumphantly successful, and there is a fragrant reward for passing pedestrians who pause to admire it.

Avenues of trees make an important structural addition to the design, and if they are scented there is an additional layer of pleasure. Limes and walnuts are well suited to this role, but the garden has to be large. The fruity scent from the leaves of the common walnut can be very strong on a still, damp day. Lilacs are tempting for the smaller garden. The colourful frothing flowerheads (sweetly fragrant at their peak, sickly afterwards) are irresistible in early summer but are very dreary afterwards; the suckers are also a problem. An avenue

of robinias would be cheerful and, like limes, they do not object to regular pruning. But for the small garden, the queen of scented trees has to be laburnum. Its attractive, airy foliage casts little shade and, whether free-growing or trained into tunnels and arches, it is a sensational sight when in bloom.

Structural Evergreens

We use hedges on the garden's boundary and as internal partitions. They can be formal and neatly clipped, imposing order on the ground-plan and countering the casual shapes and patterns of shrubs and border plants; or they can be informal, keeping the lines of the composition soft and natural and helping the garden to blend with the countryside beyond.

For a tall, formal hedge the first plant that springs to mind is yew. It is neat, evergreen, dense and dark, and grows at a manageable speed. But where is its scent? Lawson cypress and Leyland cypress are better endowed; though they are so fast-growing that they must be pruned twice a year to keep them tight. But for a really pleasant scent the top prize goes to western red cedar, *Thuja plicata*. The leaves smell of pear-drops and ask to be tweaked every time you pass. It is fresh green in colour, dense and hardy. The dark form 'Atrovirens' is the best foil for flowers.

For a small formal hedge there is no competition: box. Some people think it smells of cats, but others find it reminds them of nothing but other gardens, summer weather, and happy hours spent pottering. Borders edged in box always have an air of respectability, even if there is chaos within – as in a herb garden. The edging helps to contain floppy plants – box does not object to being buried in flowers and foliage all summer – and in winter, the outline is especially welcome. The most sophisticated use of box is, of course, the knot garden. For those who dislike the smell of box, box honeysuckle (*Lonicera nitida*) could be substituted; it has fruitily sweet, cream flowers.

Flowering hedges are rarely good backdrops for mixed flower borders; the pull between the military and civilian use of plants is confusing. But seen behind a velvet lawn, in front of rolling countryside, or behind flowerbeds uniformly planted (with a monochrome scheme of wallflowers or Hybrid Tea roses, for example), they look marvellous. There are many scented plants which can be used. For taller hedges, evergreen honey-scented barberries, powerfully sweet osmanthus, elaeagnus, and phillyrea are worth considering, and, in milder areas, resinous escallonia, musky olearia and rosemary. Deciduous mock oranges and shrub roses are also beautiful. The scent from a line of Rugosa roses is intense, and at Kiftsgate Court in Gloucestershire, England, there is a spell-binding hedge of striped Rosa Mundi. Other evergreen flowering plants for low hedges and edging work include lavender, santolina and germander.

Mixed hedges are still less formal, especially when casually clipped, with certain plants being allowed to grow tall. Hawthorn, elder and privet can be used but their heavy scents do not win universal appeal. Weaving in honeysuckles (*Lonicera periclymenum* varieties and evergreen *L. japonica* 'Halliana'), dog rose and perhaps vanilla-scented *Clematis flammula* will add sweetness. Wildlife will thank you for a hedge such as this.

Evergreen shrubs grown singly or in groups will also add structure to the garden. Those of striking shape, like pencil-slim cypresses and junipers, spiky yuccas, pyramidal arborvitae (thuja) and topiary box, attract attention and act as focal points and lynchpins in the design. Diagonally ascending junipers are adept at disguising weak junctions in the design, such as where a grass bank meets a stone wall or a flight of steps. Other evergreens form mounds and hummocks, cushions and clouds, and give the garden a relaxed winter furnishing. Deciding how many you need is always difficult: plant too few and the winter garden looks patchy; plant too many and in summer the garden feels heavy. It is a matter of giving every vista a balanced pattern of winter shapes and making sure that there continue to be focal points and justifications for the corners and bulges in the flowerbeds even after most plants have gone into hibernation.

Deciduous shrubs lend their support in spring, summer and autumn. They add bulk to the design, height and substance to border schemes and, through their cycle of expanding young growth, flowers, mature foliage, autumn colour and tracery of bare branches, they bring the full flavour of each season to all parts of the garden.

Designing with Scented Shrubs

In winter, when the majority of perennials are tucked snugly underground, shrubs and trees have a special importance. Evergreens come to the fore; we suddenly become aware of shapes; we notice the colours and textures of trunks and branches. Most of the winter-flowering shrubs are tolerant of shade, but flowers only really come to life, in this gloomy season, when they are caught by a shaft of sunshine. A witch

hazel stretching its limbs in the afternoon sun is quite a different sight from one sitting in the shadows. Perhaps you can find places for them where they are shaded in summer by a deciduous canopy or screen which drops in the autumn.

The winter viburnums are perhaps the most valuable of this season's deciduous shrubs. They produce their honey-scented, pink and white flowers on bare branches from autumn until early spring. An erect-stemmed clump is striking when silhouetted against evergreens or lawn, or against a clear sky. The winter cherry, *Prunus × subhirtella* 'Autumnalis', will pick up the pink colour in the distance; and underneath you might plant a sheet of snowdrops.

Sarcococcas are also honey-scented. These are first-class short evergreens which ought to be far better known. Their scent is breathed freely into the winter air, and at Oxford Botanic Garden in England, they front a bed of different coloured – but scentless – hellebores, so that there is pleasure for the nose as well as the eye. *Mahonia japonica* is planted on the corner and adds lily of the valley to the dominant scent of honey. As spring advances, the sarcococcas cease flowering and the mahonia scent takes over.

The various witch hazels provide a succession of warm colours from mid-winter onwards, blooming, like the viburnums, on bare stems. The yellows are sweeter than the others; the reds and oranges have a mustier, fruit-spice scent that is exactly the smell of parrots. The yellows are lovely when underplanted with green *Helleborus foetidus* and clumps of orange-berried *Iris foetidissima*, whose leaves are fragrant of roast beef.

In a rough corner of the garden you might find space for the cornelian cherry dogwood (*Cornus mas*) and willows such as *Salix aegyptiaca*, *S. triandra* and *S. pentandra*, which will provide a succession of spicy, honey and almond scents through the late winter and into the spring. Under trees, on lime-free soil, corylopsis are now displaying their lemon and primrose scented tassels, and evergreen pieris their panicles of cream, pitcher-shaped flowers, fragrant of lily of the valley and vanilla.

Spring is the climax of the shrub year and a wealth of colours and scents are on offer. The majority of spring-flowering shrubs are tolerant of some degree of shade, so the main display may still be under trees, in the shadow of walls and on the garden's fringes, the more open sites being left free for later plants that really need plenty of sunlight. *Mahonia aquifolium* has one of the most potent honey scents of early spring. I suggest placing the odd plant in various insignificant spots (it is tolerant of deep shade and dry soil) so that the entire garden is bathed in a rich background fragrance. Honey and its related flavours are breathed by many winter and spring flowers, and it is a scent which seems to enhance all others. For close association with mahonias there are skimmias, fothergillas and orange and yellow barberries, and, as underplanting, primroses and early daffodils.

Pink and white schemes, infused with almond and spice, can be orchestrated using *Magnolia* × *loebneri* 'Merrill', scented cherries like *Prunus* × *yedoensis* and 'Jo-nioi', and, of course, viburnums. The white-flowered viburnums that carry us through the spring have a different scent from the earlier varieties. A rich, usually penetratingly sweet, clove fragrance replaces the honey and almond and at this time of year it is my favourite scent. You get the best value for money from *V.* × *burkwoodii* and its clones, because they are evergreen, bloom over a long period and even provide a splash of autumn colour. But *V. carlesii* and *V.* × *juddii* must be found homes too. A short avenue of these shrubs would be a scented treat you would never regret.

Many clove-scented daphnes are in bloom now, including the excellent *D.* × *burkwoodii* 'Somerset'. You might use them to pick up the colour of crab apples, whose pink, white and red blossom often surprises you with a violet or rose scent. The dwarf pink lilacs, like *Syringa microphylla* 'Superba', might also contribute. And, if you have acid soil, so might sun-loving *Rhododendron trichostomum*. This small, dainty shrub looks very much like a daphne and its pink flowers have a strong, but not sweet, clove scent.

A different, fruity fragrance comes from the azaleas. In my view, *Rhododendron luteum* is unrivalled, both in appearance and in the potency of its fruit-cocktail scent. Its yellow flowers and lime green young leaves create patches of sunlight in the woodland shadows and it has a natural charm that has been lost in many of the brilliantly coloured hybrids. I am planting a sweep of it in front of two large copper beech trees and am encouraging bluebells to colonize from the adjacent rock garden (where they ought not to be). In mild climates, tender white rhododendrons like 'Fragrantissimum' and 'Lady Alice Fitzwilliam' are among the woodland garden's spring delights; they are fruitily scented with a dash of nutmeg. More of us can enjoy the hardier Loderi clones that bear heavy trusses of pink and white, lily-scented flowers. They are such imposing shrubs that companions need to be chosen with care. Giant Himalayan lilies (cardiocrinum) coincide usefully with the large rhododendrons of early summer, such as 'Albatross' and *R. arborescens*.

As spring ebbs into summer, the emphasis begins to shift from shade-tolerant to sun-loving shrubs. Brooms, lilacs and laburnums will help to awaken the herbaceous border. Early roses like 'Frühlingsgold' and *R. pimpinellifolia* (*R. spinosissima*) are in flower, filling the air with the scent of the cottage-garden mock orange, *Philadelphus coronarius*. It is a fragrance that can drown all others, so it needs a position on the boundary where it can reach you in wafts.

The other mock oranges are more restrained and can be planted freely. Their fruity mock-orange fragrance combines deliciously with the sophisticated scents of shrub roses and their pure white and maroon-smudged flowers blend well with the roses' crimson velvet, white damask and pink silk cockades. *Buddleja alternifolia* will contribute its lilac streamers and there is a host of purple, violet and pale yellow perennials available to provide the appropriate carpet.

In sheltered, sun-baked borders, cistuses will be flowering. The gummy scents from their evergreen leaves provide entertainment on and off all year, but in the heat of summer, when many varieties are flush with sticky young growth, the fragrance is at its richest. The leaves of rosemaries and thymes add spice to the scheme, New Zealand daisy bushes (olearia) a touch of musk and *Umbellularia californica* a dash of fruit. And flowers come forward at intervals to provide complementary top notes: honey-scented tree heathers (*Erica arborea* and its cousins) and *Helichrysum ledifolium* (*Ozothamnus ledifolius*); almond-scented *Colletia armata*; and vanilla-scented Spanish broom, *Spartium junceum*.

As a supplement to the herbaceous plants of high summer there are some excellent shrubs, that are visually exciting and scented. Mount Etna broom, *Genista aetnensis*, and tree lupin, *Lupinus arboreus*, are ideal in the perennial border. Though tall, the thinly clad broom casts little shade; while the lupin is in flower continuously until the autumn. Their yellow flowers have sweet-pea scents that you often catch in the air. Buddlejas are also quite at home here, and like their herbaceous companions are cut to the ground in spring. *B. davidii* and *B. fallowiana* provide a range of blue, purple and white blooms, while *B.* × *weyeriana* 'Golden Glow' is apricot-yellow. They have a flowery honey scent. And for prominent corners of the border there are the spectacular candelabras of yuccas.

The flowers of *Clerodendrum bungei* do carry a trace of the unpleasant meaty scent, so evident in the leaves. But their overriding sweetness, their size and the brightness of their pink make amends and earn the plant a prominent place in my late summer border. Bright pinks are very welcome at this time when the garden is becoming enveloped in tawny and misty shades. Its cousin, *C. trichotomum fargesii*, is more

at home in light shade. The scent is a touch less sweet, re-sembling that of fading jasmine flowers, but is powerful and carries well. It is a valuable plant for bringing autumn interest to the woodland garden. The white flowers and turquoise fruits, set in crimson calyces, always catch the eye.

The sugary sweet scent of *Elaeagnus × ebbingei* ('Salcombe Seedling' is an especially good form) is strong on a warm autumn evening. This is often decried as a dreary evergreen but, planted in the sun and hard pruned in spring, the silvery young growth contrasts strikingly with the gold of the dying old leaves, and the white flowers are generously borne. I have it growing beside the front drive and the scent stops all visi-tors in their tracks. For more ornamental use, the golden variegated forms of *E. × ebbingei* and *E. pungens* are stunning.

Above *A sunny walled corner is an ideal spot for a seat and a collection of fragrant shrubs. Here the leaf aromas of lavender, sage and artemisia blend, in early spring, with the clove-shaded flower scents of viburnum and daphnes. A rosemary blooms within easy reach of the seat.*

As autumn progresses, the early mahonias reveal their erect racemes of yellow flowers; these varieties are not as potently fragrant as the later species but the delicate flavour of lily of the valley is welcome all the same. *Osmanthus armatus* also offers a sweet bubblegum scent. But the fragrance I most look forward to, as the leaves turn, is the caramel of the Katsura tree (*Cercidiphyllum japonicum*) which, if conditions are right, is the accompaniment to a spectacular display of autumn colour.

Trees

Abies

Like most conifers, the firs release a resinous or fruity scent when the leaves are bruised. The bark is often resinous, too. Most make big evergreen trees, mainly conical in shape, but they are often slow-growing. For smaller gardens, the Korean fir, *A. koreana* (Z5), is a good choice; it achieves about 3m/10ft in its first 20 years, eventually reaching 12m/40ft, and bears remarkable purplish blue cones from an early age. For large gardens, the Caucasian fir, *A. nordmanniana* (Z5), is one of the most desirable; it has bright green fruit-scented foliage and green cones, and grows more than three times as high and fast as the Korean fir. The following two species have the most distinctive strong scent:

A. balsamea, balsam fir or balm of Gilead, has dark green, glossy leaves with a powerful balsam fragrance; young foliage and the undersides of the leaves are a beautiful grey. The balsam fir makes a tall tree away from its cold homeland of North America, but is at its best when young, and I would be tempted to fell it on its 25th birthday; it would then be 6m/20ft high. The cones are purple. It has a miniature (60cm/2ft) form, *hudsonia*. Lime-free or neutral soil. Z3

A. grandis, giant fir, also has dark leaves which are powerfully and sweetly resinous of grapefruit. But it is vigorous and makes a large tree. It has olive-green young shoots and bright green cones. It is more tolerant of shade and alkaline soils than many other fir trees.
Sun or light shade. Moist, well-drained soil. 15m/50ft in 20 years. Z6

Aesculus

A. californica. Some of the horse chestnuts have scented flowers, including the common horse chestnut, *A. hippocastanum*. For garden use, the best species for scent is *A. californica*. This makes a wide-spreading, small tree or large shrub with small, fingered, metallic grey-green leaves and, throughout the summer, dense, erect heads of white, rose-tinged flowers. It makes an attractive and unusual low lawn specimen and is quite hardy away from the Sunshine State. It may be hard to find in nurseries.
Sun or light shade. 3–9m/10–30ft. Z7

Betula

B. lenta, sweet or black birch, native to the eastern United States, is uncommon and less vigorous in Britain. It makes an upright tree with typical ovate, toothed leaves which turn bright, clear yellow in the autumn. The bark is smooth and black when young but becomes flaky with age. The shoots have a scent like wintergreen, or a medicinal rub, when bruised. It bears catkins in spring.
Sun. 9m/30ft in 20 years; ultimately 24m/80ft in the United States, but smaller in Europe. Z3

Carya

C. tomentosa, mockernut or bigbud hickory, is, like most of the hickories, rare in cultivation. This is because the group will not tolerate root disturbance and can be difficult to transplant. But if seed is sown *in situ* or seedlings are transplanted when very young, they will prosper. The mockernut is a beautiful tree, and is the most fragrant of the hickories. The foliage has a sweet resinous scent; sometimes it carries in the air but at other times it must be coaxed by hand. The compound leaves are exotically long and composed of seven or more leaflets; they turn yellow in the autumn. The large buds are of interest in the winter.
Sun. Good loamy soil. 6m/20ft in 20 years; ultimately 24m/80ft. Z4

Catalpa

C. bignonioides, Indian bean tree, is one of the most impressive specimen trees for the lawn of a large garden. It is rounded in shape and wide-spreading and the leaves are very large, heart-shaped and fresh light green in colour. Sweetly scented white flowers, marked in yellow and purple, are carried in showy, erect panicles in summer and are followed, in hot seasons, by slender seed pods. Hybrids between this species and *C. ovata*, grouped under *C. × erubescens*, usually have a glorious lily scent.
Sun. Deep, moist soil. 15m/50ft. Z4

Far left *Abies koreana*
Left *Aesculus californica*

Cedrus

The cedars infuse the air with a warm, resinous, blackcurrant scent on hot days but the fragrance is generally not as strong in the foliage as in other conifers. There are three main species, all of which make very large, evergreen trees; they begin pyramidal in shape and later become wide-spreading. There are few finer and more stately lawn specimens for the largest gardens.

Sun. Moist, deep, well-drained soil.

C. deodara, the deodar, has a particularly graceful, pendant habit which distinguishes it from its cousins. There is a popular form called 'Aurea', which is smaller and slower-growing and which is golden yellow in spring; and, for the rock garden, a semi-prostrate golden form called 'Golden Horizon'. The species itself is often planted in small gardens because of its attractive appearance when young, but it soon outgrows its allotted space.

14m/45ft in 20 years; up to 60m/200ft. Z7

C. libani, the cedar of Lebanon, is the familiar, majestic tree of parks and stately homes with great horizontal, spreading branches. It is slower-growing than the Atlas cedar.

9m/30ft in 20 years; ultimately 36m/120ft. Z6

C. libani atlantica, Atlas cedar, is almost identical to the cedar of Lebanon. It is fast-growing when young but takes a number of years for its branches to assume a horizontal poise. 'Glauca', its grey-blue form, is very popular and is known as the blue Atlas cedar.

12m/40ft in 20 years; ultimately 36m/120ft. Z6

Cercidiphyllum

C. japonicum, the Katsura tree, from the Far East, is one of the most exciting trees for autumn colour and, as its leaves drop, a mouthwatering scent of caramel fills the air. The leaves are heart-shaped and glaucous green. It is most frequently seen as a multi-stemmed tree, but with judicious pruning it can be trained to a single stem. The young leaves are susceptible to spring frosts so a sheltered position is needed in colder areas.

Cercidiphyllum japonicum

Crataegus laevigata and *C.l.* 'Paul's Scarlet'

Cladrastis

C. lutea, yellow wood, is a highly ornamental, round-topped, deciduous tree from the south eastern United States. It has beautiful and exotic, lettuce green, pinnate leaves that turn a clear yellow colour in the autumn. But the sweet vanilla scent comes from the white pea-flowers that open in wisteria-like, dangling panicles in early summer; these seem to appear only on the more mature plants.
Sun. Acid soil. 9m/30ft in 20 years; ultimately 12m/40ft or more. Z3

Crataegus

I cannot pass over the hawthorns without mentioning their heavy scent that is so evident in the British countryside in late spring. At best it is a sweet musty fragrance, at worst the odour of decaying fish. The common hawthorn or may, *C. monogyna*, has a most unappealing scent; it can be sweet on the air but gives a nasty shock on close contact. Another species, *C. laevigata* (*C. oxyacantha*) (Z6), is no better but scent is more or less absent from its heavily coloured forms such as 'Paul's Scarlet'. The species that have the sweeter scents are the least visually attractive and are also considerably more obscure.

There is a sensational weeping form called 'Pendulum'.
Light shade. Rich, deep, moist soil. 12m/40ft in 20 years; 30m/100ft in the wild. Z5

Chamaecyparis

The false cypresses are among the most cultivated of conifers and have foliage which is pungently resinous-scented when bruised. As trees they are conical in shape, most becoming more spreading with age. Many make good screens and tall hedges, but they grow vigorously and many forms may need pruning twice a year.
Moist, loamy soil.
C. lawsoniana, Lawson false cypress, makes a large tree with leaves held in flat, ferny sprays. It is one of the best tall screens and hedges. It has given rise to many excellent clones, including: 'Columnaris', a narrow blue-grey column, 7.5m/25ft; 'Ellwoodii', a slow-growing, dark blue-green column, dense and compact, 7.5m/25ft; 'Erecta Viridis', a deep green, compact column,

wonderfully neat and formal but best when comparatively young, 9–27m/30–90ft; 'Fletcheri', a feathery, juniper-like, blue-grey, bushy cone, slow-growing, 6–12m/20–40ft; 'Green Pillar', a superb rich green column, 7.5m/25ft; 'Kilmacurragh', a pencil-slim, dark green column, 7.5–12m/25–40ft; 'Lane', a golden pyramid, 7.5m/25ft; 'Pembury Blue', a glaucous blue-grey cone, slow-growing, 3.5–9m/12–30ft; and 'Pottenii', a grey-green cone, 9m/30ft. Z5
C. obtusa, Hinoki false cypress, has rich green foliage, horizontally borne in feathery sprays, and also makes a broad conical tree. ('Crippsii' is a good bright golden yellow form, a third smaller in size.)
Moist, lime-free soil. 7.5m/25ft in 20 years; ultimately 23m/75ft. Z5
C. thyoides, white false cypress, has glaucous green foliage with a pungent spicy scent. It makes a pleasing compact cone.
Lime-free soil. 7.5m/25ft in 20 years; ultimately 6–15m/20–50ft, 24m/80ft in the wild. Z5

Cupressus

The cypresses release a fruity, resinous scent when bruised. In warmer areas, and near the sea, the Monterey cypress, *C. macrocarpa* (Z7), is a useful, fast-growing shelter and hedging tree; it has many good golden forms, and grows 14m/45ft or more in 20 years, ultimately 18–30m/60–100ft. The slim, dark green, Italian cypress, *C. sempervirens*, will also thrive in warmer areas and there is no better vertical column for the garden's design; 11m/35ft in 20 years, ultimately 24m/80ft.
Sun. All but waterlogged soils.
C. arizonica (*C. glabra*), smooth Arizona cypress, is one of the hardiest species. It is a beautiful, ghostly tree, feathery and conical with attractive peeling, reddish brown bark. The form 'Pyramidalis' is outstandingly compact and blue. The scent is vaguely reminiscent of grapefruit.
7.5m/25ft in 20 years; ultimately 9m/30ft or more. Z6

Cydonia

C. oblonga, the common quince, has some of the most deliciously and distinctively scented fruit imaginable; a scent to send the taste buds into ecstasy! It is a small, round-topped, deciduous tree and makes a characterful, sometimes gawky, lawn specimen. The dark green leaves have woolly grey undersides, and blush pink flowers – large and saucer-shaped – appear in spring. The fruits, which are in evidence in early autumn, are yellow and pear-shaped and are used for making quince jelly. 'Vranja' is a superior form. Like most fruit trees, it is rather a martyr to pest and disease.
Sun. Good, fertile soil. 7.5m/25ft. Z5

Eucalyptus

The gum trees always attract attention outside their Australian homeland. Most, alas, are not hardy away from the milder and coastal areas, though research is under way to find more winter hardy candidates. Apart from their obvious visual beauty, a main attraction is their incredible speed of growth. The evergreen foliage has a juvenile and adult phase; the leaves usually begin shorter and more rounded, and later become slender and pointed. Their medicinal scent is evident when the leaves are rubbed. They are easy to grow from seed, and are best established when very small. They generally form erect, narrow specimens, thinly clothed in foliage. The flowers are generally richly honey-scented.
Sun. Well-drained soil preferred.
The following are relatively hardy:
E. coccifera, Tasmanian snow gum, has greyish green leaves which begin heart-shaped and turn into narrow sickles. When crushed, these release a scent of peppermint. The smooth trunk begins white and fades to grey.
17m/55ft in 20 years; ultimately 21m/70ft. Z9
E. dalrympleana is proving a most attractive and reliable species for gardens. It has larger leaves than *E. coccifera* and a beautiful smooth trunk which is a patchwork of cream, grey and light brown.
17m/55ft in 20 years; ultimately 24–36m/80–120ft. Z9
E. glaucescens, Tingiringi gum, has foliage with a delicious fruity aroma. It has juvenile

leaves of a very intense silver-blue and retains a fine glaucous colour in adulthood. It has creamy, peeling bark.
12m/40ft in 20 years. Z9
E. gunnii, cider gum, is the most popular species. Its round young leaves are a glaucous silver-blue, and its adult leaves green and sickle-shaped. The bark fades from light green and cream to brown and grey. A particular glory of this species is its juvenile foliage and it is very effective as a coppiced shrub.
23m/75ft in 20 years; ultimately 30m/100ft. Z9
E. niphophila, snow gum, is the queen of eycalypts and is also, by happy chance, the hardiest. It has rounded green juvenile foliage and leathery, grey-green adult foliage. Its smooth trunk is truly one of the world's floral wonders, a bloomy pure white, patterned in green and grey. It has a mild, fruity scent.
6m/20ft in the wild; in gardens achieves up to 15m/50ft in 20 years. Z8

Fraxinus

F. ornus, flowering or manna ash, is an interesting addition to the garden. It is not the best of the flowering ashes – that title goes to *F. sieboldiana* (*F. mariesii*) – but it wins the prize for scent which comes from its foamy heads of cream flowers in spring and is overpoweringly, though not always agreeably, of honey. It has pinnate leaves and makes a round-topped deciduous tree.
Sun. 12m/40ft in 20 years; ultimately 15m/50ft. Z5

Halesia

H. carolina, Carolina silverbell, is a pretty plant for the larger garden, particularly in a woodland clearing where it can be given a dark background. The branches drip with pure white bells during spring, and these are softly but sweetly scented. The leaves are more or less oval and turn yellow in the autumn, coinciding with small winged fruits. It is often seen as a multi-stemmed tree.
Sun or light shade. Moist, well-drained soil, preferably acidic. 4.5m/15ft in 20 years in Europe; makes a 9m/30ft-round-topped tree in the United States. Z5
H. monticola, mountain snowdrop tree, is altogether larger and even more impressive

Eucalyptus dalrympleana

Fraxinus ornus

Juglans nigra

in flower and fruit than *H. carolina.* Again it is often seen as a multi-stemmed tree.
Sun or light shade. 7.5m/30ft in 20 years. Z5

Juglans
The large pinnate leaves of walnuts are fruitily resinous and this scent can often be enjoyed in the air, especially in the autumn; the scent is more pungent when the leaves are rubbed by hand. The two species commonly cultivated are susceptible to wind and to late frosts, so a sheltered site should be found. They also resent disturbance and should be established when very young, even from seed. They are both deciduous.
Sun or light shade. Good, loamy, acid or alkaline soil.
J. nigra, black walnut, is the more ornamental of the two species commonly grown but is less strongly scented. As a lawn specimen it is impressive and tropical in appearance, for its leaves are particularly long. Do not use it in mixed plantings, since it produces toxins which may kill other plants. It forms a round-topped, pyramidal shape, and is fast-growing. The nuts are tasty.

11m/35ft in 20 years; ultimately 24m/80ft or more. Z4
J. regia, English or Persian walnut, is grown mainly for its nuts and soft fruits; particularly good clones can be bought from fruit tree specialists. It makes a smaller tree. The scent is strong and fruity and often hangs in the air.
7.5m/25ft in 20 years; ultimately 18m/60ft or more. Z6

Juniperus
The junipers have feathery evergreen foliage that is pungently resinous. The majority of interesting varieties are too small for inclusion here and are listed under 'Shrubs'.
Sun or light shade. All but waterlogged soils.

Laburnum
Among the most elegant garden trees, the laburnums produce their long, pendant racemes of golden yellow flowers in early summer. The scent from the flowers is sweet but, as with many scented members of the pea family, also rather heavy and claustrophobic.
Sun or light shade. Any soil.
L. alpinum **'Pendulum'** makes an interesting lawn specimen. It is a particularly fine form of the Scotch laburnum, with a pronounced weeping habit. It is small, slim and slow-growing (unless grafted) and a much more sensible choice for suburban gardens than a giant weeping willow. The racemes are well over 30cm/1ft long and the trifoliate leaves are a shining deep green.
3m/10ft; 6m/20ft, if grafted. Z5
L. × *watereri* **'Vossii'**, is the form most people choose for its immensely long racemes of flowers. It is spectacular when trained over a pergola. As a free-standing tree, it has a more conventional, rounded shape; though unremarkable when out of flower, it is by no means unattractive.
7.5m/25ft in 20 years. Z6

Magnolia
The majority of scented magnolias are treated in the chapter on 'Shrubs' and, in the case of *M. grandiflora*, under 'Wall Shrubs'. Two species are included here: one which is powerfully fragrant and another with striking foliage.
M. denudata, the yulan or lily tree, forms a large shrub or small tree of rounded shape

Laburnum × *watereri* 'Vossii', *Wisteria sinensis* and *Allium aflatunense*

and bears large, pure white, fleshy-petalled, lemon-scented blooms from early spring. Like all the spring-flowering magnolias, it is best planted where its frosted buds will not be caught by the early morning sun; an open or lightly shaded position facing west or southwest is ideal. It is one of the glories of the spring garden.
Neutral or lime-free soil. Usually up to 9m/30ft. Z6

M. hypoleuca produces huge, creamy, saucer-shaped flowers in early summer; these have a prominent central knob of crimson stamens and a strong fruity scent, in which the principal flavour is ripe melon. Scarlet fruits follow in autumn. It is

deciduous with very long and leathery leaves that are a beautiful shade of glaucous green. It is hardy and fast-growing, upright in habit, and makes a glorious feature for the woodland garden. The fragrance carries far.
Sun. Rich, moist, acid or neutral soil. 9m/30ft in 20 years; ultimately, 15m/50ft or more. Z5

M. kobus is a hardy deciduous Japanese magnolia, which forms a single or multi-stemmed medium-sized tree. It is notoriously slow to flower, but the loose white blooms are fragrant. They appear in spring, before the small dark leaves, and on a mature plant the display is spectacular.
Sun (avoid shade). 9m/30ft or more. Z5

M. × *loebneri* **'Merrill'** always impresses me

with its scent when I come across it in other people's gardens. It bears a mass of spidery white flowers in early spring. 'Leonard Messel' is a pink version. They are superb shrubs.
Sun. Fairly lime tolerant. 8m/25ft. Z5

M. salicifolia is a small tree distinguished by its willowy leaves. The scent comes not just from its white flowers, which are carried in spring, but from its leaves and bark, which release a sharp, spicy lemon and aniseed fragrance when bruised. It is a beautiful plant, and has a small, larger-flowered, broader-leaved clone called 'Jermyns'.
Sun or light shade. Neutral or lime-free soil. 6m/20ft or more. Z6

Magnolia × *loebneri* 'Merrill'

A hybrid crab apple

Pinus nigra

Malus

Crab apples often have scented flowers and make very characterful trees, ideally suited to a cottage garden setting. Those with bicoloured blossom – white flowers from deep pink buds – are among the most beautiful of spring-flowering trees. They are deciduous and the leaves are fragrant when crushed. Many, however, are susceptible to the same diseases as apple trees.
Sun or light shade. Most well-drained soils.
M. coronaria **'Charlottae'** has large, semi-double, shell-pink flowers with an unusually strong violet scent; they open in early summer. It makes a wide-spreading tree and the oval leaves often take on pleasing colours in autumn.
7.5m/25ft in 20 years; ultimately 9m/28ft. Z4
M. **'Golden Hornet'** is a popular variety grown mainly for its golden fruits which last well through the winter. But its white flowers, from pink buds, are also eyecatching and noticeably fragrant. It makes a stiff, upright tree. The red-fruited 'John Downie' also has scented white flowers.
7.5m/25ft in 20 years; ultimately 9m/28ft.
M. hupehensis also makes an upright tree and is second only to the Japanese crab, *M. floribunda*, in floral beauty. A cloud of white

flowers appear in spring from pink buds. In scent it is superior to the Japanese crab. 7.5m/25ft in 20 years; ultimately 9m/28ft or more. Z4

Nothofagus

N. antarctica. One of the hardiest of the southern beeches, this is a fast-growing deciduous tree from Chile, whose small, rounded leaves are powerfully scented, especially in the spring. The fragrance is resinous, rather like pumpkin pie. The leaves turn yellow in the autumn. The flowers, borne in late spring, are also aromatic. It makes an attractive tree of open, usually spreading habit. It needs protection from wind.
Sun. Acid, well-drained soil. 10.7m/35ft in 20 years; ultimately 15.2m/50ft. Z8

Paulownia

P. fargesii is less common than *P. tomentosa* (below). It has large rounded leaves and tall, erect panicles of tubular flowers in early summer, which are pale lilac, stained with yellow, and scented of fruit and honey. It is a spreading, deciduous tree, ideal as a lawn specimen, though it needs a sheltered position.

Sun. Well-drained soil, not chalk. 12m/40ft in 20 years; ultimately 18m/60ft. Z7–8
P. tomentosa, the empress or foxglove tree, has darker flowers and lobed leaves; otherwise, it is similar to *P. fargesii*. It is an exotic feature wherever it is planted and is often grown simply for its tropical sized leaves; several plants are grown in a group and cut back to within 5cm/2in of the old wood in spring. But this routine is of no interest to the scent-loving gardener! The tree is hardy, except when very young, but, unfortunately, the flowers are often caught by late frosts; so an annual fragrant feast of fruit and honey cannot be guaranteed.
Sun. Well-drained, slightly acidic soil. 12m/40ft in 20 years; ultimately 15m/50ft. Z6

Picea

The spruces are similar to the firs in appearance, immediately distinguishable by the layman only when bearing cones: the cones of firs stand erect, those of spruces are pendant. They are evergreen and their foliage has the typical resinous scent associated with conifers. They are not suitable for shallow or alkaline soils, or hot, dry climates.
Sun. Moist, deep soil.

Pinus

The pines have resinous-scented foliage and cones, and provide a further range of valuable garden evergreens. They are distinguished by their long, needle-like leaves which are borne in bundles of between 2 and 5. Of the large, less ornamental species, the beach pine, *P. contorta*, and the maritime pine, *P. pinaster*, are useful on sandy soil, the latter for fixing sand dunes; the Austrian pine, *P. nigra*, is one of the best windbreaks, even on chalk and at high altitudes, as is, in maritime areas on acidic soil, the rapid-growing Monterey pine, *P. radiata*.

Many pines are tolerant of alkaline soil. Full sun. Well-drained soil.

P. ayacahuite, Mexican white pine, is a dreamy tree, of spreading habit, for warmer gardens. The leaves are long and glaucous green, and the cones pendulous and resinous.

9m/30ft in 20 years; ultimately 30m/100ft. Z7

P. bungeana, lace-bark pine, has one of the most beautiful barks of any tree, a peeling patchwork of colours like a python's skin; however, this only becomes evident after many years of growth. It makes a compact, upright, oval tree. Its scarcity in nurseries and slow growth have combined to keep it an uncommon tree.

7m/25ft in 20 years; ultimately 12m/40ft or more. Z5

Populus

Few trees are as powerfully fragrant as the balsam poplars. In spring, and occasionally later, the air is filled with an extremely sweet, balsam scent, for the buds are sticky with fragrant resin. The scent, mouthwatering in moderation, is cloying in quantity, so a position on the garden's boundary should be sought.

Sun or shade. Any soil.

P. balsamifera, balsam poplar, makes a very tall, suckering tree in its native North America but does not perform as satisfactorily in Europe as *P. trichocarpa*. The oval leaves are green above and whitish below.

15m/50ft in 20 years; ultimately 30m/100ft. Z2

Populus balsamifera

P. 'Balsam Spire' (Tacatricho 32) This hybrid is an excellent, fast-growing balsam poplar with a narrow habit and a superb scent. It is not as prone to canker as its parents.
18m/60ft or more in 20 years; ultimately 60m/200ft.
P. × *candicans* **'Aurora'** is a form of balm of Gilead poplar whose young leaves are splashed with white and pink. It is immensely popular but in my view its freakish colouring makes it one of the most hideous of all trees.
15m/50ft in 20 years; ultimately 30m/ 100ft. Z2
P. trichocarpa, black cottonwood. One of the finest of the balsam poplars, this makes a fast-growing, pyramidal tree. In scent, it is every bit as potent as *P. balsamifera* and it, or 'Balsam Spire', is an essential ingredient for the larger scented garden.
18m/60ft or more in 20 years; ultimately 60m/200ft. Z5

Prunus

You can detect a honey or almond scent in the flowers of many members of this group, but it is usually extremely faint. I record here only the most potent varieties, though even they are always restrained in their outpourings. They are all flowering cherries and are small enough trees for most gardens. A dark evergreen backdrop shows off the white blossom perfectly, as does a clear blue sky.

Prunus 'Jo-nioi'

Sun or light shade. All but waterlogged or very dry soils.

P. conradinae **'Semiplena'** is difficult to find in nurseries and it is rather vulnerable to late frost and bud-stripping by birds. (A west-facing position, where there is much human traffic, may help solve these last problems.) I include it because it really is the loveliest early wild cherry; the white blossom is borne over a long period, usually beginning in winter, and there is a good almond scent. It makes an elegant, spreading tree. 7.5m/25ft in 20 years; ultimately 11m/35ft. Z6

P. padus, bird cherry, is a European native with striking flowers. The white, almond-scented blossom is borne on long, slender, drooping racemes rather than in a foaming mass. The bark has an acrid smell. The species itself is pretty in the wild garden or in woodland, but for gardens I would choose its clone 'Watereri', which has longer racemes. It makes an open, spreading tree. 9m/30ft in 20 years; ultimately 15m/50ft. Z4

P. × yedoensis, Yoshino cherry, is a beautiful, spreading cherry which produces its clusters of white, almond-scented blossom in early spring, just before its young green leaves expand.
9m/30ft in 20 years; ultimately 12m/40ft. Z6

Japanese flowering cherries. A number of these popular ornamental cherries are delicately almond-scented. Among the most fragrant are 'Amanogawa', a slim, columnar variety with semi-double, pink blossom in spring, 7.5m/25ft; and 'Mount Fuji' ('Shirotae'), a spreading tree with large, semi-double, white flowers in early spring, 7.5m/25ft. But the prize for fragrance goes to 'Jo-nioi', a lovely cherry of spreading habit; it bears its single white flowers in spring, 11m/35ft. Z6

Pseudotsuga
P. menziesii, Oregon Douglas fir, is a fast-growing timber tree and too large for most gardens but it is powerfully and fruitily resinous. It is broadly conical in shape and has attractive corky, deeply fissured bark. It is unsatisfactory on alkaline soils.
Sun. Moist, well-drained soil. Ultimately up to 30m/100ft; 90m/300ft in the US. Z4–6

Prunus padus

Ptelea trifoliata

Ptelea
P. trifoliata, the hop tree, is an unusual and highly desirable ingredient for the scented garden. Its clusters of small, greenish flowers, borne in summer, have a powerfully sweet, honeysuckle scent. According to one authority, they are probably the most fragrant flowers of any hardy tree. The light green leaflets are also covered in oil glands and release a pungent scent, vaguely reminiscent of hops, when bruised. Winged green fruits follow the flowers, and there is good yellow autumn colour from the foliage. It is fast-growing and makes a low, spreading, rounded tree or large shrub.
Sun or shade. Any soil. Ultimately 6m/20ft. Z5

Pterostyrax
P. hispida, epaulette tree, is an unusual deciduous tree or large shrub that deserves to be grown more often. It has oval, toothed leaves, whitish underneath, and panicles of white, sweetly scented flowers in late spring or early summer; these are followed by spindle-shaped fruits. It is fast-growing and hardy.
Sun and heat. All but shallow and chalky soils. 4.5–9m/15–30ft. Z6

Robinia
R. pseudoacacia, false acacia or black locust, has some of the freshest green, most handsome foliage of any garden tree and I wish people would plant it instead of its golden form, 'Frisia'. A delicate, sweet, pea scent comes from the wisteria-like racemes of white flowers, borne in early summer. This deciduous tree can be difficult to establish, but once growing it is vigorous. A sheltered position should be sought as it is vulnerable to wind damage.
Sun or light shade. Most soils. 12m/40ft in 20 years; ultimately 24m/80ft. Z3

Stewartia sinensis

Tilia × euchlora

Salix

S. pentandra, bay willow, has broad, glossy leaves like a bay laurel; these are sweetly aromatic when bruised and in spring the scent hangs in the air. It is the last willow to produce its catkins; they appear in early summer, the male catkins being bright yellow. It is an attractive and useful tree, slow-growing for a willow.
Sun. All but dry soils. 13.5m/45ft in 20 years; ultimately 18m/60ft.

Stewartia

S. sinensis is the most scented member of a valuable group of trees and shrubs for acid, woodland conditions. The sweetly fragrant, white, cup-shaped flowers are borne singly among the oval, bright green leaves in late summer. It also has fiery autumn colours. Above all, it has spectacular bark, which changes from smooth orange-brown in the summer to purple in the autumn, and then peels in strips during the winter. It makes a pyramidal tree that does best in a sheltered position.
Sun. Deep, moist, peaty soil. 9m/30ft in 20 years; ultimately 15m/50ft. Z6

Styrax

S. japonica, Japanese snowbell, is among the most elegant flowering trees for small gardens. Its white, slightly scented flowers hang on long stalks along the slender branches in early summer; with the bright green, oval leaves the effect is crisp and refined. It is deciduous and makes a spreading tree. Being vulnerable to late frosts, it prefers a site protected from the morning sun.
Light shade. Light, moist, loamy, neutral or acid soil. 6m/20ft in 20 years; ultimately 7.5m/25ft.
S. obassia is a more fragrant but much less common species that makes a narrow, erect tree, with larger leaves; its white flowers are borne in drooping racemes. It is no less beautiful and desirable than *S. japonica*. It enjoys the same conditions.
9m/30ft in 20 years; ultimately 11m/35ft. Z5

Thuja

T. koraiensis, Korean arborvitae, is variable in the wild, and can be seen in gardens either as a shrub or a small tree. It is identified by the silvery undersides to its leaves and its scent, which some compare to that of a rich fruit cake.
To 7.5m/25ft. Z5
T. plicata, western red cedar, is a superb evergreen tree for the largest gardens; it also makes a fine, feathery hedge. The dark green leaves have a deliciously fruity, pear-drop scent when crushed, which makes hedge-pruning a delight. Specimen trees are pyramidal in shape and their rusty orange-brown bark is spectacular.
Sun or shade. All but dry soils. 14m/45ft in 20 years; ultimately 30m/100ft or more. Z5
T. standishii, Japanese arborvitae, is uncommon but notable for having foliage sharply scented of lemon. It makes a spreading, conical tree with yellowish green leaves and deep red-brown bark.
5.5m/18ft in 20 years; ultimately 18m/60ft or more. Z6

Tilia

The limes have extremely powerfully scented flowers, and they would be planted more often if they did not drip honeydew (the result of aphid infestation) and their pollen did not contain a narcotic element that stupefies bees. Paths become sticky, plants become spotted with black mould and bees become a serious hazard. But the sugary sweet fruity scent in the air is delicious. Limes are deciduous.
Sun or light shade. Any soil.
T. cordata, small-leaved lime, has clusters of very scented, yellowish flowers in high summer. It makes a neat, pyramidal tree.
9m/30ft in 20 years; ultimately 30m/100ft. Z4
T. × euchlora, Crimean lime, is one of the best of the limes for scent and it does not drip honeydew; bees remain a problem, however. It has attractive glossy green, heart-shaped leaves and makes a pleasing, rounded, rather pendulous specimen.
6m/20ft in 20 years; ultimately 15m/50ft or more. Z6
T. 'Petiolaris', weeping silver lime, is a popular and attractive weeping tree. It has white-felted undersides to its leaves and very scented flowers, but honeydew and bees pose problems.
11m/35ft in 20 years; ultimately 24m/80ft. Z6

Shrubs

Aesculus

A. parviflora, bottlebrush buckeye, is a shrubby relative of the horse chestnut. It has typical fingered leaves and erect panicles of creamy white flowers. The scent is heavy and sweet, sometimes a little sickly, and can fill the air. It is particularly useful in woodland borders where, with hydrangeas, it ensures interest through late summer.
Sun or light shade. 2.5–4.5m/8–15ft. Z5

Berberis

Many of the barberries surprise you with a honey scent. They make dense neat shrubs and some can be marshalled into service as fragrant evergreen hedges. The flowers are borne in spring and the scent hangs in the air on warm days.
Sun or shade.
B. candidula is a low arching shrub, suitable for the front of the border or the rock garden. Its small, shiny evergreen leaves have white undersides and are protected by thorns. The bright yellow flowers are solitary and dangle on short stems.
1–1.2m/3–4ft. Z6
B. julianae, one of the hardiest of the evergreen barberries, makes an erect shrub with long slender leaves. The protective needles are conspicuous and extremely sharp. The flowers, which are pale yellow, are spaced in tight clusters along the branches. *B. sargentiana* is similar to *B. julianae* but slightly smaller and with reddish young shoots.
3m/10ft. Z6
B. verruculosa is closely related to *B. candidula* but is larger (2m/6ft) and has glaucous rather than white undersides to its leaves. It blooms in mid-spring and its golden yellow flowers are honey-scented.
Z5

Buddleja

Buddlejas provide the summer garden with some delicious honey scents. But the fragrance is not freely released into the air and you will want to position them where your nose can reach. They are deciduous.
Sun.

Buddleja alternifolia and *Allium schoenoprasum*

B. alternifolia is a graceful shrub whose narrow, grey-green leaves and arching growth look decidedly willow-like. But in early summer the pendant branches turn into colourful streamers, so thickly studded are they with clusters of lilac flowers. It can be trained as a weeping tree or against a warm wall as a fan. It needs little pruning. There is a smaller form with silver leaves called 'Argentea'.
3–4.5m/10–15ft. Z6

Buddleja globosa

Buxus sempervirens

B. davidii is the familiar butterfly bush of late summer. It grows vigorously and flowers on the current year's wood, so it should be hard pruned every spring. In the border it can be underplanted with daffodils and tulips, whose dying growth it will quickly conceal as it expands. 'Black Knight' is dark purple; 'Empire Blue' is violet-blue; 'Ile de France' is pure violet; and 'Royal Red' is reddish purple. 'Harlequin' has reddish purple flowers and white-edged leaves. The nanhoensis/'Nanho' forms, in blue, purple and white, are only 1.5m/5ft high. 3m/10ft. Z6

B. fallowiana **'Alba'** is the buddleja to choose if you want white flowers. They are set off to perfection by grey leaves and white stems. In appearance it resembles *B. davidii* but, unfortunately, it is not as hardy. It is only worth risking in the open if a sheltered sunny situation can be found. Otherwise, it can be treated as a wall shrub. It grows to 2.5m/8ft. 'Lochinch', a *fallowiana* hybrid, is my favourite butterfly bush and combines hardiness with delicate colour. It has grey leaves and lilac plumes and is a vision of pastel beauty. 3m/10ft. Z9

B. globosa, the orange ball tree, is a distinctive buddleja with panicles of orange drumsticks in summer. The proportion of flowers to coarse foliage is rather disappointing, and I would not recommend it for the small garden, but the scent is good. It grows relatively slowly and needs little pruning. 3m/10ft. Z8

B. × weyeriana **'Golden Glow'** is a much better golden-yellow buddleja which is a later-flowering version of *B. globosa*. The balls of flower are looser and they are a softer colour. It begins blooming in high summer and goes on until the first frosts. It is a first-rate ingredient for late summer's hot colour schemes. 3m/10ft. Z8

Buxus sempervirens

Common box is a mainstay of formal gardens. Being evergreen and growing in a dense compact manner, it is a good structural ingredient and lends itself well to hedge, topiary, knot garden and edging work. It can also be left to form a natural shape as part of the shrub border. It thrives in any aspect, but is slow-growing. The scent of the leaves is pleasantly pungent to my nose but others find it reminiscent of cats. Queen Anne is said to have removed the box parterres at Hampton Court because she disliked the smell so much. The inconspicuous flowers that appear in spring are honey-scented.

There are many cultivars with different attractions. 'Handsworthensis' makes the best large specimen or hedging plant. 'Suffruticosa' is a dwarf box and the best for box-edging. And 'Elegantissima' is a fine cream-variegated box.
Sun or shade. Tolerates poor soil, grows faster in fertile ground.
1.2–2m/4–6ft. Z6

Calycanthus

C. floridus is the most desirable of the American allspices. It is a deciduous shrub, unremarkable in appearance but distinctively scented in all its parts. The oval leaves, which are rough and dark on top and pale and downy underneath, smell of camphor when rubbed, as do the roots and the wood. The tiny crimson flowers, resembling miniature waterlilies, smell deliciously of fruit cocktail and are produced in summer.
Sun or light shade. 2.5m/8ft. Z5

Camphorosma

C. monspeliaca is a small evergreen shrub that looks like a grey heather with slender, woolly leaves and inconspicuous flowers. The scent, which is of camphor, is released by the young shoots when they are rubbed. It is a plant for the hot, dry border, and for coastal gardens.
Sun. 60cm/2ft. Z8

Caryopteris

C. × clandonensis is a collective name for a group of hybrid caryopteris raised in Surrey, England. They are ideal for the late-summer border, providing a range of violet-blue flowers to set beside the yellows of that season. A turpentine scent comes from the grey leaves when they are rubbed. 'Arthur Simmonds', the original clone, is pale violet-blue. 'Heavenly Blue' is similar but more compact. 'Ferndown' and 'Kew Blue' are richer in colour. Cut back each spring.
Sun. 1m/3ft. Z8

Chionanthus

C. virginicus, fringe tree, is a deciduous shrub or small tree from the eastern United States. It has narrow, oval leaves and panicles of pure white wispy flowers in summer; these are quite fragrant. It is a curious and entertaining shrub that deserves to be planted more often.
Sun. Moist, loamy soil. 3–9m/10–30ft. Z4

Cistus

No scent evokes the Mediterranean more surely than the aroma of rock roses. It is a resinous fragrance, called ladanum, that clings to the young shoots and leaves, and which, on hot days, fills the air. The best cistus glisten with sticky gum and if they produced no flowers at all I would still grow them. As it is, their flowers are sumptuous, great white and pink saucers, often stained with yellow and blotched with crimson or chocolate. Individual flowers last no more than a day but they are borne in profusion in summer. Cistus are not the hardiest of shrubs, but they grow easily and quickly from cuttings. They are evergreen and need shelter from wind.
Full sun. Well-drained soil.
C. × aguilari and its dramatically blotched form 'Maculatus' produce huge white flowers on upright plants. They are probably the most visually impressive rock roses, but they are invariably killed in a severe winter.
1.2m/4ft. Z8
C. × cyprius is one of the hardier rock roses and will fill out into a sizeable shrub. It is extremely beautiful. Its white flowers have crimson blotches and its green leaves take on a pleasing leaden blue caste in winter.
1.2m/4ft or more. Z8
C. ladanifer is especially well coated in resin, and is known as the gum cistus. The rich green foliage is a fine backdrop for the blotched white flowers, which are slightly crisper in colour than in *C. × cyprius*.
1.2m/4ft or more. Z8
C. laurifolius is reliably hardy and produces white flowers all summer. A good standby.
1.2m/4ft or more. Z8
C. palhinhae is a small compact shrub with exceptionally large pure white flowers that look stunning against the glistening dark foliage. But it is not very hardy.
60cm/2ft. Z8

Calycanthus floridus

Cistus × aguilari

Cistus × purpureus 'Alan Fradd'

Cistus 'Peggy Sammons'

Clerodendrum bungei

C. **'Peggy Sammons'** is a bushy evergreen shrub with pink flowers and grey-green foliage.
1m/3ft. Z7–9
C. × purpureus is an excellent plant for bringing colour into the Mediterranean border. It is a hybrid of two very gummy species and does not disappoint in its scent. 'Alan Fradd' is a white-flowered version.
1.2m/4ft or more. Z8
C. **'Silver Pink'** is a popular hardy hybrid with lilac-pink flowers and greyish foliage.
60cm/2ft. Z7

Clerodendrum

C. bungei sends up an embarrassing quantity of attractive purple stems and needs to be sited with care. The large heart-shaped leaves have a fetid odour and should be avoided. But the domes of sugary pink flowers are wonderfully sweet; they appear from rosy buds and make a valuable splash of clear soft colour for late summer. It appreciates shelter from wind.
Sun. 1–2m/3–6ft. Z7
C. trichotomum is a deciduous species that makes a proper shrub or small tree, rather sparse in habit and clothed in soft ovate leaves. The foliage has a fetid odour when bruised. The white flowers smell like jasmine and are carried in loose heads in late summer; they have prominent crimson calyces and the bicoloured effect is pleasing. Later, turquoise blue (ultimately black) fruits appear which are startling against the persistent crimson calyces. Its drawback is that it is susceptible to cold winds and is very slow-growing; but it is a splendid late performer for the shrub border or woodland garden. The variety *fargesii* is hardier and more vigorous.
Light shade. 3.5m/12ft or more. Z6

Clethra

C. alnifolia, the sweet pepper bush, is an interesting deciduous shrub for the woodland or bog garden. The sweet, viburnum-like scent comes from the slender spikes of fluffy white flowers that open in high summer. It forms an erect suckering plant and is clothed in toothed leaves. It is useful for its late flowering and its tolerance of wet soil. 'Paniculata' is a superior form.
Sun or shade. Acid soil. 2.5m/8ft. Z4

Colletia

C. armata is a strange leafless, and, to all intents and purposes, evergreen, tangle of thorns for the hot, dry border. It looks rather like a gorse bush but the flowers are waxy and white. It billows with blossom all through the autumn and the scent is of almonds. But be careful when you are sniffing it.
Sun. 1.2–2.5m/4–8ft. Z8
C. paradoxa (*C. cruciata*) is even more extraordinary than *C. armata*. The grey-green spines are broad, flat and triangular and give the plant a unique appearance. The tiny flowers are creamy white and sweetly scented but unfortunately are not produced very freely outdoors.
Sun. 1.2–2.5m/4–8ft. Z8

Comptonia

C. peregrina, the sweet fern, is a distinctive, small deciduous shrub for the woodland and bog garden. It has suckering growth and produces downy, fern-like leaves and, in spring, brown catkins. A spicy fragrance rises from the foliage on hot days, and can be captured if the leaves are dried.
Sun. 60cm–1.2m/2–4ft. Z2

Cornus

C. mas, the cornelian cherry dogwood, emits a penetrating spicy fragrance that can fill a garden in late winter. The problem is that it is a very big shrub or small tree that looks dull for most of the year. The tufts of yellow flowers appear on bare stems and the effect is rather like that of a witch hazel.
Sun or light shade. 6–12m/20–40ft. Z5

Corylopsis

This group of shrubs has a delicate beauty that would probably pass unnoticed if they flowered in summer. But because they bloom in early spring, and look so well with that season's blue-flowered bulbs and perennials, they are worth a place in gardens. They produce short dangling racemes of pale yellow flowers on their bare, spreading branches, and these are delicately scented of cowslips.
Light or medium shade. Acid soil.
C. calvescens veitchiana (*C. veitchiana*) has flowers with striking reddish anthers.
2m/6ft. Z7

C. pauciflora makes a low shrub and probably has the best flowers.
1.2–2m/4–6ft. Z6
C. sinensis sinensis (*C. willmottiae*) is even taller and makes a fine specimen. Its young leaves are tinged with purple, and there is a form with purple stems called 'Spring Purple'.
Up to 3.5m/12ft. Z6
C. spicata is larger, and is the species most commonly seen.
2m/6ft or more. Z6

Cytisus

C. × praecox **'Warminster'**, the Warminster broom, is the most powerfully scented of the large hardy brooms. It has a heavy, suffocating odour, which many find disagreeable but which, to me, is very much a part of the late spring garden. Its cream pea-flowers are borne in such profusion that the spectacle will take your breath away if the scent does not. There is a good deep yellow form of *C. × praecox* called 'Allgold', and a white form called 'Albus'. They are deciduous shrubs, fast-growing but short-lived.
Sun. Acid or neutral soil. 1.2m/4ft. Z6

Corylopsis pauciflora

Cytisus × praecox 'Warminster'

Daphne bholua

Daphne odora 'Aureomarginata'

Daphne × *burkwoodii* 'Somerset'

Daphne pontica

Daphne

The daphnes give the garden some of its most sophisticated perfume. It is a gloriously sweet scent, often shaded with clove. They have a reputation for being difficult to grow and unpredictable, but this should not put you off.

Light shade. Well-drained (but not dry) acid or neutral soil.

D. bholua is a variable shrub, which can be deciduous or evergreen and can produce flowers in any shade from purplish pink to blush white. 'Gurkha' is a fine deciduous selection with purple-stained white flowers, and 'Jacqueline Postill' is a splendid evergreen. Since this daphne blooms through the winter, the evergreen and deciduous forms produce quite different effects.
2.5m/8ft or more. Z8

D. × *burkwoodii* '**Somerset**' is one of the easiest and most beautiful daphnes with a delicious clove scent. Its clusters of pink starry flowers are produced in spring, and have an excellent backdrop in its small bluish-green young leaves. It makes an upright, semi-evergreen shrub. There are gold and silver variegated forms.
1.2m/4ft. Z6

D. laureola, spurge laurel, is a useful small evergreen with tiny yellow flowers that are buried in the shiny foliage and make no visual impact. They open in late winter and early spring and play tricks with their perfume; sometimes they fill the cool evening air with fragrance, but more often than not they are scentless.
Shade. Moist, fertile soil. 1m/3ft.
The variety *philippi* is 30cm/1ft smaller. Z7

D. mezereum, mezereon, is a familiar daphne in gardens and seems tolerant of alkalinity. In late winter its naked vertical stems are studded with reddish purple stars. 'Alba' is a good white form; 'Bowles' White' is even better.
1–1.2m/3–4ft. Z5

D. odora '**Aureomarginata**' is a hardy form of *D. odora*, and has golden-edged evergreen leaves. It is one of the more popular and reliable daphnes. It makes a neat bush but is not spectacular in flower, for the tight clusters of pinky purple stars are sparsely borne. They appear in late spring.
Any well-drained soil. 1.2m/4ft. Z7

Deutzia × *elegantissima* 'Fasciculata'

D. pontica flowers a month or so later than *D. laureola* and has narrower leaves, but is otherwise similar.
1–1.5m/3–5ft. Z7

Deutzia

The deutzias are a colourful group of deciduous shrubs that flower in early summer. They are dreary after flowering, but a plant in bloom is a fine sight. They are attractive either in the border, with shrub roses and hardy geraniums, or in the less formal parts of the garden.
Sun or light shade. Moist, fertile soil.

D. compacta has billowing heads of small white stars that emerge from pink buds in high summer. The scent is of almonds.
1.5m/5ft. Z6

D. × *elegantissima* bears its panicles of sweet, rose-pink flowers in early summer. There is a form in deeper pink called 'Rosealind' and one in pale pink called 'Fasciculata'.
1.5m/5ft. Z6

Dipelta

D. floribunda is a deciduous shrub that resembles weigela in its foliage and funnel-shaped flowers, though it is more upright in growth. The sweet-scented flowers are white,

Dipelta floribunda

Erica arborea alpina

tinged with pale pink and yellow, and are carried in generous heads during spring. It thrives in woodland conditions.
Light shade. 3–4.5m/10–15ft. Z6

Elaeagnus

E. angustifolia caspica is a superior form of the oleaster or Russian olive. In fact, it is arguably the best silver-leaved shrub in cultivation. The slender leaves are a sparkling silver and the plant develops an extremely graceful shape. The scent, which is piercingly sweet, comes from the minute yellowish flowers which hide under the foliage in early summer. As the centrepiece of a grey border or as a bright contrast to a purple-leaved shrub, it has no equal.
Sun. 4.5m/15ft. Z4

E. commutata (syn. *E. argentea*) is more commonly offered, is very similar and is hardly less desirable.
3m/10ft. Z2

E. × ebbingei makes a much coarser plant, but is useful for being evergreen and fast-growing; it can also be used for hedging. It is tolerant of shade, though there is a freer production of flowers in the sun. On warm evenings in autumn, the fruity sweetness from the tiny, concealed, white funnels will fill the air. The leathery green leaves have metallic silver undersides, and are an extraordinary sandy grey when young. Its parent, *E. macrophylla* (Z8), is a more elegant shrub and deliciously fragrant, but it is less vigorous and less easy to find. The yellow variegated forms of *E. × ebbingei*, 'Gilt Edge' and 'Limelight', are outstanding.
3m/10ft. Z7

E. pungens is another quick evergreen. It is less stiff in growth than *E. × ebbingei* and its leaves are smaller, with wavy margins and duller undersides. The sweet-scented flowers are also white and produced in autumn. The species itself is seldom grown, for its variegated forms – including the best-selling 'Maculata' – always steal the show.
Sun or shade. 3.5m/12ft. Z7

Elsholtzia

E. stauntonii looks spectacular in autumn, when it opens its mauve-pink bottlebrushes. It is not grown much but makes an interesting latecomer for the wild garden, where its unrefined appearance is not out of

Elaeagnus × ebbingei

Eucryphia lucida

place. The leaves release a minty scent when crushed. It is usually killed to ground level each winter, but it should in any case be cut hard back in spring to the lowest pair of buds on each stem.
Full sun. Good soil. 1–1.5m/3–5ft. Z5

Erica
E. arborea, the tree heath, brings stature to the heather garden and a welcome contrast in shape to Mediterranean schemes of cistus and lavender; it balances a specimen of rosemary rather well. In spring it is a mass of white flowers whose honey fragrance carries far. It is fairly hardy. There is a shorter, hardier variety called *alpina* (Z7).
Sun. Acid soil. 2m/6ft in cold areas, over 6m/20ft in mild areas. Z9
E. erigena (syn. *E. mediterranea*) is another excellent spring-flowering heather. Its flowers are rosy red and scented of honey. It is tolerant of lime.
Sun. 2–3m/6–10ft.

There is a lovely pink-flowered form called 'Superba'. And there are many dwarf, compact varieties for the rock garden, among which rose-coloured 'Brightness' and white 'W. T. Rackliff' are exceptional.

60cm–1.2m/2–4ft. Z8
E. × veitchii '**Exeter**' is a superb, vigorous heather for gardens in milder areas. In spring it produces huge plumes of white flowers with a delicious honey scent.
Sun. Acid soil. 2–3m/6–10ft. Z9

Escallonia
This is a useful group of shrubs that carry heads of white, pink or red blossom at intervals throughout the summer. They are evergreen and have glossy leaves and young shoots that are sticky to the touch and sweetly, if not altogether pleasantly, resinous. They are susceptible to cold and in inland gardens must be given sheltered locations. But they are tolerant of salt-laden wind and are familiar coastal hedging plants.
Sun or light shade. 3m/10ft. Z8

The pungent aroma of *E. illinita* has been compared to that of a pigsty.

'C. F. Ball' is an impressive escallonia bearing masses of large crimson-red flowers all summer. It is vigorous, forms a slightly arching shrub, and is well endowed with fragrance. 'Donard Beauty' has rather large leaves and quantities of rose-red flowers. 'Donard Gem' not only has aromatic foliage

but scented flowers as well. They are pale pink and delicately sweet. It is a graceful small-leaved shrub. 'Ingramii' is a good deep rose-pink with large leaves.
Sun or light shade. 3m/10ft.
E. rosea is not reliably hardy inland without wall protection, but is interesting for its white, sweetly scented flowers.
E. rubra macrantha (syn. *E. macrantha*) has still not been superseded as a hedging plant. It has rosy-red flowers and attractive, fragrant foliage.
Z9
E. rubra glutinosa is a low-growing shrub, with red flowers and the stickiest, most aromatic foliage of all.

Eucryphia
The eucryphias are among the most exciting large shrubs or small trees for the late summer garden. They are popular with owners of rhododendron woodland, who are looking for shrubs to extend the season. The large, single, pure white flowers, which have a shimmering boss of stamens, breathe a honey scent. But plants may take a number of years before starting to bloom. They are columnar or pyramidal in shape and need a position sheltered from the wind. They are not suitable for very cold gardens.
Light shade. Cool, moist, acid soil.
E. glutinosa is the hardiest species, but although it is visually spectacular, its scent is less strong than in other eucryphias. It is deciduous and takes on fiery tints in the autumn. It flowers in high summer.
6m/20ft or more. Z8
E. × intermedia '**Rostrevor**' is a vigorous, fairly hardy hybrid that blooms in late summer. Its yellow-centred flowers are smaller than in *E. glutinosa* but a shrub smothered in bloom is a glorious sight and has a fine scent. It is evergreen.
6m/20ft or more. Z9
E. lucida is trustworthy only in milder regions but is one of the prettiest evergreen eucryphias. Its white flowers are pendulous and are especially heavily scented.
Ultimately 12m/40ft. Z9
E. × nymansensis '**Nymansay**' is the most popular eucryphia in England and would always be my first choice. Fast-growing, fairly hardy and evergreen, it has an advantage over 'Rostrevor' in its tolerance of limy soil.

The white flowers and honey scent are superb and are enjoyed in high summer. Ultimately 12m/40ft. Z8

Fothergilla

The fothergillas are deciduous shrubs that help awaken the woodland garden in spring. They produce little cream bottlebrushes as their leaves are expanding. These give off a sweet scent flavoured with hops. Their oval leaves are unremarkable until the autumn when they assume a variety of magnificent, rich colours.

Light shade. Acid soil.

F. gardenii is a dwarf spring-flowering fothergilla for the front of the shady border. 1m/3ft. Z5

F. major, a slow-growing shrub, is the best species and makes a plump erect subject for squeezing between colourful rhododendrons. It has good glossy foliage, which turns yellow in the autumn, and plenty of scented flower spikes in spring. 2–3m/6–10ft.

F.m. **Monticola group** This is generally more spreading than the usual form of the species. In autumn, the foliage becomes a bonfire of scarlet, orange and gold. Z5

Gaultheria

The gaultherias provide a number of evergreen ground-cover plants for the desperate gardener. At best they are quietly interesting, at worst (*G. shallon*), monstrous invaders.

Sun or shade. Peaty, acid soil.

G. forrestii has dark, leathery, oblong leaves and spreads by suckers. Its attraction lies in its fragrant white waxy flowers, which are carried on white-stalked racemes in spring. 30cm–1.5m/3–5ft. Z6

G. procumbens, the wintergreen or partridge berry, is a carpeting plant to grow under rhododendrons and azaleas. It is neat and dwarf, with tiny blush-white lampshades in high summer that are followed by red fruits. It is a little dull for the small garden but particularly useful in large areas of woodland. The aromatic 'wintergreen' scent is evident in all its parts. 15cm/6in. Z3

Genista

G. aetnensis, the Mount Etna broom, develops into a tree-like specimen and makes a fine arching focal point for a summer herbaceous border, a waterfall of clear brassy yellow for a hot colour scheme. The flowers have a sweet scent and this wafts gently. It is fast-growing but, unlike the cytisus brooms, long-lived. It is perfectly hardy.

Sun. All but waterlogged soils. 4.5m/15ft or more. Z8

G. cinerea is a broom that provides a mass of golden yellow flowers at mid-summer, which have the typical fragrance of the pea family. Its specific name refers to the greyish caste of its foliage.

Sun. Well-drained soil. 2–3m/6–10ft. Z7

Hamamelis

The witch hazels produce their sea-anemone flowers on bare twigs in winter, and are perhaps the most interesting shrubs of that season. The flower scent in the yellow varieties is fruitily or spicily sweet, and becomes more pungent and less sweet in the hotter colours. They develop long outstretched branches, and it is sensible to train one of these vertically to establish early height. The leaves are oval and hazel-like and have a yellow, autumnal colouring.

Sun or light shade. Peaty, acid or neutral soil. Ultimately 4.5m/15ft.

H. × *intermedia* varieties provide some lovely red and orange flowers (notably 'Diane' and 'Jelena') but generally lack strong scent. Pale yellow 'Moonlight' is an exception but it is very rare. Z5

H. japonica **'Zuccariniana'** is a splendid late-flowering witch hazel, with small pale lemon-yellow flowers and a powerful scent. It is distinctly erect when young and has good yellow autumn colour. Z6

H. mollis, the Chinese witch hazel, is the commonest and most popular species. It is very beautiful and floriferous, bearing its clusters of large, golden-yellow flowers through winter and early spring. It has a strong scent which it passes on to its clones. 'Brevipetala' is a vigorous, upright form with orange-yellow flowers; 'Coombe Wood' has rich yellow flowers, slightly larger than in the species, and a more spreading habit, but is rare; 'Goldcrest', also rare, has yellow flowers suffused with red. Z6

H. **'Pallida'** is my favourite witch hazel. It makes a spreading shrub with large sulphur-yellow flowers and is wonderfully luminous

Fothergilla major Monticola group

Hamamelis japonica 'Zuccariniana'

Hamamelis 'Pallida'

when silhouetted against sombre evergreens.
Z6

H. vernalis gives us some small-flowered
witch hazels in copper, orange and orange-
yellow. But only one is easy to find. 'Sandra'
has cadmium-yellow flowers which, like
those of its parent, have a particularly
pungent scent. Its foliage is more
entertaining than most, being purple-tinged
in spring and fiery orange and scarlet in
autumn.
Z5

Hebe

Like chrysanthemums and dahlias, the large
hebes have an unmistakable smell, and yet I
would not really classify them as scented
plants. The smell, which will be especially
familiar to owners of coastal gardens where
these evergreen shrubs are much used as
informal hedges, is hard to pinpoint and
describe. But it is warm, green and
wholesome and can also sometimes be found
in the flowers of skimmias. In fact, one or
two large hebes do have scented flowers but
theirs is a different and sweeter fragrance.

H. cupressoides is one of a number of hebes
that look decidedly un-hebelike and in its
grey-green branches, this species resembles a
miniature cypress. The foliage even gives off
the resinous scent of cedar to complete the
mimicry. It is a neat, small evergreen for
combining with heathers and conifers at the
front of the border or in the rock garden. The
heads of tiny pale blue flowers, produced at
high summer, are not very exciting.
Full sun. Fertile, well-drained soil. 60cm–
1.2m/2–4ft. Z8

H. **'Midsummer Beauty'** is a popular hebe
with long racemes of sweetly scented mauve
flowers all summer and autumn. It makes a
mound of long slender evergreen leaves and
is hardy except in the coldest inland gardens.
Full sun. Well-drained soil. 1.2m/4ft. Z8

H. **'Spender's Seedling'**. This hardy hebe
carries racemes of white, sweetly scented
flowers during the summer.
Sun. 1.2m/4ft. Z8

Helichrysum

H. ledifolium (*Ozothamnus ledifolius*) is an
interesting small dense evergreen for the
sheltered sunny border. The young shoots
and the undersides of the small leathery

Hebe cupressoides

leaves have a sticky yellow covering which smells strongly of fruit cake. It is also inflammable and gives the shrub the name of 'kerosene bush' in its native Tasmania. The heads of murky white flowers are powerfully honey-scented at mid-summer.
Sun. Well-drained soil. 1m/3ft. Z9

Illicium

I. anisatum is a fleshy-leaved evergreen whose foliage releases the spicy scent of aniseed when crushed. It is not a plant for cold climates but in a sheltered spot in a mild area, in peaty woodland conditions, it does well. The curious spidery flowers are greenish yellow and are produced in spring. It is slow-growing.
Light shade. 2–6m/6–20ft, depending on locality. Z8
I. floridanum has a fruitier, spicy fragrance and is smaller and more compact. The flowers are maroon-purple and appear in early summer. This American species is even less hardy than its Japanese cousin, but it is most definitely worth trying against a warm

wall in mild areas.
Sun. Acid soil. 2–2.5m/6–8ft. Z9

Juniperus

The junipers have a distinctive, pungently fruity scent. Their value lies in their contribution to the garden's evergreen backbone. Not only are they more versatile and tolerant than other conifers but they also come in all shapes and sizes, and a variety of colours.
Sun or light shade. Acid or alkaline soil.
J. chinensis, the Chinese juniper, has forms with good columnar and conical habits. 'Pyramidalis' is a fine glaucous blue form over 2m/6ft high.
Z4
J. communis, the common juniper, provides a range of evergreens with very different habits: 'Compressa' makes a compact miniature cone for the rock garden or alpine trough; *depressa* and 'Depressa Aurea' make prostrate ground-cover in green or gold respectively; 'Hibernica', the Irish juniper, is the garden designer's favourite, a dense dark

column which gradually attains 3m/10ft or more; and 'Hornibrookii' is an excellent carpeter.
Z3
J. 'Grey Owl' is an excellent semi-prostrate juniper with smoky grey-green spreading branches.
J. horizontalis provides more creeping junipers in various colours.
Z3
J. × media gives those interesting spreading junipers with ascending branches, so useful for growing on awkward corners and concealing weak junctions in the garden's groundplan. 'Pfitzeriana' is the most familiar green form; 'Old Gold' is one of the best yellows.
1m/3ft or more. Z3
J. procumbens 'Nana' is a fine, fresh green, prostrate juniper for covering banks.
J. sabina, the savin, is the most pungently scented of all the junipers. The species itself is an attractive, short spreading shrub, up to 1.2m/4ft high; 'Hicksii' has ascending branches of grey-blue; and 'Tamariscifolia' is

Helichrysum ledifolium

Illicium anisatum

a good prostrate blue-green form. Z3–7
J. scopulorum **'Skyrocket'** is a superb, slim, vertical juniper, like a blue-grey pencil stroke in the landscape. It grows to 3m/10ft. Z6
J. squamata **'Meyeri'** is a popular, semi-erect, blue juniper.
4.5m/15ft or more. Z5

Ledum

L. groenlandicum, the Labrador tea, is a useful dwarf evergreen for damp sites. Its dark oval leaves, rust felted underneath, have the potent scent of rotten fruit. But it is an attractive-looking shrub, and bears clusters of white flowers in late spring.
Sun. Lime-free soil. 60–90cm/2–3ft. Z2

Ligustrum

The heavy, musty-sweet scent of their flowers is not one of the main attractions of the privets. Luckily, when they are grown as hedges, they are prevented from flowering by summer pruning. Those that are given their freedom can always be sited away from paths and from positions where the wind is likely to carry the scent towards you – variegated and golden forms of *L. ovalifolium*, *L. lucidum* and *L. sinense* are highly ornamental as foliage shrubs; green-leaved *L. quihoui* is a valuable late-flowering shrub, with impressive feathery white plumes in autumn.

Lindera

L. benzoin, the spice bush, is remarkable mainly for the powerful spicy scent released when the foliage is crushed. It does have other ornamental qualities – its large, rounded leaves turn yellow in the autumn, and, on female plants, the undistinguished greenish flowers are followed by red fruits in the autumn. It grows best in the woodland underdry.
Sun or shade. Lime-free soil. Up to 3.5m/12ft. Z5

Lomatia

L. myricoides is one of the hardier members of a lovely group of scented Southern Hemisphere evergreens. It makes an airy spreading shrub, sparsely clothed in long narrow leaves, and in mid-summer it bears clusters of cream, jasmine-like flowers which are wonderfully sweetly scented. It needs a

Ledum groenlandicum

sheltered spot, and is not suitable for cold areas. It is very distinctive in habit and a fine contrast to leathery-leaved evergreens, but it is seldom grown or offered.
Sun. Acid soil. 1.8m/6ft or more. Z9
L. tinctoria is a dwarf suckering shrub with pinnate leaves that bears its creamy, heliotrope-scented flowers towards the end of summer. But it likes similar conditions to *L. myricoides* and is almost as hardy.
60cm–1m/2 3ft. Z9

Lonicera

The shrubby honeysuckles are rarely as generous with their scent as the climbers, nor are they so visually spectacular. But many do have fragrant flowers; even that evergreen hedging honeysuckle, *L. nitida* (especially good in the clone 'Fertilis'), and the ground-covering species *L. pileata*, can surprise you with their fruity sweetness. For garden ornament, the most interesting are the winter-flowering sorts, and those with unusual foliage.
L. fragrantissima, *L. standishii* and their hybrid *L. × purpusii* are all very similar and it is hard to decide which is the best. They produce tiny clusters of small cream flowers all through the winter on more or less deciduous stems; bare branches are clearly an advantage in displaying the flowers, and *L. fragrantissima* usually loses out on this score, although it seems to be the most floriferous. They are all ungainly in summer, being inelegant of habit and clothed in large coarse leaves, and only detract from their companions in the border. Nevertheless I always grow one to fill a winter vase indoors and usually choose *L. × purpusii*.
Sun or shade. 2m/6ft.
L. syringantha is the prettiest of the fragrant summer-flowering shrubby honeysuckles. Its blue-green leaves, reddish-purple stems and arching habit make it a lovely foil for pink flowers in the sunny border, and in early summer it bears its own clusters of small lilac funnels; they seldom make much of a show but they have a delicious hyacinth scent. To encourage fine foliage, prune it hard.
Full sun. Up to 2m/6ft. Z5

Lupinus

L. arboreus, the tree lupin, is a much-neglected shrub. Easily raised from seed and fast-growing, it provides a wonderful contrast in form for the summer garden, making a mound of fingered, evergreen leaves and producing its erect racemes of yellow, pea-scented flowers for a full four months; their fragrance carries on the air. It looks as well in the shrub border as it does on a bank silhouetted against grass. Unfortunately, it is short-lived.
Sun. Well-drained, fertile soil. 2m/6ft. Z8

Magnolia

The scent of magnolia flowers is as exotic as their appearance. Many have the fragrance of tropical fruit with a subtle shading of eastern spice, but it varies from one variety to another. The commonly grown star magnolia, *M. stellata* (Z4), which produces spidery white flowers on bare branches in early spring, is relatively poorly endowed as are many of the popular tulip- and lily-flowered forms of *M.* × *soulangeana* (Z5) and *M. liliiflora* (Z6). But there are also some notable scented hybrids:
M. **'Charles Coates'** is a superb hybrid whose flowers resemble those of *M. sieboldii*, but

they are held erect instead of nodding. They have a fruity fragrance.
9m/30ft or more. Z6
M. **'Jane'**. This upright hybrid bears reddish-purple starry flowers, white inside, in late spring and has a rich scent.
Sun. Retentive, acid soil preferred. Z5
M. **'Maryland'**, an evergreen hybrid between *M. grandiflora* and *M. virginiana*, has lemon-scented creamy flowers in late summer.
Sun. Z6
M. **'Picture'** is a vigorous soulangeana hybrid with a good scent. The white goblets are flushed with purplish pink.
Sun. Z5
M. **'Sundew'**. This seedling from 'Picture' has fragrant creamy-white flowers.
M. **'Susan'** bears fragrant, purplish pink, starry flowers on its bare branches in mid-spring.
Sun. Retentive, acid soil preferred. Z5
M. sieboldii is an attractive spreading magnolia whose white scented cups appear on and off throughout the summer. These have prominent dark rose stamens and nod on long stalks. The crimson fruits are also eyecatching.
Sun or light shade. Neutral or lime-free soil. 3.5–4.5m/12–15ft. Z6

M. sieboldii sinensis is my favourite summer-flowering magnolia. Its laundry-white cups, with their boss of crimson stamens, are downturned, and looking up through their branches is an experience to be savoured. The flowers have a deliciously rich fruity scent in which lemon is the dominant note. *M. wilsonii* is similar but has narrower leaves and smaller flowers.
Sun or light shade. All but very alkaline soils. 6m/20ft. Z6
M. virginiana, the sweet bay, is one of the mainstays of gardens in the eastern United States. It likes heat and performs best in warm regions, where it produces its scented flowers for many weeks in late summer.
Full sun. Retentive soil that is not strongly alkaline. 18m/60ft or more in the southeastern United States; up to 9m/30ft in Europe. Z5–10
M. × *wieseneri* (*M.* × *watsonii*), another magnolia for warmer regions, has one of the most powerful scents of all – a glorious tropical fruit cocktail. The large, upward-facing flowers are creamy-white with rose-crimson stamens, and appear at mid-summer among the sizeable leathery leaves.
Sun or light shade. All but strongly alkaline soils. 6m/20ft. Z6

Mahonia

M. aquifolium, the Oregon grape, provides useful evergreen ground-cover for shade, though for ornament I always choose its bronzy form 'Atropurpurea' or the hybrid 'Undulata' in preference. Its polished, holly-like leaflets are burnished with purple in winter, and in spring the dense heads of yellow bells make a bright contrast. The scent is of honey and it fills the air. Blue-black berries succeed the flowers.
Sun or shade. Any soil. 1–2m/3–6ft; 'Undulata' is taller. Z5
M. japonica has a lily-of-the-valley scent. This comes from lax racemes of yellow flowers, borne from late autumn until early spring. It is one of the best winter performers with evergreen holly-like foliage. It differs from 'Charity' in shape as well as flower: it is dense and spreading, rather than gaunt and upright. *M. japonica* Bealei group is similar to *M. japonica* but its racemes of flowers are shorter and more or less erect (Z4).
Sun or shade. 3m/10ft. Z7

Magnolia × *wieseneri*

Lupinus arboreus

Osmanthus × burkwoodii

M. lomariifolia is, without doubt, the aristocrat among mahonias, though its scent is weak. It is erect in growth and bears erect racemes densely packed with flowers in early winter. But its main attraction lies in its evergreen foliage which is finer, with smaller leaflets, than in other species. It is not completely hardy, alas, and outside mild areas is often grown as a wall shrub. *MM. × media* 'Lionel Fortescue' and 'Buckland' are only slightly coarser and are good substitutes for colder gardens.

Sun or shade. Up to 3.5m/12ft. Z9

M. × media 'Charity' is the most popular of those early winter-flowering mahonias in Britain that give more or less erect racemes of yellow flowers, scented of lily of the valley. It makes a vertical, architectural shrub and, although it is not as elegant in leaf as *M. lomariifolia*, *M. × media* 'Lionel Fortescue' and *M. × media* 'Buckland', it is a useful evergreen feature.

Sun or shade. 3m/10ft or more. Z8

Myrica

M. cerifera, the wax myrtle, is a large, more or less evergreen shrub with narrow, glossy, aromatic leaves. Its white winter fruits have a covering of wax which is used to make fragrant candles.

Sun. Damp, acid soil. 9m/30ft or more. Z6

M. gale, the sweet gale or bog myrtle, is the best known of its genus, and is useful for damp spots on acid, preferably peaty, soil. The whole plant releases a sweetly resinous aroma when bruised. It is a deciduous shrub, with narrow tapering leaves. Tiny golden-brown catkins, males and females on separate plants, are borne on the bare stems in early spring.

Sun. 1–1.2m/2–4ft. Z4

M. pensylvanica, the bayberry, is useful for a very different problem site: arid soil, especially in coastal areas. It is a bigger plant than sweet gale, with oblong aromatic foliage and grey fruits in winter, but is also deciduous.

Sun. Acid soil. 2m/6ft. Z3

Olearia

Most of the Australasian daisy bushes are too tender to be grown outdoors except in the mildest areas. Those listed here are the hardier sorts, ideal for sheltered sunny borders or, in coastal regions, for hedges. The evergreen foliage is usually scented of musk, but the flowers often have a sweet hawthorn fragrance.

O. × haastii is the hardiest and thus the most commonly seen daisy bush in Britain. It is a bushy evergreen with small, dark, leathery leaves that are white-felted underneath. It produces its scented white flowerheads in high summer. This is a useful hedging plant on the coast.

Sun. Well-drained soil. 1.2–2.7m/4–9ft. Z8

O. ilicifolia is an attractive species with grey-green, toothed leaves, white-felted underneath, which bears heads of scented white flowers at mid-summer. Its foliage has a strong musk scent. It is reliably hardy in many areas and is more impressive than the commoner *O. × haastii*.

Sun. Well-drained soil. 3m/10ft. Z9

O. macrodonta, the New Zealand holly, is a vigorous shrub with glossy, silvery green, holly-like leaves scented of musk and generous heads of fragrant white flowers in summer. It is an excellent screening plant for maritime areas.

Sun. Well-drained soil. 2.7m/9ft. Z9

O. nummulariifolia is a distinctive species with small, stubby, yellow-green leaves. Its white flowers, borne in mid-summer, although not as eyecatching as in other species, have the delicate scent of heliotrope.

Sun. Well-drained soil. 2.7m/9ft. Z9

Orixa

O. japonica, Japanese orixa, is an unusual deciduous shrub of spreading habit, whose bright green leaves have a spicy orange scent when crushed. It is at its most lovely in the autumn when the foliage turns the palest shade of yellow; the flowers, green and borne in spring, are less impressive.

Sun or light shade. Any well-drained soil. 2.5m/8ft. Z6

Osmanthus

This is an invaluable genus of evergreen shrubs. The small-leaved species can be clipped into quite formal shapes and can also be used as hedging. They thrive in nearly all soils and all positions and some are reliably hardy to Zone 6. The scent comes from their clusters of white jasmine-like flowers and is normally piercingly sweet.

O. armatus has long, slender, dark, leathery leaves with prominently toothed edges and is quite distinct from its cousins. Funnily enough, this autumn-flowering species is seldom grown, offered or discussed; but it is a most attractive shrub. The scent is of bubblegum.
Sun or shade. 2.5–4.5m/8–15ft. Z7

O. × burkwoodii (formerly × *Osmarea burkwoodii*), a popular hybrid osmanthus, has a dense habit and small, dark leaves. The flowers appear in spring and are deliciously sweet: the mixture of honey and vanilla fills the air on a warm still day. It is an easy, though slow-growing plant, reliable even on thin chalk.
Sun or shade. To 3m/10ft. Z7

O. decorus (formerly *Phillyrea decora*), an excellent spring-flowering shrub, is distinguished by its large untoothed leaves.
Sun or shade. 3m/10ft. Z7

O. delavayi is a parent of *O. × burkwoodii* and is very similar. It produces a mass of white blossom in spring, with the unmistakable scent of suntan lotion.
Sun or shade. 3m/10ft. Z8

Perovskia atriplicifolia

O. heterophyllus has holly-like leaves. There are a number of coloured versions of this species, which flowers in autumn. It is very beautiful and its dense, slow-growing habit lends it to hedge work.
Sun or shade. 3m/10ft. Z7

O. yunnanensis produces flowers in late winter but its main attraction is its superb foliage; the leaves are long, exotic and toothed. It is faster growing than many of its cousins but is less hardy, and is suitable only for warmer areas.
Sun or shade. Often 9m/30ft or more. Z9

Perovskia

P. atriplicifolia, Russian sage, is treated much like a herbaceous perennial in that it is cut to the ground in early spring. You then get erect, fresh white shoots, clad in grey, finely cut leaves which are scented of turpentine. In late summer they are topped with tall, thin plumes of violet flowers. You need a group to make any real impression and you will have to stake gently, but it is worth treating this plant seriously because it can give an excellent late show. There are few better companions for red and purple fuchsias, such as the hardy 'Mrs Popple'. 'Blue Spire' is a superior hybrid.
Full sun. Good soil. 1m/3ft. Z6

Philadelphus

The heady, fruity, mock-orange scent of philadelphus is one of the fragrant highlights of the year. There are so many desirable species and varieties available that it is hard to make a choice, but in your deliberations about relative heights and patterns of flower, you might also consider strength of scent. Some are truly overpowering and are not for the sensitive nose; others are much more subtle. They all flower around mid-summer. For the rest of the year they are somewhat dull, having a relaxed habit and unremarkable foliage (except in the golden and variegated forms of *P. coronarius*). Old flowering shoots should be pruned to within 2.5cm/1in of the old wood immediately after flowering.
Sun or medium shade. All soils, even chalk.

P. **'Avalanche'** has pure white, single flowers, profusely borne and richly scented. It makes a semi-erect shrub and has small leaves.
1.5m/5ft.

Philadelphus 'Manteau d'Hermine'

P. **'Beauclerk'** has large, single, broad-petalled flowers that are white with a central flush of pink. They have a delicious scent that is not too strong. It makes a spreading shrub.
2.5m/8ft.

P. **'Belle Etoile'** is one of the best varieties. It has a measured fragrance and is very free with its white, crimson-flushed flowers.
1.5m/5ft.

P. coronarius, the familiar 'mock-orange' of cottage gardens, has an overwhelming fragrance. Plant it on the garden's boundary so that it reaches you in moderation. It makes a large, upright shrub (to 3.7m/12ft) with single, creamy white flowers. The golden ('Aureus') and white-variegated ('Variegatus') forms are among the best coloured foliage shrubs; they are smaller, easier on the nose, and best in light shade. Z5

P. **'Manteau d'Hermine'** is a superb, short, compact philadelphus for the front of the border. It has small leaves and pure white,

Philadelphus 'Beauclerk'

double flowers and is deservedly one of the most popular varieties.
1–1.2m/3–4ft.
P. *microphyllus* is an attractive species with small leaves and richly scented, single white flowers in early summer. It makes a compact, bushy shrub.
Full sun. 1m/3ft. Z6
P. 'Sybille' has almost-square flowers, arching branches and white, crimson-stained flowers. Its fragrance is delicious.
1.5m/5ft.
P. 'Virginal' bears pure, double white flowers and has a magnificent scent. It is large and erect.
2.7m/9ft.

Phillyrea
The most valuable species for scent, *P. decora*, is now listed under *Osmanthus*, but the two other species are worthy of wider publicity. Both are interesting, more or less hardy, large evergreens.
Sun or shade. All soils.
P. *angustifolia* makes a compact dome of narrow, dark leaves and bears clusters of sweetly scented flowers in early summer.
3m/10ft. Z8
P. *latifolia* has dull white, less fragrant flowers. But it bears small glossy leaves on arching branches, and is an excellent foliage feature, resembling a dwarf holm oak.
4.5m/15ft or more. Z8

Pieris
This is a genus of attractive, lime-hating evergreens for the shady border. They are very useful in rhododendron woodland, contributing panicles of pitcher-shaped flowers in spring that look like those of lily of the valley. The scent shades from lily of the valley to vanilla. The foliage is slender, dark and leathery and in many varieties is brilliant red when young. They need a location that is well protected from the cold winds of spring.
Light shade. Peaty soil.
P. 'Forest Flame' is one of the hardiest and more vigorous varieties with striking new red growth in spring. It produces large

Pieris japonica 'Christmas Cheer'

Pieris japonica 'Fire Crest'

drooping panicles of scented flowers.
3m/10ft or more. Z7
P. formosa forrestii is probably the best
pieris, with brilliant young foliage and long
panicles of flowers. It is not for cold gardens,
however. There are two excellent selections
in 'Jermyns', with particularly rich colouring
of new growth and flower inflorescence, and
'Wakehurst', which has broader foliage.
3m/10ft or more. Z8
P. japonica is a beautiful foliage shrub,
glossy-leaved with its young growth tinged
with copper. Its flowers hang in elegant
panicles. But its young shoots are quite
susceptible to frost damage, and gardeners in
cold areas should plump for its variety
'Christmas Cheer' with rose-flushed flowers.
'Fire Crest' is a superb variety.
1.5–3m/5–10ft. Z6

Poncirus
P. trifoliata, the Japanese bitter orange, is a
thorny deciduous shrub at its peak in spring
when it carries its large, white starry flowers
on bare green branches. The scent from the
flowers is the sweet bubblegum scent of the
citrus family. In mild areas these are followed
by small downy oranges. It is perfectly hardy
and makes a very interesting feature or it can
be clipped and used as an impenetrable
hedge.
Full sun. Fertile, well-drained soil. 2.4m/8ft
shrub to 6m/20ft tree. Z8

Rhododendron
This important genus provides the garden
with some wonderful scents, sweet, spicy and
aromatic. For spring colour and diversity of
size and form, it has no rivals. However, the
large hybrids, with their huge, exotic heads
of flowers, and the richly coloured species
are seldom scented. Scent is concentrated
mainly among the deciduous azaleas and a
range of white-flowered species. Many of the
latter are tender, and have been listed under
Conservatory and Tender Plants.
Light shade. Retentive but well-drained,
lime-free, peaty soil.
R. arborescens is a large deciduous azalea
which blooms usefully late, in early to mid-
summer. The funnel-shaped flowers are
white, tinged with pink and with protruding
red stamens, and are fruitily sweet-scented.
The foliage is glossy and often has good

autumn colour. It is not grown very much
but it is extremely attractive.
6m/20ft. Z5
R. atlanticum is an attractive deciduous
azalea from the eastern United States with
small white, often pink-tinged flowers borne
in spring which have a rich, spicy, rose scent.
It is stoloniferous and makes a large clump
under ideal conditions.
Sun or light shade. Deep, damp soil. Up to
1.5m/5ft. Z6
R. auriculatum flowers in high summer. It is
an evergreen rhododendron with very large,
dark, leathery leaves and huge trusses of
large white flowers that are spicily sweet. It
needs shade from strong sunshine, and
grows best in mild climates, where a long
growing season ensures that the young
shoots ripen properly before the early frosts.
Its sensational white-flowered hybrid 'Polar
Bear' is even more desirable; Argosy, white
with a crimson basal stain, is also good.
4.5m/15ft or more. Z6
R. ciliatum is a pretty rhododendron with
hairy, oval leaves and clusters of bell-shaped
flowers in spring. The flowers open pink
from rose-red buds and are spicily sweet. It
makes a neat evergreen dome for the front of
the shady border, but needs protection from
cold winds and early frosts.
1–1.2m/3–4ft. Z8
R. decorum, a splendid large evergreen
rhododendron with leathery leaves,
produces impressive lax trusses of white or
pale pink, fruitily scented flowers in early
summer. It is a variable species and some of
the best forms are rather tender.
Up to 7.5m/25ft. Z7
R. fortunei bears clusters of pale lilac-pink,
scented, bell-shaped flowers in spring. It is
an attractive rhododendron, well worth
growing, but for southern gardens its
subspecies *discolor* is even better; this has
huge trusses of blush pink flowers from early
summer. Both have given rise to some truly
splendid hybrids which have inherited their
parents' scent, among which 'Albatross', a
magnificent large shrub with lax trusses of
richly scented white trumpets, and the Loderi
clones, listed below, stand supreme.
3m/10ft or more. Z7
R. glaucophyllum is interesting for its
resinous scented foliage, reminiscent of
saddle soap, but it is not in the front rank of

rhododendrons. It makes a bushy evergreen shrub with slender dark leaves, white beneath, and produces heads of rosy flowers in springtime.
1–2m/3–6ft. Z8

R. heliolepis has strongly aromatic, evergreen, glossy leaves but its rosy-purple, crimson-marked flowers, borne in small clusters in early summer, are unscented. Its subspecies *brevistylum* is similar but blooms slightly later.
3m/10ft. Z8

R. Loderi (R. Kewense) is the most exciting of the large scented rhododendrons and it is probably at its finest in the clone 'Loderi King George'. This makes a substantial, vigorous, evergreen shrub clad in large, mid-green leaves and in spring bears huge trusses of funnel-shaped flowers. These are white, blush pink in bud, and have a marvellous spicy, fruity fragrance. 'Loderi Pink Diamond' is an excellent pale pink version. The Loderi hybrids are best planted alongside a path and encouraged to arch over, so that you can reach up to the flowers. The bare stems are beautifully coloured and flaked.
Light shade, sheltered from cold winds.
Up to 7.5m/25ft. Z8

R. luteum is the yellow deciduous azalea commonly encountered in British woodland gardens. Its fruity honeysuckle fragrance fills the spring air and comes from beautiful heads of tubular, bright yellow flowers. It is a deciduous shrub and in autumn its slender

Above and right *Rhododendron luteum*

Rhododendron trichostomum

leaves assume crimson and orange tints. In spite of a deluge of rival hybrid azaleas, this remains one of the glories of the spring garden.
Sun or light shade. 2.5m/8ft. Z5

R. moupinense, an attractive short evergreen rhododendron, is ideal for the front of the border or the rock garden. It bears its large white or pink, sweetly scented flowers singly or in small clusters in late winter and although they are frequently spoilt by frost, they are lovely in a mild spell. The leaves are leathery and oval.
Up to 1.2m/4ft. Z7

R. mucronatum makes a small spreading evergreen rhododendron and produces pure white, sweetly scented, funnel-shaped flowers in spring.
Up to 1.2m/4ft. Z6

R. occidentale is a deciduous shrub valuable for extending the azalea season well into early summer. It has cream or pale pink flowers, stained in yellow, and a delicious honeysuckle fragrance. It gives good autumn colour. In its best forms this is a lovely

species, which has been much used for hybridizing.
2.5m/8ft. Z6

R. prinophyllum (*R. roseum*), the roseshell azalea, is another desirable species of deciduous azalea, but this time with clear deep pink flowers in spring and a scent of clove.
2.5m/8ft. Z3

R. rubiginosum, a large, upright rhododendron, has aromatic, lance-shaped leaves and pink or rosy-lilac flowers in late spring.
6m/20ft. Z6

R. saluenense is a small aromatic evergreen rhododendron with small, dark, glossy leaves. It produces clusters of rosy purple flowers in spring.
Up to 1.2m/4ft. Z6

R. serotinum is one of the last rhododendrons to flower, in late summer. It is a lax-growing evergreen with large, sweetly scented, bell-shaped flowers, tinged and spotted with pink.
3m/10ft or more. Z8

R. trichostomum is a favourite of mine. Often mistaken for a daphne, it has small narrow leaves and tight heads of tubular flowers in spring. These can be white, pale pink or rose and are strongly scented of clove. This evergreen enjoys a sunny spot and is so dainty and so unlike a rhododendron that it can easily be accommodated in mixed plantings.
Up to 1.2m/4ft. Z7

R. viscosum, the swamp honeysuckle, is a bushy deciduous azalea with a magnificent spicy sweet fragrance. It performs late – in early summer – and produces clusters of white, pink-flushed, funnel-shaped flowers. It usually colours well in the autumn. It tolerates but does not need damp ground.
2.5m/8ft. Z3

R. yedoense poukhanense, the Korean azalea, is a spreading deciduous shrub bearing small clusters of sweetly scented, rosy purple flowers in spring. It also gives good autumn colour.
1.2m/4ft. Z5

Azalea hybrids

There are a huge number of colourful deciduous azalea hybrids and many have the delicious sweet honeysuckle scent. The Ghent group usually have elegant, long funnelled flowers, good autumn foliage and strong scent: 'Daviesii' is white with a yellow centre; 'Nancy Waterer' is a rich golden yellow; and 'Narcissiflorum' is a double, clear yellow and a first-rate, compact plant. They are reliable, hardy shrubs.
1.5m/5ft.

The Knap Hill group have impressive trumpet-shaped flowers and good autumn foliage. The flower colours are generally much more vivid than the Ghents but the scent is usually weak or absent: 'Lapwing', in creamy yellow, flushed pink, and 'Whitethroat', a fine double white with compact growth, are notable exceptions.
1.5m/5ft. Z5

The Mollis group bear striking large trumpet flowers in late spring. But they invariably disappoint the nose and they are also susceptible to late frosts.
1.2m/4ft.

The Occidentale group have round full trusses of flowers which are especially well scented though not usually of brilliant hue. They have a long flowering period in early summer and good autumn foliage: 'Exquisitum' is flesh pink with an orange flash; 'Irene Koster', the best variety, is smaller-flowered, pink-flushed white.
1.5m/5ft. Z7

Azaleodendrons are hybrids between deciduous azaleas and evergreen rhododendrons. They have the habit of azaleas but are semi-evergreen. Some have a good fragrance, notably 'Govenianum', an erect, compact shrub with lilac-purple flowers, and 'Odoratum', a small bushy shrub with pale lilac flowers, which is now extremely rare. They flower in summer.
1.2–1.5m/4–5ft.

A new race of late-flowering azalea hybrids is just coming into circulation. Bred by Mr Denny Pratt of Cheshire, England, some inherit strong scent from *R. viscosum* and *R. occidentale*, while colour is furnished by *R. bakeri* and the Knaphill hybrids. So far I have only met 'Anneke', in gold and yellow, and 'Summer Fragrance', in cream and yellow, both of which are richly and fruitily fragrant. They bloom around mid-summer.
2–2.5m/6–8ft.

Rhus

R. aromatica is sometimes grown in gardens in its native eastern United States but is uncommon in Britain. Its chief attraction is its handsome, three-fingered leaves, which release an appealing resinous aroma when bruised, but the dense clusters of yellowish flowers in spring are also of merit. It makes a spreading, deciduous shrub.
Sun. 1–1.5m/3–5ft. Z3

Ribes

R. odoratum, the clove currant, is quite unlike the common flowering currant, described below. It makes a lax, erect shrub clothed in shiny, fresh green, lobed leaves which take on fiery autumn tints. Its scent comes from the golden yellow flowers, which appear on short racemes in spring, and is of clove. It makes an attractive and unusual addition to the border.
Sun or light shade. 2–2.5m/6–8ft. Z5

R. sanguineum, the flowering currant, haunts every old shrub border and I find its minty-sweet, sweaty leaf scent, which hangs in the air, extremely unpleasant. I cannot imagine anyone choosing this shrub specifically for its fragrance, but the dangling racemes,

Rhus aromatica

Ribes odoratum

which appear in spring, are highly ornamental and come in pink, red, crimson and white; the flowers are scentless. It is deciduous and shade tolerant.
2–2.5m/6–8ft. Z6

Rubus

R. odoratus, flowering raspberry, suffers from having an excess quantity of large, vine-like leaves in proportion to its heads of flower; it is also a vigorous colonizer. But for the wild garden, this deciduous shrub is a desirable ingredient. The single, bright pink flowers, which are carried in clusters atop the stems for a long period during the summer, are mildly fragrant, while the young shoots have a scent of resin.
Sun or shade. 2.5m/8ft. Z4

Salix

S. aegyptiaca (*S. medemii*). You may not think of willows as being a likely source of garden scent, but some have aromatic foliage (the bay willow, *S. pentandrà* – described under Trees – and the rare balsam willow, *S. pyrifolia*, for example) and some have scented catkins (including the almond-leaved willow, *S. triandra*, used for basket-making). Of the latter, the musk willow, *S. aegyptiaca*, is the most potently sweet. Perfumed drinks were made from its male catkins and they were even eaten as sweetmeats. The catkins are conspicuously large and bright yellow and are produced on the bare greyish twigs in late winter. It is a large, vigorous shrub, with lanceolate leaves.
Sun or light shade. All but dry soils. 4.5m/15ft. Z6

Sambucus

Elder flowers have a heavy musky scent that will not appeal to all noses. Elders are very useful, fast-growing, deciduous shrubs which thrive anywhere. In the wildlife garden the common elder is an important specimen or hedgerow plant, popular with insects when in flower and with birds when in berry. Elsewhere, it is the coloured and cut-leaved varieties that are most valuable, as background foliage to fleeting border flowers.
Sun or shade. All soils.

S. nigra, the common elder, has large flat heads of cream flowers in early summer, followed by generous bunches of black berries. It comes in many leaf colours, including a bewitching sombre purple and a striking golden-variegated form, and in a good ferny form called 'Laciniata'.
From 3m/10ft to small tree size. Z6
S. racemosa **'Plumosa Aurea'** is the finest of the golden-leaved elders and arguably the best golden shrub in cultivation. It has beautiful cut foliage, tan when young, and puffs of yellow flowers in early summer; these are occasionally followed by a splendid show of scarlet berries. The foliage scorches in strong sunlight so a lightly shaded position is best.
2.5m/8ft. Z5

Sarcococca

The sweet or Christmas boxes should be in every garden. They are unassuming dwarf or small evergreens that produce tufts of flowers in late winter. The flowers are inconspicuous but release a powerful rich honey scent into the air. They are good

Sarcococca hookeriana digyna

Sarcococca humilis

Skimmia japonica

companions for hellebores and mahonias, which flower simultaneously, and are handy for tucking into narrow beds.

Shade. All but very dry soils.

S. confusa makes a bushy spreading shrub. It has long, slender, pointed leaves, dark and glossy, and creamy flowers followed by small black fruits.

1.5m/5ft. Z6

S. hookeriana digyna is one of the more commonly offered forms. It has slender, purplish-green leaves borne on upright branches. The flowers are pink-tinged and are followed by black fruits.

Up to 1.2m/4ft. Z6

S. humilis, another popular form, is a dwarf suckering shrub with beautiful dark shiny foliage that makes cushions of greenery for the front of the shady border. The creamy flowers are followed by black berries.

Up to 60cm/2ft. Z6

S. ruscifolia. The variety *chinensis* is preferable to the species itself, being more vigorous. It is similar in appearance to *S. confusa* but the berries are red.

1.5m/5ft. Z8

Staphylea colchica

Skimmia japonica 'Rubella'

Skimmia

This group of small evergreens make good plants for shady borders and tubs, but they dislike strongly alkaline soils. Gardeners on chalk or lime can grow them in ericaceous compost and water them with rainwater. Skimmias have narrowly oval, leathery leaves and make neat, dense, dome-shaped shrubs. The panicles of flowers carried in spring are scented – the fragrance shades from lily of the valley to one reminiscent of hebes. On female plants the flowers are followed by prominent clusters of scarlet fruits in the autumn. You need a male plant in the group for berries to be borne.

S. japonica has produced an array of excellent plants. *S. japonica* 'Veitchii' (usually sold as *S.* 'Foremanii') is a vigorous female with fine fruits; 'Nymans' is also good. The males produce the best flowers and, for sweet scent, 'Fragrans' is the clone to choose; 'Rubella' is an interesting colour variant, with red-budded flowers.

1m/3ft. Z8

S. laureola, in a male form, has good greenish-cream fragrant flowers. The leaves are very pungent when crushed.

Usually under 1m/3ft. Z8

S. reevesiana is hermaphrodite so the crimson-red berries always appear after the cream flowers. It is smaller still, about 60cm/2ft high. Z9

Spartium

S. junceum, Spanish broom, is popular for its long summer flowering and its tolerance of hot, dry conditions. It does particularly well by the sea. It makes an erect, often leggy shrub but can be kept neat and bushy by spring pruning. The blast of bright yellow, pea flowers begins in summer and continues until autumn; the flowers are scented of vanilla.

Sun. 2.5m/8ft or more. Z8

Staphylea

S. colchica, bladdernut, is an erect deciduous shrub that bears panicles of white flowers in spring; the famous plantsman and author E. A. Bowles likened their scent to that of rice pudding. Conspicuous inflated seed capsules follow.

Sun or light shade. Loamy soil. 3m/10ft or more. Z6

Syringa

The lilacs are the heralds of summer and a mainstay of the late spring garden. The larger forms, the size of small trees and bearing great plumes of flowers, are deciduous background plants for the sunnier parts of the shrub border and for the wild garden; while the smaller forms, which are less obtrusive in leaf and often longer flowering, can be slipped into the mixed herbaceous border to provide early flowers. The flower scent is distinctive enough to be described as 'lilac' but varies within the group from very sweet to unpleasantly heavy.

Sun or light shade. All but very alkaline soils.

S. × chinensis, the Chinese or Rouen lilac, is a pretty but uncommon shrub with arching panicles of pale lilac-coloured flowers with a good scent. It makes a bushy but often rather lax plant.

3m/10ft. Z3

S. × hyacinthiflora is a variable hybrid from which many attractive clones have been selected. It is similar to the common lilac but makes a more spreading shrub and has looser heads of flower; it also blooms earlier in the spring. 'Clarke's Giant' is a fine lilac-blue with large heads; 'Esther Staley' is a splendid pink, red in bud.

3.5m/12ft. Z3

S. × josiflexa **'Bellicent'**, an exceptionally beautiful large lilac, produces long plumes hung with drooping flowers. These are a pale, clear pink and sweetly scented. It is quite stunning when at its peak – if you only have room for one sizeable lilac, this is the one to choose.

3m/10ft or more. Z5

S. meyeri **'Palibin'** is a commonly grown short lilac with small leaves and loose panicles of sweetly scented, lilac-pink flowers borne in early summer.

Up to 1.5m/5ft. Z5

S. microphylla **'Superba'** is the best of the small lilacs and one of the most desirable small scented shrubs. It blooms over a very long period – after its spring burst, intermittently until autumn. The flowers, which appear from rosy buds, are clear pink and are carried in rounded heads. I would not be without it.

1.2m/4ft. Z4

Syringa microphylla 'Superba'

Syringa × *persica* 'Alba'

S. × *persica*, the Persian lilac, is more delicate in appearance, with graceful sprays of flowers and slender leaves. The flowers are nicely scented and pale lilac; there is an even lovelier white form called 'Alba'.
2m/6ft. Z5

S. × *prestoniae*, another variable hybrid, gives a range of large lilacs in different colours. They extend the lilac season well into summer. Many have fine heads of drooping flowers and all are scented. 'Elinor' in lilac-pink is the most freely available, but 'Audrey' in deep pink and 'Isabella' in lilac-purple are also good.
4.5m/15ft. Z2

S. sweginzowii is definitely the connoisseur's choice, with its elegant, arching branches and long panicles dripping with sweetly scented, pale pink flowers.
3.5m/12ft. Z6

S. vulgaris, the common lilac, is available in such a quantity of single and double-flowered cultivars, in all colours, that it is hard to make a choice. Here is a selection: 'Charles Joly', a double dark reddish-purple; 'Firmament', a single clear lilac-blue; 'Katherine Havemeyer', a double lavender-

purple; 'Madame Lemoine', a double white; and 'Andenken an Ludwig Späth' ('Souvenir de Louis Spaeth'), a single wine-red.
4.5m/15ft. Z4

Thuja

The fruity scent of their foliage makes thujas appealing conifers for the fragrant garden. Their role is as specimen evergreens, of various sizes, or as backdrops, screens and hedges; *T. plicata*, the western red cedar (described under Trees), makes one of the best evergreen hedges, and the best-scented one.

T. occidentalis, the American arborvitae or white cedar, gives a range of conifers of all shapes and sizes, though mainly dense and conical. The most popular are 'Danica', a dwarf, dark green globe which turns bronze in winter; 'Ericoides', a dwarf, grey-green cone, also bronze in winter; 'Holmstrup', a pleasing, dark green pyramid which grows slowly to 2–3m/6–10ft; 'Rheingold', a 1.2m/4ft dome which changes its shade of gold each season; 'Smaragd' ('Emerald'), a bright green pyramid, 3m/10ft high, and a fine hedging plant; and 'Sunkist', a golden pyramid, slowly reaching 1.2m/4ft.
Sun. Z3

T. orientalis, the Chinese arborvitae, has also produced many good garden conifers, though fewer than the above species. But they are invariably less fragrant.
Sun. Z5

T. plicata, the western red cedar, passes its scent on to its clones, of which these coloured forms are the most popular: 'Rogersii', a dwarf golden globe, which in winter assumes good bronze tones; 'Stoneham Gold', a broad, bright golden cone, slowly growing to 1m/3ft; and 'Zebrina', a broad, golden-variegated pyramid, ultimately tree size.
Sun. Z5

Umbellularia

U. californica, California laurel, is a large, aromatic, evergreen shrub or small tree, whose oval, leathery leaves are pungently fruity when crushed. It is said that prolonged sniffing causes headaches and sneezing and can even render a person unconscious! Small umbels of yellowish flowers are produced in spring, and are occasionally followed by

fruits. It needs a warm situation, sheltered from early frosts.
Sun. Well-drained soil. Z9

Viburnum

This group of shrubs gives the garden some of its most fabulous scent. The fragrant varieties (by no means all viburnums are scented) fall into two categories: those which flower on bare stems during the late autumn, winter and early spring; and those which flower during spring. All need to be within reach of the nose. Plant them in the shrub border in front of deciduous trees.
Sun or light shade. Most soils.

V. × *bodnantense*, in a good form, is the finest winter-flowering viburnum, producing its rose-pink clusters of flowers, which are surprisingly frost-resistant, on and off from autumn until spring. The scent is honey sweet, suffused with almond, and on warm days carries in the air. 'Dawn' is a superb

Viburnum × *bodnantense* 'Dawn'

Viburnum carlesii 'Diana'

Viburnum × *juddii*

Viburnum × *burkwoodii*

vigorous selection, with large pink flowers and large foliage; 'Deben' is white from pink buds, lovely but damaged by bad weather. They are deciduous and have an upright habit.
3m/10ft. Z7

V.* × *burkwoodii is a semi-evergreen with wonderfully glossy leaves, some of which take on lively autumn tints. The dense, rounded clusters of pure white flowers appear mainly in spring; the sweet scent, like a clove carnation, carries well. It is a lovely backbone plant for the flower border. Several excellent forms and hybrids are available, notably 'Anne Russell', with pale pink flowers; 'Fulbrook', with larger white flowers, distinctive foliage, and a graceful habit; and 'Park Farm', a magnificent, vigorous plant with larger leaves and larger white flowers.
2.5m/8ft. Z5

V.* × *carlcephalum, fragrant snowball viburnum, is a popular, spring-flowering,

deciduous viburnum, but rather coarser than *V. carlesii* and, in my view, less desirable; the leaves are larger and the heads less elegant, bigger and more compact. But the scent is sweet and potent.
2.5m/8ft. Z5

V. carlesii has the best scent of the spring-flowering deciduous viburnums: a sweet clove fragrance and far-reaching. It is a rounded shrub with dull greyish green foliage and white flowers. Its three clones are even better than the species: 'Aurora' has red flower buds which open pale pink; 'Charis' is particularly vigorous, also red-budded but with white flowers; and 'Diana' has red buds and more reddish flowers than 'Aurora'.
1.2–2.5m/4–8ft. Z5

V. farreri (*V. fragrans*), a much-loved constituent of the English cottage garden, blooms on and off on bare branches all winter. The flowers are white, tinged with pink, and are scented of almond. In old age it is usually more spreading than *V. × bodnantense* but in youth it is equally upright. It is deciduous.
3m/10ft. Z6

V. × juddii is another outstanding spring-flowering deciduous shrub. It is similar to *V. carlesii* but bushier and neater. The heads of white flowers are also usually a touch bigger. The scent is sweet but with an extra dash of spicy clove.
1.2m/4ft. Z5

V. odoratissimum is included here for convenience, but it is really only successful in milder regions. It would make an interesting plant for a large conservatory, or possibly a wall that receives full sun. It is an evergreen, with large leathery leaves; these sometimes turn bronze during the winter. The conical panicles of pure white flowers are produced at an unusual time, in late summer.
3–7.5m/10–25ft. Z8

V. tinus, laurustinus, is a commonly grown evergreen shrub and one with which I have a love–hate relationship. Its attractions are that it makes a neat, bushy background plant (or informal hedge), is tolerant of quite deep shade, and is winter-flowering. Its drawback is that at no moment in the year does it really give you a thrill. Unless, of course, you catch a waft of honey scent, but this is very unpredictable. Often there is not a trace or it

is only very faint. The white flowers appear from pink buds on and off from autumn to early spring. In some years they are succeeded by blue fruits. 'Eve Price' is a compact, smaller form with bright pink buds and pink-tinged flowers.
Shade. 2–3.5m/6–12ft. Z8

Weigela

A few weigelas take you by surprise with a honey scent, though most of the genus are scentless or very faintly scented. Weigelas are popular deciduous shrubs for early summer, producing masses of tubular flowers along the previous year's shoots; flowering shoots should be pruned hard after the blossoms fade. They have rather uninteresting foliage, except for the coloured-leaved forms, so they need to be given positions where they can be unobtrusive after flowering.
Sun or light shade. Any soil.

W. **'Mont Blanc'** is one of the best white weigelas; it is vigorous, with large flowers, and has a good scent. But it is not commonly offered.
2.3m/7ft.

W. praecox **'Variegata'** is a cream-variegated hybrid of strongly scented *W. praecox*. It has rose-pink flowers.
2.3m/7ft.

Yucca

Most of us think of yuccas as border perennials but since they are strictly shrubs I include them here. The spiky clumps of sword-shaped, evergreen leaves strike a tropical note in the planting, and the tall stems hung with cream bells combine wonderfully with yellow kniphofias (red-hot pokers) and blue agapanthus. As architectural specimens on corners of borders or growing in paving cracks, they have few equals. But bear in mind their dangerous, dagger-sharp leaf tips, which are at eye level for children and dogs. The flowers have a sweet scent.
Sun. Well-drained soil.

Y. filamentosa, Adam's needle, has more or less stiffly erect, grey-green leaves with curly threads at the margins. The loose, broad panicles of flowers are borne in high summer.
Up to 2m/6ft. Z5

Y. flaccida has narrower, greyer leaves which are more lax and generally bent downwards from the middle. The flowers are borne on shorter panicles. 'Ivory' is a superb free-flowering selection.
1–1.2m/3–4ft. Z5

Y. gloriosa, Spanish dagger, flowers less freely, often not at all. But when the bells do appear they are on massive narrow panicles. The foliage is stiff and dangerous.
Up to 2.5m/8ft. Z7

Zenobia

Z. pulverulenta is an attractive, small deciduous shrub for association with rhododendrons. Clusters of bell-shaped, white flowers appear in summer and these have a scent of aniseed. The ovate leaves are glaucous when young and in autumn assume fine red tints. It is a very desirable plant.
Sun or shade. Moist, acidic soil. 1.2–2m/4–6ft. Z6

Yucca gloriosa

Herbaceous Borders and Ground-Covering Plants

In the depths of winter, the scents of border plants and bulbs are best savoured indoors. On the whole, these flowers are less resilient than those of shrubs and outside, assaulted by wind, frost and rain, they are often spoiled, while their fragrances are lost in the cold air. Some bulbs are worth growing in pots to be kept outside in a cold frame or plunge bed (a bed of sand in which the pots are sunk to their rim) and brought into the warmth of the house as the flower buds become visible. In the autumn I always plant up potfuls of crocuses, narcissi, violet-scented *Iris reticulata* (with me, this iris is not a reliable performer outdoors, anyway) and forced hyacinths, to enjoy by my desk from Christmas onwards.

Other plants can be cut as they come into flower. Snowdrops, especially the large 'S. Arnott', bunched in jars surprise you with the potency of their honey scents, and Algerian irises, forms of *I. unguicularis*, deliver some sophisticated sweet perfumes. Pale lavender 'Walter Butt' has a particularly good cowslip scent. The famous English plantsman and gardening writer E. A. Bowles gives detailed advice on the picking of Algerian irises in his book *My Garden in Spring* (1914). In frosty weather he suggests pulling the buds as soon as the coloured parts of the flower are visible above the spathes, and placing them immediately in water up to their necks. This prevents them drooping, and as they lengthen and burst open they are transferred to a display vase.

As winter wanes and serious gardening begins again, you can enjoy more scents in the open. Sheets of snowdrops and spring snowflakes, with *Crocus tomasinianus* for colour, may now be revealing themselves under bare-stemmed shrubs like spicy Cornelian cherry dogwood (*Cornus mas*) and sweetly scented willows. The stinking hellebore, *H. foetidus*, is also in bloom. It does not stink unless you bruise it, and even then not much; but in some forms, notably 'Jekyll's Form', a lily-of-the-valley fragrance can be detected in the flowers. *H. foetidus*, with its evergreen fingered leaves, is an ideal foil for snowdrops and will seed itself among them, and on shady banks is a natural companion for primroses. The purplish winter leaves of *Tellima grandiflora rubra* are also excellent with snowdrops and primroses, but its sweetly scented flowers do not appear until early summer.

As spring advances, the garden really gets into its stride. The shrub season has begun, and the chief role of the early bulbs and perennials is to provide a multicoloured understorey. Sweet violets, primroses, grape hyacinths and daffodils are among the scented candidates that require or tolerate a degree of shade, and can be massed under magnolias, cherries, ornamental quince (chaenomeles) and acid-loving woodlanders like winter hazel (corylopsis) and fothergilla. But the more scented daffodils, the jonquils and tazettas, perform better when they are nurtured in sunny, sheltered sites. At their peak of flowering, the piercingly sweet scents will make your eyes water. The sinister snake's head, *Hermodactylus tuberosus*, is an interesting companion bulb for them; its velvet-black and lime-green harmonizes well with the different shades of yellow, orange and white and it has a delicate clove scent. There are also dwarf, honey-scented tulips around to fuel the scheme.

In late spring, while flowering shrubs and trees continue to offer a feast for eye and nose, the bulbs start to give way to perennials and biennials. In shady, and often sunny borders too, lily of the valley is now displaying its tiny white bells. It

Right *Scents are not abundant among the traditional ingredients of high summer's herbaceous borders. Shrubs, lilies, annuals and other plants may therefore need to be woven into the composition to inject extra fragrance. Here climber and bush roses contribute notes of sweetness, while an edging of box gives a background aroma.*

has a habit of thriving just where you are sure it won't and of not thriving just where you are sure it will; so the answer is to try a few roots everywhere. The scent can be elusive outdoors so it is worthwhile bringing a few stems into the house every few days.

Wallflowers are a luxury I would not want to be without. I say luxury because I buy my plants each autumn. My local garden centre raises such good plants that there does not seem much point in troubling to do so myself. Their warm spicy scent echoes the eastern image conjured up by their sumptuous colours, and I wish I had room to plant carpets of them. In my congested borders they have to be arranged in small groups. I have mixed-colour groups here and there, and single colour groups teamed with foliage like bluish catmint and, more particularly, fennel. There is more than a trace of aniseed in wallflower scent, and the green and bronze fennels, also aniseed-scented, are happy bedfellows. Sunny borders that are predominantly herbaceous are probably a little short of colour at this time of year, unless they are swathed in tulips, and wallflowers give them a fillip. Other scented plants that can help are *Iris* 'Florentina', stocks, perennial honesty (*Lunaria rediviva*) and false Solomon's seal (*Smilacina racemosa*). The smilacina's creamy plumes really are an eyecatching feature – they look well with lime-green euphorbias and tulips; you expect a heavy meadowsweet scent from them but in fact they have a refreshing lemon fragrance.

By mid-summer, the garden is awash with pastel colours. This is the season for all those favourite perennials of the cottage garden – peonies, irises, lupins and pinks among them – and the air is infused with the scent of roses, honeysuckles and mock orange. Pinks have the most potent scent of the perennials and if your soil is dry and limy enough, you can use them freely to line paths, spill from raised beds, and bulge out of paving cracks. Their warm clove scent hangs in the air.

All sorts of fruity and vanilla scents may be detected in bearded irises; lavender-blue *I. pullida pallida* (*I.p. dalmatica*) is one of the best. Other irises worth having are *I. hoogiana* and *I. graminea*. Both are exceedingly beautiful, the former in lavender-blue and the latter in violet-blue and rosy purple, and have remarkable scents. *I. hoogiana* smells of roses and *I. graminea* of stewed plums and greengages.

Peonies and lupins will prosper in light shade so they are the perfect plants to set in the shadows of your shrub roses. Peonies and roses were made for each other; they share a rounded, petal-packed shape, a pinky colour range and a sweet scent. The lupins provide a rocket-shaped note of con-

trast. Lily-scented daylilies like yellow *Hemerocallis lilio-asphodelus* (*H. flava*) provide useful splashes of colour early in the season and at mid-summer their rushy leaves add foliage interest.

It is on warm early summer evenings, when you are strolling between the borders, that you begin to take in the fragrances of night-scented plants. One of the most delicious is that of the sweet rocket, *Hesperis matronalis*. The white and pale lilac heads of this tall, self-sowing biennial glow in the half-light and waft a clove fragrance for yards around.

Annual tobacco flowers are essential in the garden, especially the night-scented whites, with their powerful fragrance, exotic enough to transport you to tropical climes, where breezes are laden with the scent of frangipani. For visual drama, choose giant *Nicotiana sylvestris* with its drooping funnels. This year I have also been much enjoying the scent of white verbenas, which I planted in pots with deep purple heliotrope and *Argyranthemum frutescens*, a scentless tender perennial that creates a haze of glaucous blue leaves and is always studded with white daisies. I could not get over the strength and sweetness of the verbena scent in the evening and kept popping out of the back door just to drink it in. Night-scented stocks and almond-scented *Schizopetalon walkeri* will contribute further layers of fragrance.

A fruitier night-scented scheme can be orchestrated using lemon-scented annual *Mirabilis jalapa* and biennial evening primroses – pale yellow *Oenothera stricta* (*O. odorata*) is a favourite of mine – with petunias contributing a touch of vanilla.

Lilium regale is also powerful at night and is the best and easiest of the mid-summer lilies. It is worth having bulbs in pots on the patio as well as growing in the border; for a later show you might plant a pot of spicy-sweet *Lilium auratum*. In the border *L. regale* looks well in silvery schemes of white roses and artemisia and beneath crimson and yellow roses that pick up the shading on its reflexed trumpets. If your soil is not too acidic, you should also try the Madonna lily, *L. candidum*; it enjoys the rough and tumble of the flower border and a scattered drift is a ghostly sight at dusk.

The most entertaining plant on a still warm mid-summer's evening is burning bush, *Dictamnus albus* (*D. fraxinella*). You can ignite the fragrant volatile oil on the flowerheads with a match, and an orange flame flickers up each stem, releasing the resinous scent of lemon into the air. No damage is done to the plant. Success can never be guaranteed – it never works when you have an audience – for conditions have to be exactly right.

Crambe cordifolia and the giant Himalayan lily, *Cardiocrinum giganteum*, also have visitors gasping. Like a giant gypsophila, crambe releases a cloud of tiny white, honey-scented flowers from stems 2m/6ft high. It is lovely with roses and strongly coloured perennials like scarlet Maltese cross, *Lychnis chalcedonica*; but I have it all alone on a shrubbery corner, leaning over grass. Seen from the lawn it shimmers against the shadows of an old copper beech tree, but as you come around the corner from the rock garden, its flowers, billowing at head height, give you a momentary fright. Elsewhere, in our paved garden, its relative the sea kale is also in bloom. The honey scent is probably stronger but you have to bend down to savour it.

Cardiocrinum is at home in woodland clearings and in bays between rhododendrons. I cannot look at it without thinking of that bizarre photograph in Gertrude Jekyll's *Wood & Garden* that shows a clump of these plants towering over a cowled monk. The monk turns out to be her Head Gardener in disguise. 'The scent seems to pour out of the great white trumpets, and is almost overpowering', she writes, 'but gains a delicate quality by passing through the air, and at fifty yards is like a faint waft of incense.' Sadly, I never have big enough groups to notice this.

Scented perennials are comparatively few and we must rely on annuals to boost the fragrance of the herbaceous border. The multi-coloured strains of sweet sultan and snapdragon and the extraordinary poached eggs of *Limnanthes douglasii* bring a carnival spirit to the garden and always remind me of seaside holidays and promenades planted with riotous bedding schemes. Snapdragons and limnanthes are good at self-sowing, as is that other favourite, sweet alyssum. It does not have to be grown in a straight line, alternating with blue lobelia; it can be allowed to appear where it likes, taking you by surprise with its thick honey fragrance.

Queen of the scented annuals is the sweet pea. It is a labour-intensive plant but provides so much cutting material for the house that it remains a favourite. In the best varieties its French perfume pierces the nostrils. The trellises and wigwams erected for it can be useful design features, not only in the kitchen garden but in the border too; naked evidence of the gardener's craft, here in the form of canes lashed together with twine, attracts attention, particularly in this age of *laissez-faire* gardening, and can serve as a counterweight to the informality of the rest of the planting.

Among the stalwarts of the herbaceous border in high summer only the phloxes are generously scented. They can contribute great swathes of colour and, with monkshoods and

Above *In a garden setting, the more delicate fragrances may be hard to catch, especially when the air is chilly and there are more forceful neighbours around. Here the musty scent of broom dominates; the primroses and bluebells will be better appreciated if picked and brought into a warm room.*

Japanese anemones, provide a backdrop for dashing individuals like tiger lilies and fuchsias. The fragrance is sweet and peppery, and in the cool of the evening becomes quite strong on the air. An attractive companion for it is the herbaceous, non-climbing clematis, *C. heracleifolia davidiana*. 'Wyevale', with violet-blue flowers and a good sweet scent, is the best form to date but I am told that richer blue varieties are about to be introduced.

Phloxes are still going strong when galtonias appear. These bulbous plants flower in late summer and their fragrant white bells are perfect with blue agapanthus and orange and yellow kniphofias. In sunny beds, on good deep soil, they will seed themselves about. And do not overlook the sweet-scented *Verbena bonariensis* whose skeletal shapes pop up in unexpected places – in sunny borders and between paving cracks – and present their mauve flowers for months on end.

Tender perennials, lifted or propagated from cuttings each year and overwintered in a frost-free greenhouse, make an important contribution in extending the season of the summer border. Many, like argyranthemums, fuchsias and osteospermums, flower non-stop from the time they are planted out until the first frosts. Others, notably many of the salvias, come into bloom just as numbers of hardy perennials are tiring. Those that contribute scent as well as colour are doubly welcome.

Cosmos atrosanguineus, with its blood-black, chocolate-scented flowers, is a sumptuous perennial that no one would want to be without. It will often survive outdoors under a covering of peat, bracken or pulverized bark, but I find it prefers a nomadic existence; it is lifted in the late autumn and spends the winter in the border of my unheated greenhouse. Salvias are one of my favourite groups of plants and I grow so many that it is hard to find them winter accommodation. Useful for late colour, and possessing fragrant leaves, are meat-scented *S. confertiflora*, with wonderful rusty red flower spikes, blackcurrant-scented *S. microphylla*, and minty *S. uliginosa* in kingfisher blue. Again, with protection, they will survive winters in the milder areas; but it is sensible to take cuttings in early autumn as a precaution.

To round off the year, there is a flush of scented pink and white-flowered bulbs. In sunny borders there are the great trumpets of crinums followed, a little later, by the pink stars of *Amaryllis belladonna* that have the pleasant but rather synthetic scent of peach soap. Late-flowering hostas are also a feature now, displaying their white funnels, sweetly scented but with a hint of mothballs, over fresh green foliage; they associate well with pink and white colchicums.

In the shade, tucked around the boles of deciduous trees, *Cyclamen hederifolium* are in flower. To have carpets of these in the autumn garden should be the ambition of every gardener. Not only are they in bloom for a long time but their patterned leaves remain in evidence throughout winter and spring, making another lovely foil for snowdrops. To encourage a wider colonization you can transplant seedlings in the early spring; one gardener I know scatters the seed by going over the seedheads with a strimmer as they are opening, and this has proved highly successful.

Left *Late summer borders rely largely on annuals and tender perennials to maintain the display. Here cosmos and penstemons fuel the pink colour scheme, with scents provided by artemisia, box and a mass of sweet Williams. Beyond the path, lavatera and roses carry the colour up into the trees.*

Perennials

Adenophora
A. liliifolia, common ladybell, is a close relative of the campanulas, and an unusual perennial for the border. It bears loose panicles of pale blue, delicately scented bells in high summer. It should be propagated from seed, as it has fleshy roots which resent disturbance.
Sun or light shade. All but very dry soils. 46cm/18in.

Agastache
A. foeniculum (*A. anisata, A. anethiodora*) has leaves strongly scented of aniseed when rubbed. The young foliage also has an attractive purplish caste, which makes a good foil for early summer flowers, especially pale yellows. Its own flowers – chunky violet spikes that appear in late summer – are rather disappointing.
Sun. Any fertile soil. 90cm/3ft.
A. mexicana is unreliable in cold areas, but is

another interesting perennial with aromatic leaves. Its sage-like flowers, borne in high summer, vary in colour from rose-pink to crimson.
Sun. 60cm/2ft.

Anthemis
A. punctata cupaniana makes a fine silvery mat for the front of the border, and its foliage has a camomile scent. White daisies appear in early summer. It is at its best when young and should really be divided and replanted each spring.
Sun. Well-drained soil. 30cm/1ft.

Artemisia
The artemisias give the garden some of its laciest and most shimmering silver foliage but the flowers of these species are worthless. They are superb in front of pink shrub roses, with blue irises, and among white flowers. The leaves are pungently – to

my nose usually unpleasantly – scented when rubbed.
Full sun. Well-drained soil.

Asphodeline
A. lutea, asphodel, is an ancient garden plant and one of the most characterful perennials. The straw-yellow stars open on the erect flower spikes in early summer, are delicately scented and have the perfect foil in their grassy, bluish foliage.
Full sun. Well-drained soil. 90cm/3ft.

Calanthe
C. discolor is a terrestrial orchid from the Far East that is hardy outside in a sheltered spot except in very cold areas. It has large, oblong leaves and its tall stems carry up to 20 chocolate-brown flowers with pale pink lips; these are sweetly scented and appear in early summer. Plant shallowly under a leaf-mould mulch in a peat bed.
Light shade.

Clematis
C. heracleifolia davidiana is a herbaceous clematis whose pale violet-blue flowers have a deliciously sweet scent. The flowers resemble those of a hyacinth and appear in whorls up the stems in late summer. It has broad, dark foliage and makes a good clump. 'Wyevale' is a superior selection with stronger colour and an equally strong scent.
Sun or light shade. Well-drained, fertile soil. 1.2m/4ft. Z3
C. recta 'Purpurea' is a floppy herbaceous clematis for training through a shrub; mine grows through the white shrub rose 'Madame Hardy'. Its main attraction is its purplish foliage, but this varies in intensity among seed-raised plants. Cream blossom, often with a heavy scent, is borne at mid-summer and is followed by silver seedheads.
Sun or light shade. 1.2m/4ft. Z7

Far left *Agastache foeniculum*
Left *Clematis heracleifolia* 'Wyevale'

Convallaria

C. majalis, lily of the valley, is an indispensable member of the scented garden. Its small, white bells hang on a short raceme above the broad leaves in late spring and can fill the air with their piercingly sweet scent; more often, though, the scent is elusive outdoors. It resents disturbance and can be a difficult plant to establish; once settled, it will colonize readily, even along the base of a hedge. 'Fortin's Giant' is a fine, large-flowered form; 'Variegata' has cream stripes; and the mauve-pink variety *rosea* has reputedly the sweetest scent of all.
Sun or shade. All soils. 23cm/9in.

Cosmos

C. atrosanguineus is one of the most coveted of plants. Its sumptuous, velvet red flowers are almost black on opening and are produced in late summer; they breathe the mouthwatering scent of bitter chocolate. Outside the warmer regions, it is best protected with a mulch; alternatively, it may be lifted and stored like a dahlia. Growth begins very late, in spring, and it is easy to presume too soon that your plants have perished.
Sun. 60cm/2ft.

Crambe

C. cordifolia produces a cloud of tiny white flowers, like a giant gypsophila, in early summer and these have a strong honey scent. It is a large plant but the real bulk – the huge, green, heart-shaped leaves – is low down, while the top is airy and transparent. It can be grown happily at the back of the herbaceous border, but to enjoy the scent, you will have to grow it where the nose can reach, such as on a shrubbery corner.
Sun. 2m/6ft, and as much across.
C. maritima, sea kale, is grown outside the kitchen garden mainly for its broad, glaucous blue, cabbage-like leaves. These are a

Crambe cordifolia

Convallaria majalis

Cosmos atrosanguineus

Dictamnus albus

splendid foil for flowers of all colours and have good purplish tints when young. But its stiff, tight heads of white blossom are also richly honey-scented. Unless you keep cutting the leaves for flower arrangements, it needs plenty of room to luxuriate. It comes readily from root cuttings.
Sun. 60cm/2ft.

Delphinium
D. brunonianum has comparatively large flowers for its diminutive stature; they are pale purplish blue and borne on branching racemes in early summer. The scent, which is of musk, comes from the kidney-shaped, hairy leaves. It is ideal at the front of the border or in the rock garden.
Sun. 46cm/18in.
D. leroyi (*D. wellbyi*) is a rare and rather tender delphinium with the most sophisticated spurred flowers in greenish blue; they are sweetly scented and appear in high summer. It may be tried outside in the warmer areas.
Sun. 90cm/3ft.

Dictamnus
D. albus, burning bush, is an unusual perennial whose flowerheads can be ignited with a match on a warm, still summer evening; they are covered in a volatile oil,

fragrant of lemon, like the foliage. The pinnate leaves and wispy flowers are very attractive; they are white in this species and purplish in *D.a. purpureus*. They are sometimes difficult to establish and should not be disturbed when happy.
Full sun. Well-drained or dry soil. 60cm/2ft. Z3

Dryopteris
D. aemula, a British native hay-scented fern, is seldom grown or offered but is worth hunting down for the sake of its evocative hay scent that is particularly marked when the fronds are dying. It is an attractive, evergreen fern.
Light shade. Moist, well-drained, peaty soil. 60cm/2ft.

Geranium
G. endressii is a pretty ground-covering plant that smothers itself in cheerful, bright pink flowers all through the summer and autumn. Its foliage has a pronounced rose scent when brushed against, pleasing in small doses but cloying in quantity. There are a number of variants in different shades of pink, among which salmon 'Wargrave Pink' is perhaps the best; *G.* × *oxonianum* and its forms provide more pink flowers and fragrant leaves on bigger, more vigorous plants. These

geraniums make a fine underplanting for shrub roses.
Sun or shade. All soils. 46–76cm/18–30in. Z3
G. macrorrhizum is a lovely edging plant that is blessed by gardeners for its tolerance of dry, shady conditions. It flowers only in late spring but its comparatively brief performance is made up for by a display of fiery leaf colour in the autumn. The species itself has magenta-pink flowers and is surpassed in beauty by the pale pink 'Ingwersen's Variety' and, even better, 'Album', whose white flowers are set off perfectly by the red calyces. The foliage has a heavy rose scent when brushed against, and is a source of oil of geranium.
Shade. 30cm/1ft. Z3

Helleborus
H. foetidus has a very elusive flower scent, of lily of the valley, which is most pronounced in the rare, taller 'Miss Jekyll's Form'; it is also evident in the rather tender *H. lividus*. *H. foetidus* is an excellent perennial for the shady border with its elegant, fingered leaves, dark and evergreen, and its contrasting clusters of lime green bells. These are produced in late winter and are edged in maroon. It seeds itself freely and is lovely with snowdrops.
Sun or shade. All soils. 46cm/18in. Z6

Hemerocallis lilio-asphodelus (H. flava)

Hosta plantaginea

Hemerocallis

Numerous daylilies have scented flowers. The sweet lily scent is generally too heavily laced with fetid undertones for my liking; indoors it quickly becomes revolting. Strong scent is confined mainly to the species, especially those with yellow flowers, and some hybrids. The species do not flower for as long as the hybrids and usually have smaller blooms, but they have a poise and simple charm that the hybrids often lack. They are attractive companions for early roses and violet geraniums.
Sun or light shade. All but dry soils.
H. citrina is a night-blooming daylily with rather slim, citron yellow trumpets over dark leaves in mid-summer.
90cm/3ft.
H. dumortieri is a good early daylily, producing its rich apricot-yellow funnels from brown buds in early summer.
60cm/2ft.
H. lilio-asphodelus (*H. flava*) is the pick of the species, with clear lemon-yellow flowers in early summer.
60cm/2ft.
H. middendorfii has orange-yellow flowers from brown buds in early summer.
60cm/2ft.
H. minor has clear yellow flowers, flushed brown on the outside, in early summer.
46cm/18in.

Hosta

This group of perennials is grown almost entirely for its broad, chunky foliage, especially beloved by flower arrangers, garden designers and, of course, slugs; there are dozens of varieties available showing variations of leaf colour, size and shape, and since they are all so eyecatching for so long, it is tempting to fill every border with them. Their flowers are a much neglected quality. They are elegant trumpets, borne on erect stems, and some breathe a sweet lily scent.
Sun or shade. Fertile, retentive soil.
H. 'Honeybells' is a hybrid with a notable fragrance. It has pale lilac flowers in late summer and fresh green leaves. 'Royal Standard', with white flowers and good, light green leaves, is slightly scented. And of the newer varieties 'Summer Fragrance', with lilac flowers and cream-edged leaves, and 'Sugar and Cream', with white flowers and cream-edged leaves, have a sweet smell.
60cm/2ft. Z3
H. plantaginea is a late-summer flowering hosta that enjoys sunnier conditions than other hostas; it makes a good tub plant. It has wonderful lettuce green leaves and pure white flowers. The Japanese form, *grandiflora*, is every bit as desirable. If you can keep your plants free of slug holes, they are one of the glories of the late border.
60cm/2ft. Z3

Iris

I. 'Florentina' has sweetly scented, greyish white flowers in May; its dried rhizomes are also scented, of violets, and are the source of orris root. This is an attractive iris, its floral beauty enhanced by the grey-green fans of foliage.
Sun. Well-drained soil. 60cm/2ft.
I. foetidissima, the native British gladwin iris, is valued by gardeners for its evergreen, sword-shaped foliage and its tolerance of dry, shady positions. The wishy-washy lilac flowers are not very striking, but the seed-pods are sensational in the autumn when they crack open to reveal the brilliant orange seeds within. The scent interest comes from the leaves that have a slightly fetid odour when broken, reminiscent, to the imaginative, of roast beef. The flowers are a more attractive pale yellow in the form 'Citrina'.
Sun or shade. Any soil. 60cm/2ft. Z5
I. germanica, the common purple bearded iris. In spite of the great influx of more flamboyant hybrids, this iris with its sweetly scented flowers is still worth growing. It is reliable, early and does not require staking, which many of the newer forms do. A variety of fruity and vanilla scents can be detected in a number of the tall, intermediate and dwarf hybrids but it is difficult to compile a list; named varieties seem to come and go faster

than Hybrid Tea roses. Plants should be split and replanted every few years, during high summer.
Full sun. Well-drained soil. 60–90cm/ 2–3ft. Z3

I. graminea is called the plum-tart iris because of the fruity scent of its flowers; they are small, reddish purple and produced in early summer. This is a beautiful iris, with distinctively grassy leaves. For years I grew its broad-leaved variety, *pseudocyperus*, thinking it was the species, and wondered what all the fuss was about; the scent of this variety is elusive, usually absent. Now I have the species itself and have realized what I was missing. The scent is quite delicious.
Sun. 46cm/18in.

I. hoogiana is exceptionally handsome in flower and has a good rose scent. The blooms are lavender blue, with a yellow flash, and appear in early summer; the foliage is bluish green. It is an easily grown iris for the front of the border.
Sun. Well-drained soil. 60cm/2ft.

I. pallida pallida (*I.p. dalmatica*) is a pastel beauty, valuable as much for its fans of greyish foliage, which remain respectable throughout the summer, as for its pale lavender-blue flowers; these appear in early summer and are very sweetly scented. It is an old garden plant of the first order.
Sun. Well-drained soil. 90cm/3ft.

I. unguicularis (*I. stylosa*), Algerian iris, is an essential plant for the fragrant garden. It blooms cheerfully on and off throughout the winter months, and it can be brought indoors to sniff in a vase. It has rich violet flowers, marked in golden yellow, and these appear in quantity among the narrow, evergreen leaves. There are a number of colour variants; 'Mary Barnard' is a good strong violet and 'Walter Butt', in pale lavender, has an outstanding cowslip scent. It makes a good clump and wants roasting hot sunshine and poor, dry soil to flower well; the base of a sunny wall is ideal. It resents disturbance.
Full sun. Poor, dry soil. 60cm/2ft.

Iris 'Florentina'

Iris unguicularis

Bearded iris and white lilac

79

Lunaria rediviva

Lupinus polyphyllus

Lunaria

L. rediviva, perennial honesty or money plant, has white or pale lilac flowers, delicately scented of stocks, which appear in spring. Like the more common biennial honesty (which, incidentally, has a faint musty scent of its own), it has rice paper seedheads in the autumn and is an attractive plant for the spring border.
Sun or light shade. Any soil. 60cm/2ft.

Lupinus

L. polyphyllus, lupin, is a plant that no cottage garden can be without. The tall spires of flowers, standing erect above the fingered foliage, are one of the delights of early summer. They come in every colour of the spectrum. There are some good seed strains available but for the most outstanding you need to purchase from a specialist breeder. The flowers have the typical, heavy, peppery, pea-family scent. Cut away the spikes after flowering and disguise the presence of the plants – which become sad and mildewy – by growing something slightly taller in front, such as hardy chrysanthemums.
Sun or light shade. 1.2m/4ft.

Melittis

M. melissophyllum, bastard balm, is an interesting relative of dead nettle for the front of the shady border or woodland garden. The hairy leaves are markedly sweet-scented when dried. The tubular flowers are white with pinkish lower lips, and are borne in whorls in early summer.
Fertile, retentive soil. 46cm/18in.

Meum

M. athamanticum, baldmoney or spignel, with its spicily fragrant foliage and umbels of white or purplish flowers in summer, is a novelty plant for the sunny border.
Sun. 46cm/18in.

Morina

M. longifolia is a distinctive, evergreen, thistle-like plant that bears whorls of tubular, rose-pink and white flowers up stout stems in summer. But it is the prickly leaves that have a lemon fragrance. It contributes an eyecatching silhouette to the border and its flowerheads are popular for dried flower arrangements.
Sun. 90cm/3ft.

Nepeta

N. × *faassenii*, catmint, is one of the best edging plants, especially good lining a path under roses or running beneath a low retaining wall. The haze of greyish, aromatic foliage and lavender-blue flowers can be enjoyed for many weeks; if plants are cut back hard after their first early summer flush, they will provide a display on and off until the autumn. The young blue foliage is a striking complement to daffodils in the spring.
Sun. Well-drained soil. 46cm/18in. Z3
N. 'Six Hills Giant', is a more commonly offered form. It is larger, tougher, and generally considered preferable, especially in cold, damp areas.
90cm/3ft.
N. sibirica has dark grey aromatic leaves and rich blue flowers.
90cm/3ft.
N. 'Souvenir d'André Chaudron' is an uncommon catmint, exceptionally beautiful in flower – like a short version of *N. sibirica* – but beware: the leaf scent is fruitily fetid and quite nauseating.
46cm/18in.

Paeonia

Peonies play an important role in the early summer border and are an integral part of the cottage garden. Most people grow the Chinese hybrids, forms of *P. lactiflora*, which produce those great globes or dishes of pink, crimson or white petals; most of these have a spicy sweet scent. The species peonies, though usually hard to find in nurseries, are also of great beauty, in leaf as well as flower, and bloom a month or so earlier; some of these are scented too. The common peony, *P. officinalis*, has a rather unpleasant smell.
All peonies resent disturbance.
Deep, rich soil.
P. emodi is rarely offered but is a real gem. It has pure white, scented flowers, single and filled with golden stamens, in May, and bright green foliage.
Light shade. 90cm/3ft.
P. lactiflora is seldom used, in spite of its great beauty. It has large, white, scented flowers, single and filled with golden stamens, and excellent reddish foliage. It is hard to make a choice among the many hybrids, but among the doubles I would

Paeonia emodi

Paeonia lactiflora 'Sarah Bernhardt'

Paeonia lactiflora 'Duchesse de Nemours'

suggest, for scent, 'Duchesse de Nemours' in creamy white, 'Baroness Schroeder' in blush white, 'Sarah Bernhardt' and 'Clare Dubois' in pale pink, 'Laura Dessert' in palest lemon, 'Président Poincaré' in deep carmine, and 'Philippe Rivoire' in crimson. Among the singles, 'White Wings' and 'Pink Delight'.

The huge, single dishes of the Imperial or Japanese peonies, which are filled inside with smaller petals, have their own appeal, though many consider them vulgar; 'Calypso' in carmine and gold, and 'Crimson Glory' in ruby red have a good scent.
Sun or shade. 90cm/3ft.

Petasites
P. fragrans, winter heliotrope, is only for very brave or reckless gardeners. It is an extremely vigorous colonizer but fun to grow in a self-contained bed in the wild garden, ideally bounded by water. It has large, rounded foliage – smaller than the familiar *P. japonicus*, though – but its heads of white flowers, which have a strong vanilla scent, appear in late winter just before the leaves start to expand.
Retentive soil. 30cm/1ft.

Phlox

P. maculata is a little shorter than the more common *P. paniculata* and has cylindrical rather than pyramidal heads. It is usually seen in its lilac-pink 'Alpha' and white, lilac-eyed 'Omega' forms, which have the sweet, peppery phlox scent. They make a change from other phloxes and are very pretty.
Sun or light shade. Fertile, retentive soil. 90cm/3ft.

P. paniculata is a mainstay of the border in high summer and provides great blocks of colour in shades of pink, violet, crimson-purple, salmon and white. The peppery sweet scent carries well in the evening. 'White Admiral' and 'Fujiyama' are fine whites; 'Sandringham' and 'Balmoral' are good pinks; these tend to have better scents than the stronger colours. They are prone to eelworm (though this can be prevented by increasing from root cuttings) and mildew, and should be divided regularly.
Sun or light shade. Fertile, retentive soil. Up to 1.2m/4ft. Z4

Polygonatum

P. × hybridum, Solomon's seal, I mention because it is a favourite spring perennial of mine, but, truth be told, its scent is very slight. It drips its white, green-tipped bells from arching stems, and is a characterful subject for the shady border or wild garden. Shade. Retentive soil. 90cm/3ft. Z4

Polygonum

P. polystachyum is a tall invasive perennial for the wild garden or pond side. It is valuable for its autumn display of white, vanilla-scented plumes, though its pointed foliage, with its red veins and stems, is attractive all summer. Good ground cover, but only where its vigour will not be embarrassing.
2m/6ft.

Primula

P. veris, cowslip, is a plant that looks its best in the wildflower meadow; seedlings can be planted in the grass in autumn and thereafter annual mowing is delayed until mid-summer. The rich yellow bells have a distinctive sweet scent of their own.
Retentive, limy soil. 15cm/6in. Z5

P. vialii is a startling little primula that produces erect scarlet pokers from which hang violet bells; these sometimes have a good scent. Its foliage appears rather late in the year and although easily raised from seed, plants are neither long-lived nor easy to establish; but always a talking-point when in flower.
Light shade. Retentive soil. 30cm/1ft.

P. vulgaris, primrose, is lovely on shady banks, again in grass if possible. It is too well known to need description but a surprising number of people have never sniffed the pale yellow flowers. The scent is passed to many of the double kinds and is evident in many polyanthus.
Light shade. Retentive soil. 5cm/2in. Z5

Salvia

The salvias are a fascinating group of plants for the scent-conscious gardener. The scent comes from the leaves, and the range of flavours among the different species is staggering. Pineapple, blackcurrant, 'sage', rose, roast lamb and even old socks are present. I am not covering them all here, however. I have also listed sage under 'Herbs'; some of the tender species that are better suited to pot culture, are included under 'Conservatory and Tender Plants'. Among those I have treated as border plants,

Phlox maculata 'Alpha'

Primula vulgaris

several are too tender to survive winters outdoors and cuttings must be taken in late summer and overwintered in a frost-free room or glasshouse. It is well worth the trouble, not just for the scent but for the electrifying colours of the flowers. Anyone who thinks salvias begin and end with scarlet annuals – often grown on municipal roundabouts – is in for a surprise.
Sun. Well-drained soil.

S. confertiflora is an eyecatching plant that flowers in early autumn. It has thin, orange-brown, velvety flower spikes and large, pointed leaves scented of roast lamb when crushed. It benefits from the warmth of a wall to bloom before the frosts.
Full sun. 1.5m/5ft.

S. glutinosa, Jupiter's distaff, a hardy salvia with pale yellow, hooded flowers, blooms during late summer. The coarse, heart-shaped leaves have a fruity but rather clammy aroma. It is interesting rather than spectacular; ideal for the wild garden.
90cm/3ft.

S. microphylla is a shrubby salvia with small, fruity scented leaves and heads of crimson flowers. *S. grahamii* is closely related and has scarlet flowers; this has survived a number of years against a sunny wall in my garden, though like *S. microphylla* it is not considered reliable outside in cold areas. They bloom all summer and autumn.
60cm–2m/2–6ft.

S. uliginosa is a striking autumn perennial with branching spikes of flowers in kingfisher blue. The foliage is sufficiently minty to disguise the fetid undertones. It is not reliably hardy in cold areas.
Sun. Retentive soil. 1.5m/5ft.

Smilacina

S. racemosa looks very like Solomon's seal until it reveals its flowerheads which are frothy cream plumes instead of pendant bells. It is one of the taller spring perennials and is valuable for this reason; the blooms, which have a surprisingly sweet lemony scent, appear in spring on 90cm/3ft stems. It is good with early oriental poppies and tulips. I have also grown the shorter, colonizing *S. stellata*; it is rather too weedy for the border.
Light shade. Fertile, retentive, lime-free soil. Z3

Smilacina racemosa

Tellima

T. grandiflora rubra is a favourite of mine for the front of a shady border. It makes neat clumps of scalloped leaves that turn an attractive crimson in winter; they are an ideal foil for snowdrops. Wispy racemes of tiny greenish bells appear in early summer and their scent is piercingly sweet. I could not do without it.
Sun or shade. Any soil. 60cm/2ft.

Verbena

V. bonariensis is a distinctive perennial for the summer border. The flat heads of mauve flowers have a phlox-like scent and are presented at nose height on wiry branching stems. It seeds itself freely.
Sun. Well-drained soil. 1.5m/5ft. Z10

Viola

Scent is evident, though usually in small measure only, in many of the cultivars of viola, those smaller, more perennial counterparts to the pansy. They come in all colours, plain and with faces and perform for months on end. 'Aspasia' in yellow and cream, 'Little David' in cream, 'Inverurie

Viola 'Maggie Mott'

Beauty' in violet, 'Maggie Mott', a cream-centred mauve, and 'Mrs Lancaster' in white, are notably well endowed with fragrance. But to be able to savour violet scent in its richest dose, you must grow forms of sweet violet.
V. odorata, the British native sweet violet, is an easy plant that seeds itself about. It comes in all colours from purple and pink to yellow and white, and some of these are named; 'Coeur d'Alsace' is usually a particularly fine deep pink. The main flowering is in spring, but many perform in the autumn and, during mild spells, right through the winter.
Shade or, on retentive soil, sun. Fertile soil. 15cm/6in.

Florist's sweet violets

These are derived from *V. odorata* and the North American species, *V. obliqua*. They are hardy but because the flowers, particularly of the double varieties, are easily spoilt by wet and frosty weather, they are best suited to cold frame culture. When you lift the glass roof, the blast of scent is a real treat.
Fertile, retentive soil. 15cm/6in.

Bulbs

Amaryllis

A. belladonna flowers usefully late, in the autumn. Its clusters of large magenta-pink stars, which have a scent similar to apricot soap, are supported on dark purple stems. The leaves appear afterwards and persist through the winter. It likes a well-drained position, though not too dry. Pink and white forms are available.
Sun. 60cm/2ft.

Arisaema

A. candidissimum is a curious and hardy Chinese plant that is well worth growing. Its flowers take the form of spathes. These are pure white, striped inside with pink and outside with green; the spadix is greenish yellow. The flowers have a slight scent and appear in early summer. Large, three-lobed leaves follow the flowers.
Sun or light shade. Retentive, peaty soil. 30cm/1ft.

Amaryllis belladonna

Cardiocrinum

C. giganteum, the giant Himalayan lily, is among the most imposing of garden plants. Its tall stems are topped with as many as 20 enormous, pure white trumpet flowers, splashed inside with crimson-red. They have a cool, sweet scent. This is a plant for the woodland garden and would look wonderful growing in an open clearing between rhododendrons. Bulbs flower in high summer and die afterwards, leaving offsets which should be lifted the following spring and replanted with their noses just above the surface. Offsets take as long as 3 or 4 years to flower, and seed takes 12 months to germinate and up to 8 years to produce flowering-sized bulbs. But it is most definitely worth the wait. *C.g. yunnanense* has dark brownish stems, lime green flowers and a stronger scent.
Light shade. Deep, rich, retentive soil. 2.1–3m/7–10ft.

Cyclamen hederifolium

Crinum

C. × powellii produces its rose-pink trumpets on stout stems in late summer and these have the fragrance of lilies. The flowers are very impressive but are rather let down by the coarse, often battered and yellowish, strap-like leaves. Plant with the necks protruding above the soil. It needs protection from the wind and in very cold areas, a winter mulch will be necessary. There is a white form, 'Album'.
Full sun. Fertile soil, not too dry. 90cm/3ft.

Crocus

Crocuses can flood autumn, winter and early spring borders with colour, but to enjoy their scent you really need to grow some at nose level, on banks and in raised beds. The winter crocuses are often ruined by bad weather and it is a wise precaution to put a pane of glass over them as they come into flower. Growing some in pots in a cold frame, to bring indoors at flowering time is also well worthwhile. Outdoors they like ample moisture while in leaf.
Sun. Well-drained soil.
C. chrysanthus is the most important scented species and gives us a range of named varieties in shades of lavender, violet, purple, yellow and white; 'Cream Beauty', buttery 'E.A. Bowles', maroon-striped yellow *fusco-tinctus*, and white 'Snowbunting' are beautiful and especially rich in the thick, golden honey scent. They bloom in winter.
C. imperati, a buff and lavender species that flowers in mid-winter, has rather a nasty acrid scent but is lovely as a carpet.
C. laevigatus blooms in mid-winter and its lilac, feathered cups have a powerfully sweet scent. Its variety *fontenayi* has a buff exterior.
C. longiflorus has bluish violet flowers – paler on the outside – in autumn and a good, sweet scent.
C. speciosus is the easiest of autumn-flowering crocuses, often naturalizing in borders, under trees and thin grass. The scented flowers come in various shades of lilac-blue and white, and there are a number of named varieties. No garden should be without it.

Cardiocrinum giganteum yunnanense

Crocus chrysanthus 'Snowbunting' and 'Blue Pearl'

Sun or light shade. 10cm/4in.
C. versicolor has purple-veined lilac flowers in winter. They have a fine scent as have those of its white, purple-striped version 'Picturatus'.

Cyclamen
There are two species of hardy cyclamen with a pronounced scent, *C. hederifolium* and *C. purpurascens*; *C. coum* and its cousins, which make such a splash of carmine, pink and white in the late winter garden, are scentless. Other cyclamen worth growing for their lily-of-the-valley or honey fragrance, but requiring cold frame cultivation, include autumn-flowering *C. cilicium* and spring-flowering *C. balearicum* and *C. pseudibericum*. The frost-tender *C. cyprium* and *C. persicum* must be grown with a little heat, both are deliciously fragrant but the latter has not passed its scent to the large-flowered florist's strains.
Shade. Well-drained soil.
C. hederifolium (C. neapolitanum) produces its flowers in late summer, the first appearing just before the leaves. It comes in all shades

of pink and white. The musky sweet fragrance is often very faint, but there is a strongly scented strain in circulation. The foliage displays great variety in shape and silver marbling and remains in beauty from autumn until spring. It will colonize shady areas around the boles of deciduous trees and should be given a dressing of leaf mould during the summer.
C. purpurascens (C. europaeum) is a lime-loving species that blooms through the summer and autumn. It is usually evergreen, its leaves being circular with some patterning. It is reliable in all but the coldest areas.
Well-drained soil.

Galanthus
Many snowdrops have a pronounced scent, most noticeable when you bring them indoors. The common snowdrop, *G. nivalis*, is not well endowed; the double form is a little better. But for a strong honey fragrance, the

Right *Galanthus nivalis*

varieties to choose are 'S. Arnott', a superb and vigorous snowdrop with perfect flowers, and 'Straffan', a splendid late-blooming variety, with large flowers. Ideally, they should be planted and divided, like all snowdrops, immediately after flowering, not as dry bulbs in the autumn.
Light shade. Fertile, retentive soil.

Galtonia
G. candicans, the Cape hyacinth of southern Africa. The flower spikes drip with white, green-tipped bells during high summer; and these have a delicate scent. This is an invaluable border plant and superb in combination with agapanthus and kniphofia.
Sun. Well-drained, fertile but not dry soil. 90cm–1.2m/3–4ft.

Gladiolus
G. tristis is a far cry from the blowsy florist's gladioli and can be tried outside in the warmer regions; otherwise, it should be grown in a cold greenhouse. The large cream flowers, marked in green and maroon, are borne in spring among the slender leaves and have a sweet spicy scent, which is particularly strong at night. 'Christabel', in deeper yellow, is a fine hybrid.
Full sun. Fertile, well-drained soil. 46cm/ 18in.

Hermodactylus
H. tuberosus, snake's head, is a desirable spring bulb with a distinctive and rather sinister colour scheme: the iris-like flowers have greenish yellow standards and velvet

Hyacinthoides non-scripta

Hyacinthus 'Delft Blue' and 'L'Innocence'

Gladiolus 'Christabel'

black falls. These appear in spring and have a delicate clove scent. It needs a sheltered position.
Sun. Well-drained, limy soil. 30cm/1ft.

Hyacinthoides
H. non-scripta, English bluebell, fills whole woods with its balsam scent in spring but few gardeners are prepared to reproduce the experience at home. The problem is that bluebells self-sow prolifically and you very quickly find them poking up between every border plant. If you have your own wood or wild garden, that is another matter. The Spanish bluebell, *H. hispanica,* is more substantial, equally invasive, but almost scentless.
20–40cm/8–16in.

Hyacinthus
H. orientalis The florist's hyacinths can be grown outside or in bowls to be enjoyed indoors: for Christmas blooms, plant prepared bulbs in fibre in late summer and keep them somewhere cool until the emergent flowerheads are 5cm/2in high; then introduce them by stages into the warmth. All colours are available.
Unfortunately, as the flowers of new varieties get bigger, the scent becomes weaker; the old Roman hyacinths were very sweet, but where are they now?
Sun. Well-drained soil. 10–20cm/4–8in.

Iris
I. bakeriana is rare and lacking in vigour, but it is a beautiful dwarf iris with a violet scent and colour and purple and white markings on the falls. Outside, it should be planted in a raised bed, but it may be grown satisfactorily in pots in a cold frame.
Sun. Well-drained soil. 15cm/6in.
I. reticulata enjoys the same conditions outside as *I. bakeriana* and also needs a raised bed if you are to savour the violet scent; but there are few more rewarding bulbs to grow in pots to bring indoors at flowering time. The flowers are a rich imperial purple with a prominent orange-yellow flash on the falls. They are produced in mid-winter. To my nose, none of the named colour variants is as scented as its parent.
15cm/6in.

Leucojum
L. vernum, spring snowflake, looks much like a snowdrop but has green strap-like leaves and inner and outer segments (petals) of uniform length; the flowers resemble lampshades. This winter-flowering species is small with violet-scented flowers; the larger, more imposing, summer snowflake, *L. aestivum,* which flowers in spring, is unscented.
Sun or shade. Retentive or damp soil. 15cm/6in.

Lilium
L. auratum, the golden-rayed lily of Japan, bears large, open flowers during late summer. They are waxy white, streaked in golden yellow and speckled with crimson, and sometimes as many as 30 are carried on a stem. The scent is spicily sweet. It is not an easy lily to cultivate, being prone to virus, but is certainly one of the most stunning of the lilies. It enjoys shelter and is suitable for growing in pots. *L.a. platyphyllum* is shorter, stockier, larger in flower, and perhaps more amenable.
Dappled sunlight. Well-drained, lime-free, humus-rich soil. 1.5–2.5m/5–8ft.
L. candidum, the Madonna lily, has been in cultivation for centuries and is one of the easiest to grow. The tall stems carry numerous pure white, richly honey-scented, open trumpets during high summer. It is a

Iris reticulata

Leucojum vernum

Lilium auratum platyphyllum

Lilium regale

traditional feature of the cottage garden and thrives in the sunny border among perennials, which shade its basal foliage. It sends up new leaves in late summer so is best transplanted soon after flowering. Plant shallowly, with the nose at soil level. Unfortunately, it is a carrier of viruses and, accordingly, many lily growers choose to exclude it from their collections or grow it in isolation.

Sun. Limy or neutral soil. 90cm–1.8m/3–6ft.

L. cernuum is a dainty lily with small turk's cap flowers, that are rosy-lilac in colour and spotted. It has a sweet scent. It is not especially easy to grow nor is it long-lived, but it is an interesting plant for open positions with well-drained, humus-rich soil. It blooms at mid-summer.

Sun. Well-drained, humus-rich soil. 60–90cm/2–3ft.

L. duchartrei, Farrer's marble martagon. This beautiful lily bears umbels of small white fragrant flowers, which are spotted with purple and become reddish purple as they mature. It is stoloniferous and stem-rooting and can form large colonies under ideal conditions.

Shade. Retentive, peaty soil. 90cm/3ft.

L. formosanum pricei is the hardy, dwarf form of the tender *L. formosanum*, and can be safely grown outside in all but the coldest regions. It produces long, pure white, sweetly scented trumpets in late summer. It does well planted deeply among dwarf shrubs. Though short-lived, it comes readily from seed and flowers in its first year.

Sun or light shade. Well-drained, humus-rich soil. 30–60cm/1–2ft.

L. hansonii bears orange-yellow, lightly scented turk's caps in early summer and is among the easiest to grow. The flowers are speckled in brown and are not as recurved as other turk's cap species. In the right conditions it will persist for many years.

Light shade. Deep, fertile soil. 1.2–1.5m/ 4–5ft.

L. kelloggii is an interesting lily from north-west California with pendulous pale mauve-pink turk's caps, spotted maroon, which are honey-scented and appear in high summer.

Light shade. Retentive soil. 30cm–1.2m/1–4ft.

Lilium Pink Perfection

Lilium monadelphum

Lilium hansonii

L. leucanthum centifolium has trumpets that are white inside and a wonderful blend of green and rose-purple outside. They have a sweet fruity scent. It is an uncommon lily but well worth seeking out, as it is stunning when in flower.
Sun. Well-drained soil. 1.8–2.7m/6–9ft.
L. monadelphum produces its drooping reflexed trumpets at mid-summer. They are creamy yellow in colour, tinged and sometimes spotted with wine purple, and have a strong scent, sweet but slightly fetid at close range. It is an adaptable plant.
Light shade. Most soils. 90cm–1.5m/3–5ft.
L. parryi is an exceptionally lovely lily from the West Coast of America. The slightly reflexed trumpets are a clear lemon yellow and are borne in high summer. The scent is powerful and sweet. It is not an easy lily to grow, however, requiring dry conditions above ground and moist below; open woodland sites are sometimes acceptable. 60cm–1.8m/2–6ft.
L. regale is, with *L. candidum*, the most familiar of fragrant garden lilies. Its white, yellow-throated trumpets are slightly reflexed and are shaded rose-purple outside.

They open in high summer, sometimes 30 to a stem, and have a delicious fruity scent that carries well. A position between low shrubs suits it admirably, for its young shoots are susceptible to early frosts. It comes readily from seed and flowers in its second or third year. A fine pure white form, Album, is available.
Full sun. Most soils. 90cm–1.8m/3–6ft.
L. × testaceum, the Nankeen lily, has scented turk's caps in a delicate shade of creamy apricot. It flowers in high summer. It is an easy lily to grow but is now becoming rare.
Full sun. Deep, fertile, acid or alkaline soil. 1.2–1.8m/4–6ft.

Hardy hybrid lilies
Many hybrid lilies have been bred from scented lily species. The Oriental hybrids (O), which include strains and clones derived from *L. × parkmannii*, generally thrive in open, woodland conditions, on acid, gritty, humus-rich soil, with their heads in the sun and their roots in the shade; the trumpet and so-called Aurelian hybrids (T) usually prefer full sun and a drier soil. The following are among the best fragrant varieties.

'Black Dragon' (T) is a strong, vigorous lily with large white, recurved trumpets, stained reddish brown outside. It flowers in high summer. 1.2–1.8m/4–6ft.
'Green Dragon' (T) is similar to 'Black Dragon' but has a green reverse. They are both highly desirable lilies.
Imperial Crimson (O) is a strain of flamboyant lilies with open, white flowers, suffused and speckled with bright rose-red. They bloom in high summer. 1.2–1.5m/4–5ft.
Imperial Gold (O) is a strain of lilies which have open, glistening white flowers, striped in gold and peppered with crimson spots. They flower in high summer. 1.2–1.5m/4–5ft.
Imperial Silver (O) is similar to Imperial Gold but lacks the rich stripe.
'Limelight' (T) bears unusual greenish yellow funnels in high summer. It is a reliable and impressive variety which tolerates some shade. 1.2–1.8m/4–6ft.
Olympic hybrids (T) provide a range of splendid scented trumpet lilies, from cream to pink and yellow. 1.2–1.5m/4–5ft.
Pink Perfection (T) is a strain of bright pink trumpet lilies which flower in July. 1.5–1.8m/5–6ft.

Muscari armeniacum

Muscari macrocarpum

Narcissus recurvus

Muscari

M. armeniacum is one of the most common of the grape hyacinths. Its bright azure blue pokers appear in spring and are delicately honey-scented. It is a vigorous colonizer for the front of the border. The grassy foliage is evident throughout the winter. It is lovely with primroses.

Sun or light shade. Most soils. 20cm/8in.

M. botryoides is less vigorous than *M. armeniacum* and trustworthy among choice plants, even in the rock garden. Its china-blue flowers have a good honey scent. The white form, *album*, is commonly available. Sun. 15cm/6in.

M. muscarimi (M. moschatum) is a curiosity with flowers that change from purple to yellowish green as they age. It has the best scent of all muscari, a sweet musk fragrance which carries in the air on warm days. *M. macrocarpum*, with bright yellow flowers, is closely related.

Sun. 20cm/8in.

Narcissus

This great tribe contributes colour throughout spring. The larger daffodils are at their best at the back of the border, where their dying leaves are concealed by the growth of other plants, or in grass, where they can be left to naturalize; their foliage must not be cut down until 6 weeks after flowering. The smaller daffodils are for the front of the border, the rock garden, raised beds or even for pots to be brought indoors at flowering time; some may also be grown in grass. There is scent in most of them. Often it is pleasantly mossy and often it is nastily fetid; but in some it is powerfully sweet and these are the varieties I describe here.

N. assoanus (N. juncifolius) is a miniature jonquil with narrow leaves and small, deep yellow flowers in early spring. These have a good scent. It can be grown outside in sheltered spots but is perhaps best as a pot bulb.

Sun. Well-drained soil. 15cm/6in.

N. jonquilla, jonquil, has perhaps the sweetest scent of all daffodils. It has narrow rushy leaves and small, very shallow-cupped, bright yellow flowers. 'Queen Anne's Double Jonquil' and 'Pencrebar' are double forms with outstanding scents. There are many

Narcissus jonquilla

excellent, powerfully scented, single jonquils, derived from this and other jonquil species, including: 'Baby Moon', dwarf yellow; 'Bobbysoxer', yellow with orange cup; 'Lintie', clear yellow with orange cup; 'Orange Queen', deep orange-yellow; 'Sugar Bush', white with pinkish cup; 'Sundial', pale yellow with orange cup; 'Suzy', bright yellow with bright orange cup; and 'Trevithian' in lemon yellow. Outside, they need a sheltered position. They are superb pot bulbs.
Sun. 30cm/1ft.
N. × odorus rugulosus is a good form of the

Campernelle jonquil, and has bright yellow flowers with a deeper cup than *N. jonquilla*. 30cm/1ft.
N. poeticus recurvus, old pheasant's eye narcissus, is a lovely, unsophisticated daffodil for naturalizing in grass. It blooms at the end of the daffodil season and has white flowers with a tiny, yellow, orange-rimmed cup. There is a rare, pure white, double form called 'Plenus'; 'Actaea' is a single form, with larger flowers, a finer shape, and more vigour; and 'Cantabile' gives single flowers of perfect, exhibition quality. All have an

outstanding sweet scent.
Sun or light shade. Retentive soil. 38cm/15in.
N. rupicola is similar to *N. assoanus* but it has larger flowers, singly borne, and glaucous greyish leaves. It is also a better garden plant with a stronger scent.
Sun. Well-drained soil. 15cm/6in.
N. tazetta is a sweetly scented, bunch flowered daffodil that needs a hot, dry, sheltered site to perform satisfactorily outside. The closely related *N. canaliculatus* is more commonly offered; this has white flowers with golden cups. Fine named

hybrids of *N. tazetta* include 'Minnow', a lemon yellow dwarf; 'Geranium', white with orange cup; 'Silver Chimes' in creamy white; and white 'Cheerfulness' and 'Yellow Cheerfulness', both doubles. These are reliable outside, if given sun and shelter, and also make good pot bulbs; the popular Christmas pot tazetta 'Paper White' is unreliable outside except in mild areas. 46cm/18in.

Notholirion
N. thomsonianum is a rare plant for the connoisseur. It bears pale rose-lilac flowers that are funnel-shaped with recurving tips, like a lily. These are carried on tall stems in spring and are sweetly scented; the leaves are long and narrow. It requires a sheltered position and cool greenhouse treatment is usually necessary in colder regions.
Full sun. Well-drained soil. 90cm/3ft.

Scilla
S. mischtschenkoana (*S. tubergeniana*) is a miniature plant that produces its pale, cup-shaped flowers with its strap-like leaves in early spring. They have a sweet scent.
Sun or light shade. Well-drained soil. 5–10cm/2–4in.

Tulipa
Scent is not a quality you expect to find in tulips but a few species, and even a few tall hybrids, possess a warm sweet scent worth recording.
T. clusiana, lady tulip, is a striking species with scented white flowers, striped in crimson-pink in spring. It appreciates heat and shelter.
Sun. Well-drained soil. 30cm/1ft.
T. humilis (*T. aucheriana*) is, in its most scented form, a dwarf pale pink tulip, striped in greenish yellow with a deep golden yellow base. But it is very variable and there are many strains with magenta and purplish flowers. It is excellent as a pot plant, but short-lived outside.
Sun. Well-drained soil. 15cm/6in.
T. sylvestris is easily cultivated and one of the few tulips which can be satisfactorily naturalized in grass. It is often shy to flower though. The blooms are bright yellow with pointed segments and open in mid spring. Sun or light shade. Moist soil. 30cm/1ft.
T. tarda is a dwarf tulip for sunny rock gardens and raised beds. It produces bunches of white, starry flowers, tinged greenish yellow on the outside and filled with yellow within. These appear in mid spring and have a noticeable scent. It is easily grown and reliable.
Sun. Well-drained soil. 15cm/6in.

Hybrid tulips
The best known scented hybrids are 'General de Wet' ('De Wet'), in bright golden orange, 'Bellona' in golden yellow, and 'Prince of Austria' in bright orange red. They are good, tall-stemmed plants but 'Prince of Austria' seems to have vanished completely from bulb lists. 'Oranjezon' ('Orange Sun') and 'Lighting Sun' are, I am told, new introductions with a sweet scent; I have not sniffed them. The parrot tulip 'Orange Favourite' is also scented.
Sun. 38cm/15in.

Tulipa sylvestris

Tulipa tarda

Annuals and Biennials

Abronia

A. umbellata, sand verbena, is the best known of this group of scented Californian plants but even this species is not as common as in the past, when it was much used for hanging baskets, especially in the conservatory. It is a half-hardy annual or perennial of trailing habit. Its domed heads of rose-pink flowers appear among the kidney-shaped leaves from high summer until early autumn. They have a sweet scent which carries freely at night.
Sun. Well-drained soil. 15cm/6in.

Antirrhinum

A. majus, snapdragon, is a sweet-scented half-hardy annual that comes in a kaleidoscope of brilliant colours, as singles or doubles, and in a range of heights. It often self-sows. Rust can be a problem, and resistant varieties are available. A summer bedding favourite.
Sun. Well-drained soil. 23–90cm/9in–3ft.

Asperula

A. orientalis (A. azurea setosa), blue woodruff, is a charming, old-fashioned hardy annual for the front of the border. Its slender leaves are borne in whorls and create a hazy effect; they are topped from high summer until autumn with clusters of tubular, violet blue flowers, which have a sweet scent.
Sun. 30cm/1ft.

Calendula

C. officinalis, pot marigold, has a distinctive tangy scent in flowers and foliage. It is a medicinal and culinary plant and is as much at home in the herb garden as the flower border. The flowers are brilliant orange. Many garden varieties are available, including creams and yellows, and forms with extra large, fully double flowers. It is fully hardy, can be sown *in situ* in autumn or spring, and will seed itself thereafter. The flowers are good for cutting.
Sun or light shade. 46cm/18in.

Cheiranthus cheiri

Centaurea

C. moschata, sweet sultan, is a hardy annual now most commonly seen in its Giant or Imperialis strain. The large, fluffy flowers are borne on tall stems from high summer until early autumn and are excellent for cutting. They come in shades of rose-pink, white, purple, and lemon yellow and all have a powerful, musk-sweet fragrance. Another cottage garden favourite.
Sun. 60cm/2ft.

Cheiranthus

C. cheiri, wallflower, with its Persian carpet colours and warm, aniseed scent, is an almost indispensable feature of the spring garden. It is treated as a biennial and seed is sown outdoors in late spring. The seedlings are thinned during the summer and plants are transferred into their final positions in autumn. Wallflowers are available in single or mixed colours.
Sun. Well-drained soil. 46cm/18in.

Dianthus

D. barbatus, sweet William, is usually grown as a biennial; seed is best sown early, under glass, in mid to late spring. The flowers are borne in generous heads during early summer and contribute much to the cottage garden mood. Single and double flowers are available, in single or mixed colour collections. Some flowers have pronounced eyes, and the colour range encompasses lilac, mauve, rose and magenta pink, white and blood red. At their best, they have a superb clove fragrance, but highly selected strains often have little or no scent. The flowers are good for cutting.
Sun. 15–60cm/6in–2ft.

D. caryophyllus, carnation, can make an excellent and easy half-hardy annual. The Chabaud Giant is one of the best strains with large, double, fringed blooms usually in crimson, salmon and rose-pink. The 'Knight' series of F1 hybrids also gives fine bedding plants in a superb range of colours including yellows and whites and many with flecks. Dwarf and pendulous carnations are also

available. The clove scent is invariably powerful.
Sun. Well-drained soil. 30–46cm/12–18in.

Dracocephalum

D. moldavicum, dragon's head, is an unusual hardy annual, popular with bees. It has hooded, wide-lipped, violet-blue flowers, which are carried in whorls throughout the summer. But the scent comes from the leaves, whose fragrance is like that of lemon-scented balm. It makes an erect bushy plant.
Sun or light shade. 46cm/18in.

Erysimum

E. allionii (E. perofskianum) is a member of a botanically muddled group, closely related to *Cheiranthus*. It is a true annual with heads of rich orange flowers during the summer. Other species appear in catalogues from time to time, some under the name of 'alpine wallflowers'. All can be treated as biennials, and the majority have some degree of clove scent.
Sun. Well-drained soil. 46cm/18in.

Exacum

E. affine is a tender annual that must be grown in the greenhouse or as a house plant. Seed can be sown in early spring for summer flowering or, if a minimum temperature of 16°C/60°F can be maintained, in late summer for spring flowering. It is a compact and attractive plant whose lavender flowers have a strong and exotic scent.
15cm/6in.

Gilia

G. tricolor, birds' eyes, is an easy to grow, unusual hardy annual, that has small lavender and white flowers. These have a throat beautifully marked in maroon and yellow and breathe the scent of chocolate.
Sun. Well-drained soil. 46cm/18in.

Heliotropium

H. arborescens (H. peruvianum), cherry pie, a half-hardy annual, is usually offered in the strain called 'Marine', which has very dark leaves topped with large heads of deep violet flowers. Although visually seductive, its vanilla-like, heliotrope scent does not compare in strength to that possessed by the perennial varieties propagated by cuttings; these are described under 'Conservatory Plants'.
Sun. 46cm/18in.

Hesperis

H. matronalis, sweet rocket, is an essential plant for the cottage garden. The tall heads of white or lilac flowers, borne during the summer, really come into their own in the evening when they become luminous and fill the air with a light, sweet scent. Although a perennial, younger plants are preferable and sweet rocket is usually treated as a biennial; it will self-sow freely. Its double-flowered forms, which have to be propagated by cuttings, or, more slowly by division, have long been rare, coveted and virus-ridden, but thanks to micro-propagation, clean stock is now coming into circulation.
Sun or light shade. 1.2m/4ft.

Far left *Heliotropium arborescens*
Left *Dianthus barbatus*

Hesperis matronalis and *Rosa* 'Bourbon Queen'

Iberis

I. amara, rocket candytuft, is, for the scent-conscious gardener, a preferable species to the common candytuft, *I. umbellata*. There are different strains available; plants can be dwarf, with rounded heads, or have tall, erect heads like the Giant Hyacinth Flowered strain. All are white with a sweet scent and are treated as hardy annuals.
Sun. 15–38cm/6–15in.

Ionopsidium

I. acaule, violet cress, is a tiny lilac-flowered plant that has to be grown in a raised bed for its delicate scent to be appreciated. It is hardy, can be sown *in situ* and enjoys moisture. It will often seed itself.
Light shade. 7.5cm/3in.

Ipomoea

I. alba **(Calonyction aculeatum)**, moonflower, is a half-hardy climber, related to morning glory, that can be grown as an annual against a sheltered wall outside or in the greenhouse. At its best in the evening and early morning when the huge white saucers breathe their exotic scent, it flowers continually in summer.
Sun. 6m/20ft.

Lathyrus odoratus

Matthiola incana Brompton strain

Lathyrus

L. odoratus, sweet pea. The piercing scent of sweet peas epitomizes summer in the cottage garden. Unfortunately, the modern Spencer varieties have obtained their size, colour and perfection of form largely at the expense of fragrance, although there are some fragrant strains around. To give the nose a real feast, you have to return to the older varieties. These are usually offered in an Old-fashioned or Grandiflora mix, but sometimes you can acquire named kinds like 'Painted Lady', the oldest sweet pea variety and a carmine and white bicolour, or 'Matucana', a luxurious maroon and mauve bicolour. These are all powerfully sweet. To obtain the best plants, sow singly in 7.5cm/3in pots under glass in late winter. Plant out when large enough, in early spring. Support the seedlings with bushy twigs and then train them onto wigwams or trellises of canes and string. Feed, water and dead-head regularly.
Sun. Deep, rich soil. 2–2.5m/6–8ft.

Limnanthes

L. douglasii, poached egg flower or meadow foam, is a popular hardy annual which self-sows freely and is much visited by bees. The white, golden-centred saucers are delicately scented and appear all summer above the hazy foliage.
Sun and light shade. Any soil. 15cm/6in.

Lobularia

L. maritima (Alyssum maritimum), sweet alyssum, is one of the most popular hardy annuals, not least for the rich golden honey scent released by the lacy flowers. It blooms from early summer until autumn and the colour range encompasses white, lilac, pink, carmine and purple. Its dwarf habit makes it ideal for edging, rock gardens and raised beds. It often self-sows, but plants become less compacted and revert to white.
Sun or light shade. Well-drained soil. 10cm/4in.

Lupinus

L. luteus, yellow lupin, is the plant the scent-conscious gardener should grow as a soil improver. The tall, dense spikes of yellow flowers have a sweet, beanfield fragrance; and plants 'fix' nitrogen and can be dug back into the soil at the end of the season. Treat as a hardy annual.
Sun or light shade. 60cm/2ft.

Matthiola

M. bicornis, night-scented stock, never looks much by day, but the wispy lilac flowers open in the evening to pour out their clove scent. It is hard to believe that so insignificant a thing is so potent that it can fill the air with sweetness. Sow the seed *in situ* under windows and beside paths in order to enjoy the scent.
Sun. 30cm/1ft.

M. incana From this species are derived the annual and biennial stocks, without which no scented garden would be complete. The clove fragrance is delicious both by day and by night. Viruses can be troublesome.
The half-hardy annual stocks are available in Ten Week and Seven Week strains, comprising rather dumpy, double and single flowers; and in Giant Imperial, Excelsior and Beauty of Nice strains with erect, columnar heads. The colour range comprises crimson, rose, lilac, white, apricot and yellow.
Sun. 38–76cm/15–30in.

The hardy biennial stocks are available in the East Lothian and Brompton strains. The

Mirabilis jalapa

East Lothian stocks are sown in high summer to produce dwarf plants for flowering under glass the following spring (Beauty of Nice stocks also perform well as winter pot plants if sown in high summer); they can also be treated as late flowering annual stocks. The Brompton stocks are sown in high summer for flowering outdoors the following spring. Both have medium-sized spikes of flowers in the same colour range as the annual stocks. Sun. 46cm/18in.

M. incana 'White Perennial' persists for many years. The powerfully fragrant white flowers are set against a mound of grey leaves. The lilac version is equally desirable. Sun. 45cm/18in.

Mirabilis

M. jalapa, marvel of Peru, was a favourite plant of the Victorians. Its trumpet-shaped flowers, produced all summer, can be pink, rose red, yellow or white and are deliciously lemon-scented. They do not open until late afternoon, hence the alternative common name of 'four o'clock'. It is usually grown as a half-hardy annual.
Sun and heat. Well-drained soil. 60–90cm/ 2–3ft.

Nicotiana

N. alata is a half-hardy annual that has given rise to the various strains of coloured tobacco flowers, those popular bedding plants which have starry blooms in carmine pink and red, white and lime green. Many of them have a good scent and have the advantage over the more potent *N.a. grandiflora*, described below, in keeping their flowers open during the day. Sun or light shade. Fertile soil. 25–90cm/ 10in–3ft.

N. alata grandiflora (*N. affinis*) is the familiar white tobacco flower, whose large starry flowers fill the evening air with an exotic scent. By day it is rather weedy-looking but at dusk it glows with an ethereal beauty. It is treated as a half-hardy annual. Sun or light shade. Fertile soil. 90cm/3ft.

N. suaveolens is an unusual annual with white, tubular flowers, shaded greenish purple on the outside, which are powerfully scented at night.
Sun or light shade. 60cm/2ft.

N. sylvestris is visually the most impressive tobacco flower and is among the most architectural of annuals. It forms a bulky, leafy, bright green plant with stout stems topped with panicles of drooping, tubular, white flowers. In the evening, the exotic

Nicotiana alata

Nicotiana sylvestris

scent is released. This half-hardy annual is excellent as a specimen or in a group. Sun or light shade. 1.5m/5ft.

Oenothera

O. biennis, common evening primrose, releases a sweet, lemon scent in the evening, when it opens its bright yellow saucers. It is a popular annual or biennial which self-sows freely; indeed, it can prove too energetic, and may need to be confined to the wilder parts of the garden.
Sun. Well-drained soil. 90cm/3ft.
O. caespitosa is a very lovely, dwarf species with a superb sweet scent, slender, hairy leaves and particularly large, white flowers which by morning have faded to pink. It is usually treated as a hardy biennial, but is often perennial, and is grown ideally in a raised bed.
Sun. Well-drained soil. 15cm/6in.
O. odorata is a great favourite of mine and usually behaves as a biennial with me, self-sowing into paving cracks. The large saucers open a creamy yellow in the evening, when they breathe their lemon scent; by the next morning they have faded to a peach pink.
Sun. Well-drained soil. 60cm/2ft.
O. trichocalyx is an evening primrose of bewitching beauty and neat habit. Its large, sweetly scented flowers are pure white, and have the advantage of remaining open during the day. Although a biennial or perennial plant, it is often treated as an annual.
Sun. Well-drained soil. 46cm/18in.

Petunia

Petunias are among the most popular summer bedding plants, and it comes as a surprise to many people to discover they sometimes have a vanilla scent, most evident in the evening. But colour rather than scent has been the quality pursued by the plant breeders, and I cannot recommend any particularly fragrant strains; however, white, violet-blue and purple petunias seem to be better endowed than others. They are treated as half-hardy annuals.
Sun. Well-drained soil. 23cm/9in.

Phacelia

P. campanularia The best known of this group of Californian hardy annuals, it does have fragrant leaves but it is commonly grown for the dazzling, gentian blue flowers which it produces all summer. It is beloved by bees. Its relative, *P. ciliata*, apparently has scented, lavender blue flowers, but I have not met it.
Sun. 15cm/6in.

Proboscidea

P. louisianica (Martynia louisianica), unicorn plant, is a rare, half-hardy annual with downy, heart-shaped leaves, sticky to the touch, and large, gloxinia-like flowers. These come in shades of cream, rose and purple, are marked in yellow and purple, and have a sweet scent. The flowers are followed by strange fruits shaped like curved horns. It can be grown outside in a sheltered spot but is more reliable under glass.
Sun. 60–90cm/2–3ft.

Reseda

R. odorata, mignonette, is one of the best known fragrant hardy annuals. Alas, the scent is often elusive, but at its best is piercingly sweet, tinged with raspberry, and can be powerful by day and night. It has rather weedy-looking flowers of greenish white, but modern strains have better colouring and bigger heads. It succeeds well as a pot plant indoors – seed can be sown in late summer for spring flowering. Outside, seed can be sown from early spring onwards to ensure a succession of bloom; it makes a long-lasting cut flower.
Sun. 30cm/1ft.

Scabiosa

S. atropurpurea, sweet scabious. This upright, bushy species bears dark purple, pink or white, flat pincushion flowers on tall stems and is beautifully scented. The newer garden varieties have larger, fully double flowers with raised centres. They are treated as hardy annuals and bloom in late summer and autumn. They last well in water.
Sun. 46–90cm/18in–3ft.

Far left *Oenothera biennis*
Left *Reseda odorata*

Schizopetalon

S. walkeri is an interesting half-hardy annual whose white, fringed flowers release an almond scent in the evening. Seed must be sown either in small potfuls, to be planted out in the late spring, or directly into the ground earlier in the season.
Sun. 30cm/1ft.

Tagetes

I cannot believe anyone would choose to grow French or African marigolds because they like the scent. Even whitefly evacuate the greenhouse at the first whiff of it and indeed, many growers use marigolds to keep pests at bay. But it you like your scents good and pungent, the seed catalogues offer a tempting array of sunshine strains.

Tropaeolum

T. majus, nasturtium. The nasturtium offers sweetly scented flowers in its 'Gleam' varieties. These are semi-double, and come in shades of yellow, orange and scarlet. They are bushy and semi-trailing in habit. Nasturtiums are hardy annuals and are useful for cheering up neglected parts of the garden. They look particularly well on gravel paths and drives, where they will often self-sow, and when hoisting themselves up shrubs like *Cotoneaster horizontalis*. The flowers can be used in salads.
Sun or shade. 30cm/1ft.

Verbena

V. × *hybrida*, common garden verbena, is available in many strains and is grown as a half-hardy annual. The sweet, exotic scent, which is released in the evening, is more pronounced in the white, pink and violet shades than in the brilliant reds. It is a cheerful plant, producing its tight heads of flower all summer, and looks well in pots and in the border. 'Showtime' is a strain giving bright, compact plants.
Sun. 23–30cm/9–12in.

Zaluzianskya

Z. capensis is an unusual half-hardy annual that is powerfully fragrant at night. It bears white, starry flowers which remain closed during the daytime. *Z. villosa* has white flowers with an orange centre, and has an equally potent scent.
Sun. Well-drained soil. 30cm/1ft.

Scented verbena

Walled Gardens and Vertical Planting

Walls are prized by all keen gardeners. They offer support for a range of climbing plants and protection for a number of shrubs not hardy enough to withstand life in the open. Scent-conscious gardeners value them above all for their help in creating a warm, still, microclimate in which fragrances are richly diffused and held captive.

While few people have gardens girdled by stone and brick, most of us have house walls that can be draped in greenery. The most precious aspects are those that enjoy the strongest sunshine and shelter from cold winds. Walls that receive full sun in particular offer scope for really adventurous planting, and those gardeners who rise to the challenge are frequently rewarded with flourishing shrubs and climbers of such an exotic character that visitors rub their eyes in disbelief.

Patios and sitting-out areas should, ideally, be backed by sunny walls so that the air is warm and still as you sit, and the aromas intense. Night-scented plants ought to be present to take over from the daytime fragrances; and you will want to make sure that no unpleasant scents can disturb you in this, the fragrant garden's inner sanctum. You are unlikely to be sitting outdoors much in the coldest months of the year, so the sun-loving scented wall shrubs and climbers that perform in winter and early spring are not prime candidates for patio areas. Reserve these for summer-bloomers, if possible, and plant your early spring performers somewhere less precious.

Winter sweet, *Chimonanthus praecox*, is one of the pleasures of mid-winter and, brought into the warmth of a room, its cut stems will fill the air with a spicy lemon scent. The inner segments of the flowers are purplish but the outer segments are disappointingly translucent and you may like to partner it with the more cheerful yellow of winter jasmine; and perhaps underplant with violet winter irises. The flowers are fairly frost-proof but its wood needs a good summer ripening, which is why a wall that receives full sun is advisable.

It has taken me a long time to discover Japanese apricots. They bloom on bare stems in late winter and appreciate the shelter and warmth of a sunny wall. The perfume is wonderfully sophisticated and seems to vary greatly from variety to variety. Rose-scented 'Beni-shidare', in rich rose-pink, is my favourite apricot and would be sensational against a white-washed wall, with white 'Omoi-no-mama' ('Omoi-no-wac') for brick or grey stone. In Britain, birds usually strip the buds unless plants are protected by black cotton from autumn onwards. But in North Carolina, where for some reason birds do not seem to be such a problem to gardeners, I have seen unprotected plants flowering magnificently in the open border.

Daphne bholua might be offered a sheltered nook near a wall. This is a plant worth cosseting since it can be in bloom throughout the winter season. Deciduous forms like 'Gurkha' are generally showier than evergreen ones and the effect is not dissimilar to that of winter-flowering viburnum, to which this daphne might serve as an echo in the design. A bush of evergreen *D. odora* 'Aureomarginata' could provide some accompanying foliage and would take over the scent production from its cousin in late spring.

Azara microphylla flowers in late winter. Its scent is of vanilla, and it is thrilling to catch a cloud of it as you hurry to the front door or woodshed. A number of other vanilla and almond-scented plants are in flower at the same time or are poised to enter the stage, and it would be an appealing idea to devote one sunny corner to them. The colour scheme would be green and white and you would have flowers over many months. *Abeliophyllum distichum* opens in mid-winter,

Right *Pergolas need plants which look and smell good from underneath. Wisteria, with its pendulous racemes of fragrant flowers, is an ideal candidate. Here the swags of* W. floribunda *'Multijuga', visually one of the most impressive varieties though less strongly scented than some, are perfectly matched in colour by the lilac bearded irises beyond.*

Clematis armandii in late winter and *Choisya ternata* and *Clematis montana* in spring. The large evergreen leaves of *C. armandii* would counter the skimpy appearance of both azara and abeliophyllum and *Choisya ternata* would offer a mound of glossy foliage to clothe the ground.

Space is always short on sunny walls and choosing just a few plants among the many exciting summer performers is exceedingly difficult; it is especially tricky deciding what to have around the patio. For me, ceanothus is the sovereign of the late spring season. To have a cloud of indigo drifting across your wall or fence is a rare treat for the eye. But, though some ceanothus often have a good dose of honey scent, I have to admit that there are plants with a more enticing fragrance.

Moroccan broom, *Cytisus battandieri*, with its pineapple scent, is quite delicious, and the rich yellow cones are set strikingly against silvery leaves. But it does need a high wall. Mine is against a wall 2.4m (8ft) tall, and I am constantly having to cut it back to prevent the wind catching its top growth and ripping the whole plant from its wire supports. I should have done better to plant it as a free-standing specimen; except in very cold areas, it will thrive happily in the open in a sheltered position. Honey scents go well with pineapple and you could partner the broom with *Olearia macrodonta* and *Helichrysum ledifolium* (*Ozothamnus ledifolius*); the colour scheme would be yellow and white.

Roses are always tempting; their colour, scent and romantic associations enhance every planting scheme. But since you do not actually need a wall to grow roses, they do not top my list of candidates. The same applies to wisteria, though I dearly love the Japanese variety draped over my sitting-room window. An assortment of other shrubs and climbers are more deserving. First, there is *Carpenteria californica*, a fine evergreen shrub with large, delicately scented white saucers. It performs at the same time as the Moroccan broom and on a high wall they make excellent companions. Then there are the myrtles. You get a double dose of spicy scent from these evergreens, for both the leaves and flowers are aromatic. Some species bloom in late spring but others, including the common myrtle that is the best choice for most gardeners, perform in late summer. They are ideal candidates for the patio, since you can enjoy the fragrance of the flowers in the air and tweak the leaves as you sit.

I would want *Cestrum parqui* somewhere but not by the patio. Late at night the fragrance from the tiny greenish flowers is potently and spicily sweet, but in the daytime and early evening, when you are sitting outside, the scent is unpleasantly meaty (though, thankfully, it is not breathed into the air). *Buddleja crispa* is certainly a prime candidate for the best position. Its lilac flowers and sweet scent can be enjoyed all summer and autumn. It needs winter protection in cold areas in the form of a wire overcoat stuffed with straw or bracken and a generous mound of pulverized bark over its roots. But once you have seen it in its full glory, you will not begrudge it any amount of care. Purple heliotropes are attractive in front of it and if there is room I should allow a passion flower to rise up beside it.

Among summer-flowering climbers, one of my favourites is star jasmine, *Trachelospermum jasminoides*. Its exotic scent has the flavour of bubblegum and none of the headiness of real jasmine. It survived at −20°C/−4°F in one garden I know, so once established, it is hardier than generally supposed. In colder areas, you will also have to provide a warm wall for *Jasminum officinale*, but before you plant it near the patio, consider whether you really want to be drowned in its scent. Would it be better wafting to you on the evening breeze from another part of the garden?

Honeysuckles are essential somewhere in the vicinity of your sitting-out area, but you need not waste a sunny wall on them. If there is no fence or pergola close by, then you could grow them as standards, trained up a post. They fill the air with scent in the cool of the evening. It is usually a fruity fragrance – all forms of *Lonicera periclymenum* are delicious – but *Lonicera × americana* is distinctly clove-like.

Towering trees of *Magnolia grandiflora* are a feature of many gardens in the eastern United States, but in Britain this magnolia is usually encountered on a sunny wall, for it needs every ray of sunshine to ripen its wood. The great cream goblets open into lemon-scented waterlilies and you have to bury your face in them to enjoy a deep draught of fragrance. A few flowers are usually within your reach from the ground but your chief goal should be to be able to stretch lazily out of your bedroom window and drink from there. All wispy companions look inadequate next to this magnolia's substance and aristocratic bearing, so I should choose something with architectural presence: spiky yuccas, perhaps, whose creamy candelabras shine crisply against the magnolia's glossy, evergreen foliage; or *Pittosporum tenuifolium*, whose tiny chocolate flowers deliver their honey scent in spring, before the magnolia has begun.

In mild regions, many shrubs and climbers which I have listed under 'Conservatory and Tender Plants' can also be considered for a protected wall. Acacias, tender buddlejas, callistemons, coronillas, lemon verbena and prostantheras are among them. It may be sensible to take cuttings every year, just in case there is an exceptionally hard winter, but such supposedly tender plants are forever surprising us with their resilience and powers of rejuvenation.

Walls that are shaded and cold offer less scope for adventurous planting. But you do not have to resort entirely to ivies, pyracanthas and climbing hydrangea. Many honeysuckles are happy here, as are many clematis, including the vanilla-scented montanas; and many climbing roses will tolerate shade, including white 'Madame Alfred Carrière' and pink 'New Dawn'. The semi-evergreen honeysuckle, *Lonicera japonica* 'Halliana', which has an exceptionally strong fruity fragrance, can also be expected to thrive. Winter-flowering shrubby honeysuckles – *Lonicera fragrantissima, L. standishii* and *L. × purpusii* – may be trained against a shaded wall and their creamy, lemon-scented flowers often show up better here than in the open. *Daphne laureola* and *D. pontica* are low evergreen companions for them; their greenish yellow flowers are carried in spring, and late evening is the best time to catch their elusive scent. You might also include honey-scented *Mahonia aquifolium* – which responds well to vertical training and climbs surprisingly high – and berberis; these will inject some strong colour.

I think my favourite scented shrub for a shady wall is *Osmanthus × burkwoodii*. Its white flowers, borne in spring, are deliciously sweet and the fragrance carries well. The small, dark, evergreen leaves are a fine foil for other plants and the whole shrub is very compact and can be clipped to shape. Pieris, skimmia and *Viburnum × burkwoodii* produce their scented white flowers at the same time and are also shade-tolerant and evergreen. The autumn-flowering osmanthuses help to bring late interest to shady walls, as do mahonias such as *M. lomariifolia* and the hardier *M. bealei*. They have bold, dramatic foliage and the racemes of flowers stand erect.

You do not need walls in order to grow hardy climbing plants. These can be spun around pergolas, along fences and trelliswork, over outbuildings, up telegraph poles and trees, and across ropes and wires; they can even be used as ground-cover, under trees, down banks and over tree stumps.

If you are planning a tunnel or arch for walking under or an arbour or bower for sitting in, be sure to choose plants whose flowers you can enjoy from below. Most would display their flowers on the outside so you would find yourself under a canopy dripping only with rain. Lilac-blue and white wisterias and yellow laburnum hang downwards and are the most exciting plants for such features. In the United States, I encountered a long pergola planted with akebias; their vanilla-scented flowers do not dangle but their sausage-

Above *A delicate arrangement of golden stamens, like fine lacework, reveals itself when you examine the flowers of* Azara serrata. *The scent is fruitily sweet. Fragrant wall shrubs are wasted if marooned at the back of deep borders; they need to be close to paths or seats.*

shaped fruits do. The pendant seedpods of wisterias are also a bonus in hotter climates than Britain.

Roses, honeysuckles, jasmines and clematis are the main scented candidates for covering other areas. Cowslip-scented *Clematis rehderiana* and meadowsweet-scented *C. flammula* extend the season into late summer and autumn (also *C. terniflora* in the United States); *Lonicera periclymenum* 'Serotina' and many roses also last well. And *Clematis cirrhosa balearica* carries us through the winter.

Wall Shrubs

Abelia triflora

Abelia

The abelias are small deciduous or evergreen shrubs valuable for their long and late-flowering season. They are not stunning visually, but make attractive companions for plants with strong colour. Even the hardiest varieties appreciate the warmth and protection of a wall that receives sun, unless grown in the milder regions.
Sun or light shade. Moist, loamy soil.
A. chinensis releases a fine, sweet, honeysuckle scent from its clusters of white, tubular flowers, which appear from rose-tinted buds during summer and autumn. It is not commonly offered but is one of the best abelias for fragrance. It makes a spreading deciduous shrub.
1–1.5m/3–5ft. Z7
A. × grandiflora is the most popular abelia and one of the hardiest, being virtually evergreen, but its scent is very faint. Its clusters of white, tubular flowers come from pink buds, and are borne in summer and autumn. The small, pointed leaves are a good, bright green and it makes a loose, arching mound.
1–2m/3–6ft. Z6
A. triflora has a much stronger, sweeter scent than *A. × grandiflora*. The flowers are rose-tinged and come from deep pink buds in early summer, but cannot be relied upon to appear in quantity every year. It is deciduous and vigorous and erect in habit.
3m/10ft or more. Z7

Abeliophyllum

A. distichum wants a sunny wall in order to ripen its wood. The white flowers, vanilla-scented, are borne on the bare twigs in winter. It is well worth planting as it takes up little space and performs at a useful time. The effect is of a small, white-flowered forsythia.
Sun. 1.2m/4ft. Z4

Azara

The azaras are an extremely valuable group of evergreen shrubs or small trees from Chile which can be tried on a sunny wall. They are

Azara serrata

Buddleja crispa

not entirely hardy but some are proving tougher than previously thought.
Sun. Moist, loamy soil.

A. lanceolata has slender, bright green, toothed leaves and produces its puffs of dull yellow flowers in quantity in early spring. It grows best in cool, mild, damp climates. This interesting and unusual evergreen is half-hardy.
Up to 6m/20ft. Z9

A. microphylla, the most common azara, is reliably hardy in all but the coldest areas. It has small, dark, rounded leaves and produces its clusters of insignificant yellow flowers in late winter; the air around the plant can be thick with vanilla essence at this time.
Up to 6m/20ft. Z8

A. petiolaris has comparatively large, holly-like leaves and small racemes of pale yellow flowers in spring. It is the most beautiful azara in flower and the scent is strong and sweet. It seems to be quite reliable on a warm wall.
Up to 3.5m/12ft. Z8

A. serrata is a good glossy evergreen with puffs of mustard yellow flowers, fruitily scented, which appear in late spring.
3m/10ft. Z8

Buddleja

B. crispa is one of the most desirable of deciduous shrubs and one of the main contenders for a sunny wall. A vision of pastel beauty, it has woolly grey leaves and short, rounded panicles of lilac flowers, borne over a long period from summer until the first frosts. The scent is the honey fragrance characteristic of buddlejas. It makes a bushy, wide shrub, and a proportion of the old wood should be pruned hard back every spring to encourage new flowering growth.
Sun. 2–3.5m/6–12ft. Z9

Carpenteria

C. californica is a very aristocratic evergreen, with slender, leathery leaves, for a sunny wall. The large, single white flowers, lit by a boss of golden anthers, are produced at mid-summer and are delicately, but sweetly, fragrant. A proportion of the old wood may be removed in spring to keep the plant youthful. 'Ladham's Variety' has larger flowers but is rare.
Sun. Well-drained soil. 1.5m/5ft. Z7

Ceanothus

These magnificent shrubs, comprising the only really sizeable, truly blue-flowered plants that we can grow in gardens, are not normally praised for scent. But some do surprise you with a faint honey fragrance; some also have distinctly aromatic foliage.
C. 'Puget Blue' (Z8), which has intense mid-blue flowers in late spring and early summer, combines both these qualities.
Sun. 2.5m/8ft or more.

C. arboreus 'Trewithen Blue', also evergreen but with mid-blue flowers in quite long panicles, also has the honey scent in some measure; it grows taller and lives longer (the evergreen ceanothus are usually very vigorous but have a short life).
Z9

Cestrum

C. parqui begins to pour out a magnificent and exotic spicy-sweet perfume from its small, greenish yellow, tubular flowers in the late evening. It blooms for many weeks during the summer, though, unfortunately, in the daytime the flowers smell rather fetid. The shrub has long, narrow leaves, and is usually deciduous.
Sun. Well-drained, fertile soil. 2.5m/8ft or more, unless continually cut back by hard winters. Z8

Carpenteria californica

Cestrum parqui

Chaenomeles

The japonicas or ornamental quinces merit inclusion for their deliciously scented fruits which have a powerful, sharply sweet fragrance. These can be harvested in late summer and used for making jellies. Plants will grow happily in the open border, but they are popular subjects for a sunny or slightly shaded wall; a properly espaliered specimen is very decorative, even when out of flower. Prune back the previous season's growth after flowering. The cup-shaped flowers, produced in spring, come in a range of red, pink, salmon and white colours.
Sun or shade. 1–3m/3–10ft depending on variety. Z5

Chimonanthus

C. praecox, winter sweet, is a plant for the patient gardener, as it may take five years or more to begin flowering. But it is worth the wait. The waxy, translucent yellow bells, purple-stained inside, have a spicy sweet fragrance which is among the finest of the season; a few twigs indoors will scent a whole room. The flowers are produced on the bare branches throughout the second half of the winter. It is a dreary-looking plant in summer, though. 'Grandiflorus' and 'Luteus' are forms with better flowers, but the scent is not as good. Cut out weak shoots immediately after flowering, otherwise little pruning is required. In sunnier areas it succeeds as a free-standing shrub in an open position.
Sun. 2.5m/8ft. Z6

Choisya

C. ternata, Mexican orange blossom, is a beautiful evergreen shrub with glossy, trifoliate leaves and heads of white, starry flowers in spring. The foliage is aromatic when crushed, and the blossom has a heavy scent, reminiscent of hawthorn but without the fishy undertones. It is hardy enough to thrive in the open but resents cold winds and needs a sheltered position, so it is often grown as a wall shrub. It makes a neat, dome-shaped specimen but is at its best in youth and it is a sound policy to prune the whole shrub back to 46cm/18in every few years. It has a new golden-leaved form called 'Sundance'.
Sun or shade. 2m/6ft. Z8

Cytisus

C. battandieri, Moroccan broom, is a deciduous shrub the scent lover will not want to be without. The fragrance from its erect, golden yellow racemes is of pineapple, and no one can pass a plant in flower without wishing to reach out and inhale it. It flowers at mid-summer. Its foliage is quite untypical of brooms, being rounded, trifoliate and silvery. It is usually trained against a sunny wall, but it is big and if no suitable wall is available, it may be tried as a free-standing specimen in a sheltered spot.
Sun. 4.5m/15ft. Z8

Drimys

D. winteri, Winter's bark, is a tall evergreen shrub that needs wall protection outside milder regions. Its bark and large, grey-green leaves are attractive and aromatic when crushed, but beware: if the oil is accidentally transferred from fingers to mouth or eyes it can cause a burning sensation and even temporary blindness! The jasmine-like, white flowers are also scented; the fragrance is of milk of magnesia.
Sun or light shade. Acid, peaty soil. 4.5m/ 15ft or more. Z9

Eriobotrya

E. japonica, loquat, has enormous, coarse, dark leaves, which are ribbed and toothed,

Choisya ternata

Chimonanthus praecox

Cytisus battandieri

Drimys winteri

and it is a very popular foliage shrub with garden designers. The yellowish white flowers, produced in panicles through the autumn, are strongly scented of hawthorn; yellow, pear-shaped fruits follow but are seldom ripened outside of the mildest climates. It often comes out of a winter looking rather battered, but a perfect plant is impressive. A sunny wall is preferred.
Sun. Up to 9m/30ft. Z8

Escallonia
E. 'Iveyi' is one of the more tender escallonias, requiring the protection and heat of a sunny wall outside mild areas. It is also the most beautiful. Its glossy, dark, evergreen leaves have the fruity resinous aroma typical of escallonias but its flowers are sweetly scented too. These are pure white and are borne in panicles during late summer and autumn.
Sun. Well-drained soil. 3m/10ft. Z8

Hoheria
H. *lyallii* is an unusual deciduous shrub for a sunny wall. It has heart-shaped, grey-green leaves, toothed and downy, and in high

summer bears quantities of white, saucer-shaped flowers, that have a honey scent. This is a fine plant for a white garden.
Sun. Well-drained soil. 4.5m/15ft. Z9
H. *sexstylosa* is an evergreen hoheria of narrow, upright shape and with slender, glossy, toothed leaves. Its white flowers, which appear in high summer, are slightly smaller than those of H. *lyallii* but have the same honey scent. It is another desirable plant.
Sun. 4.5m/15ft. Z9

Itea
I. *ilicifolia* never fails to raise eyebrows when, in high summer, it turns from an unassuming holly-like shrub into a flowering waterfall. The pendant racemes of greenish white flowers, which look like sprays of millet, can be 30cm/1ft in length. They are scented of honey. The dark, glossy leaves are a good foil for other plants right through the year. It grows best against a sunny wall.
I. *virginica* (Z5), with shorter, fragrant, creamy racemes, is hardier and suitable for open positions on moist soil.
Sun. 3m/10ft. Z9

Eriobotrya japonica

Magnolia grandiflora

Myrtus communis

Jasminum

J. humile **'Revolutum'**, Italian yellow jasmine, does not have the powerful sweet scent of its climbing relatives but has some fragrance. The flowers are bright yellow and are carried in clusters among the airy foliage during high summer. It is reliably hardy against a sunny wall and is more or less evergreen; it can be tried as a free-standing shrub in all but the coldest areas.
Sun. 1.5m/5ft or more. Z8

Laurelia

L. serrata, Chilean laurel, is a rare, handsome-looking evergreen worth searching out for its spicy scent, similar to bay, released by the foliage when crushed. The long leathery leaves are bright green and serrated and clusters of yellowish green flowers appear in early spring. It grows best in a mild climate but can be tried against a sunny wall elsewhere, except in the coldest areas.
Over 15m/50ft in mild areas. Z9

Magnolia

M. grandiflora is the queen of wall shrubs. Its huge, glossy, evergreen leaves, rust-felted underneath, bring grandeur to their setting, while the great saucer-shaped flowers, creamy yellow and spicily lemon-scented, are as exotic as waterlilies. The flowers are borne intermittently through the late summer and autumn. They can be grown as free-standing shrubs in sunny climes and in the south-eastern United States they make great trees. But elsewhere they need the heat of a sunny wall to perform well. The species takes a while to settle down to flowering, and its precocious clones are preferable: 'Exmouth' has narrower leaves and is the hardiest; 'Goliath' is the best selection of all but not for very cold gardens.
Sun. Fertile soil. 7.5m/25ft or more. Z7–9

Myrtus

The myrtles have recently been savaged by the botanists and broken up into half a dozen genera. But to keep things simple, I group them all here. The larger species are usually treated as slow-growing evergreens for a sunny wall and well-drained loamy soil, but they are not reliably hardy in cold areas. The leaves are aromatic and the white blossom is spicily sweet. Both these scents fill the air on warm days.
Sun. Well-drained, loamy soil.

M. apiculata (*Luma apiculata*) has superb peeling, cinnamon and cream bark, and is at its best as a free-standing tree in mild areas. But when in flower against a wall it is also attractive. It produces its blossom over a long period in late summer and autumn. It is less hardy than common myrtle.
2–6m/6–20ft; 18m/60ft as a tree. Z9

M. communis, common myrtle, produces its flowers in late summer and in both foliage and blossom is a real feast for the nose. It does well against a wall, although it may sometimes be cut to the ground by frost. Its variegated and narrow-leaved forms, including *M. c. tarentina*, are less reliable outside. This is an interesting plant with historical associations.
2–3m/6–10ft. Z8

M. lechleriana (*Amomyrtus luma*) produces good coppery coloured young leaves and blooms early, in spring, but is not very hardy.
2–7.5m/6–25ft. Z9

M. nummularia (*Myrteola nummularia*) is the only really hardy myrtle. It is a prostrate plant for a sunny spot in the rock garden and flowers in early summer.
Z8

M. ugni (*Ugni molinae*), Chilean guava, is an erect shrub whose white flowers are tinged with pink. It flowers in spring and is hardy enough to be worth trying in all but very cold areas. Its red fruits are supposed to taste of strawberries but I cannot confirm this; Queen Victoria's favourite jam was reputedly made from them.
1–2m/3–6ft. Z9

Pittosporum

P. tenuifolium, kohuhu, is the most common pittosporum. Its dark purple flowers, borne in spring, are small and unobtrusive but they waft a thick honey scent. The fragrance is at its strongest in the evening. The evergreen foliage, popular with flower arrangers, is shiny, wavy-edged and fresh green, and the leaves are complemented beautifully by the black twigs. It may be pruned after flowering. There are many forms available with variegated, purple, silver and golden foliage.
Sun. Well-drained soil. Up to 12m/40ft. Z8

Rhaphiolepis

R. umbellata is a slow-growing evergreen for a sunny wall. It has thick, leathery, oval leaves and makes an attractive, rounded shrub. Its white flowers, borne in panicles during summer, have a sweet, bubblegum scent. It makes a nice conservatory plant in cold areas.
Sun. Well-drained soil. 3m/10ft. Z8

Romneya

R. coulteri, California tree poppy, is surprisingly sweetly scented for a member of the poppy family. It is a suckering sub-shrub, whose erect growths should be cut back to ground level in early spring if the winter has not done the job for you. The large white saucers, with their prominent central boss of golden stamens, appear from high summer until autumn and are set off perfectly by the deeply cut, glaucous grey foliage. It can be difficult to establish but afterwards the problem is its colonizing vigour. Its hybrid 'White Cloud' has bigger flowers.
Sun. Well-drained soil. 1.2–2.5m/4–8ft. Z8

R. trichocalyx is shorter than *R. coulteri* and has finer foliage. But it is even more invasive and less pleasantly scented.
Z8

Vitex

V. agnus-castus, chaste tree, is a valuable, but seldom grown, autumn-flowering shrub which needs the heat of a sunny wall. The lance-shaped leaves, grey on their undersides, are pungently aromatic and the violet flowers, borne on erect racemes, are sweetly scented. It is spreading, slow-growing and deciduous.
Sun. Well-drained soil. 2.5m/8ft. Z6

Rhaphiolepis umbellata

Romneya coulteri

Climbers

Actinidia

A. deliciosa (A. chinensis), Chinese gooseberry, is a deciduous climber grown principally for its Kiwi fruits. Its sweetly scented flowers are an unexpected bonus; they open in clusters at mid-summer, beginning white and fading to biscuit. The large, hairy, heart-shaped leaves are impressive, as is the plant's vigour. For fruits you need a female and a male plant; 'Hayward' is a popular female clone and 'Tomuri' a popular male. But this plant needs a great deal of space, and you may not think it is worth it. It dislikes strong midday sun, so a partly shaded wall or pergola that receives some sun is ideal.
All but very dry soils. 9m/30ft. Z7
A. kolomikta is a startling deciduous plant whose leaves look as if they have been dipped first in whitewash and then in raspberry juice. I cannot stand the sight of it but others swoon in admiration. The clusters of white, slightly scented flowers appear in early summer. It is less vigorous than other actinidias and may take a few years for its leaves to colour. It wants a wall that receives full sun.
6m/20ft. Z8

Akebia

A. quinata is a fascinating climber for a sheltered, sunny pergola. It has elegant leaves, composed of five rounded leaflets, and in mild winters is evergreen. In spring, curious three-sepalled, chocolate-purple flowers appear, which release a spicy scent on warm days. Even more curious purplish, sausage-shaped fruits sometimes follow. It is a vigorous climber. Often recommended for shady walls, but all the best plants I have seen have been in full sun.
9m/30ft. Z4

Billardiera

B. longiflora is an unusual evergreen climber for a sunny wall in warmer areas. It is a dainty thing, with slender leaves and small, scented, greenish yellow funnels in high summer. But it is at its best in the autumn when it is hung with rich violet-blue, oblong fruits. A novelty, not a show-stopper. It makes a good conservatory plant.
Sun. 2m/6ft. Z9

Clematis

Scent among the climbing clematis is found chiefly in the small-flowered species, not the large-flowered hybrids. These may not provide the same splashes of colour, but they have a natural charm that more and more gardeners are coming to appreciate. They look as well growing up trees and shrubs as on walls and pergolas. Clematis do particularly well on limestone and they need a cool, shady root run. Container-bought plants should have their rootballs planted 5cm/2in below soil level. Most need little or no pruning.
Deep, fertile, moist soil.
C. afoliata is an unusual clematis for a sunny, sheltered wall in warmer areas. It has tendrils instead of leaves, and bears clusters of pointed, straw-green flowers in spring, which have a daphne fragrance; the scent is elusive outdoors but pronounced when the plant is grown in a conservatory.
2.5m/8ft. Z9
C. armandii is a handsome and vigorous evergreen with long, dark, leathery leaves. The creamy flowers, sometimes flushed with pink, appear in spring and are scented of almonds. It should be trimmed lightly after flowering. 'Apple Blossom', with bronze young foliage and pinky flowers, and 'Snowdrift', with pure white flowers, are superior selections. This popular and desirable plant needs shelter from cold winds and a sunny aspect.
6m/20ft. Z8
C. cirrhosa balearica, fern-leaved clematis, has finely cut, evergreen leaves which turn bronze in the autumn and carries its bell-shaped, creamy flowers, usually speckled

Actinidia

Akebia quinata

Clematis flammula

with crimson inside, through the winter. The flower scent is elusive outdoors, but if the plant is grown in a conservatory its lemon fragrance can be properly savoured.
Sun or shade. 3m/10ft. Z8

C. **'Fair Rosamond'** is, as far as I am aware, the only large-flowered hybrid with a pronounced scent; it has been described as a blend of cowslip and violet. The flowers are white, flushed pink, and have prominent purple stamens. It blooms in early summer and can be grown in a tub.
Sun or shade. 2m/6ft.

C. flammula is a deciduous plant similar to traveller's joy or old man's beard, *C. vitalba*, but, for garden purposes, altogether superior. It is vigorous, while still being manageable, has good polished leaves, and its white flowers, produced in late summer and autumn, are powerfully scented of meadowsweet; the scent is enjoyable in the air, but overpowering at close range. Being from southern Europe, it appreciates sun and shelter from cold winds. It is excellent when trained up an outbuilding or tree.
Up to 4.5m/15ft. Z6

C. forsteri is a New Zealand evergreen species that has yellow-green starry flowers with a fair degree of lemon scent. The related species *C. petriei* is especially well endowed and is hardy and vigorous. It has green flowers in spring; they are larger on male

Clematis armandii 'Apple Blossom'

Clematis rehderiana

plants, but the females carry attractive seedheads. A sheltered, sunny position is needed; in cold areas, these make excellent plants for the cool conservatory.
Z9
C. montana is one of the glories of the spring garden. It bears its four-sepalled flowers, rather open and square-looking, in magnificent quantity. The species itself is white and has a strong vanilla scent; 'Grandiflora', which has larger white flowers, is unscented. *C. montana rubens* is a bright mauve-pink, and 'Elizabeth' is a large-flowered pale pink; both are vanilla scented. *C. montana wilsonii* blooms later in the year; it is white and strongly scented. The montanas thrive in sun or shade and because of their vigour are much used for covering unsightly buildings. They are deciduous.
6m/20ft. Z5
C. rehderiana flowers from high summer until autumn and releases a delicious primrose fragrance from its small, pale yellow bells. I think this is one of the most desirable of all clematis. This deciduous climber is lovely up a wall or tree.
Sun or light shade. 7.5m/25ft, but can be hard pruned in early spring.
Z6

C. serratifolia is worth growing for its lemon scent. It is an unusual clematis, similar in appearance to *C. tangutica* and *C. orientalis*, but with smaller, paler bells, filled with brown filaments. It blooms profusely in late summer. It is deciduous.
Sun or light shade. 3m/10ft. Z5
C. terniflora (C. maximowicziana, C. paniculata of gardens) is related to *C. flammula* and its white flowers release the same hawthorn fragrance. It is a popular clematis in the United States, but needs more sun than the British climate can provide. It is a vigorous grower and flowers in autumn.
9m/30ft. Z9
C. × triternata 'Rubro-marginata', an unusual and vigorous hybrid, between *C. flammula* and *C. viticella*, bears a mass of purple-edged white flowers in late summer and autumn. These have the flammula scent.
Sun or light shade. 3.5m/12ft. Z6

Decumaria

D. barbara is a self-clinging, semi-evergreen climber. It is similar and related to the climbing hydrangeas and schizophragmas, but its white flowers are all fertile; they are borne in small, erect corymbs during summer and are honey-scented. It can be grown up a wall or tree.
Sun or light shade. Moist, well-drained soil. 7.5m/25ft or more. Z7
D. sinensis is a rare evergreen species that enjoys exactly the same conditions as *D. barbara*. It bears pyramidal panicles of creamy flowers –that are also honey-scented – in early summer.
3m/10ft. Z6

Holboellia

H. latifolia is an unusual twining evergreen for milder gardens. It bears very sweetly scented, greenish white flowers in early spring, and these may be followed by purple, sausage-shaped fruits. The leaves are long, glossy and luxuriant. A very sheltered wall is necessary in areas subject to frost.
Sun. 6m/20ft. Z7

Jasminum

The common jasmine gives us one of our most potent evening scents. It is a heavily sweet, exotic fragrance, always delightful on the air, but overpowering, even unpleasant, in quantity. Plant this away from the house, where its scent will reach you diluted and in

Jasminum × stephanense

Lonicera × *americana*

Lonicera caprifolium

wafts; the other jasmines can be planted beside windows and doors.
Sun. Fertile soil.
J. beesianum has small, deep rose-red flowers in early summer, followed by shiny black berries. It is an interesting plant, but perhaps not among the most distinguished jasmines. It is evergreen in mild areas.
3.5m/12ft. Z6
J. officinale, common jasmine, is a vigorous, usually deciduous, climber that is beautiful when scrambling up an outbuilding, a pergola or even over a tree stump; in cold areas, though, it needs a sheltered wall that receives full sun. The pure white flowers open from pink-tinged buds throughout the summer. It is best left unpruned. *J.o.* 'Affine', Spanish or royal jasmine, is a superior form with slightly larger flowers; 'Aureum' has yellow-blotched leaves.
6m/20ft or more. Z7
J. × *stephanense* is a hybrid between the

previous two species. It is a lovely plant that bears sweetly scented pale pink flowers in summer. It is evergreen in mild areas, and its young leaves often display creamy variegation.
6m/20ft. Z7

Lonicera

The honeysuckles are a mainstay of the scented garden. In the cool of the evening or the early morning, the air will be filled with fruity or spicy sweetness; in the heat of the day, they have to be sniffed. They are usually at their best scrambling freely over fences and pergolas or up trees, rather than pinned vertically to walls; little pruning is then necessary. They are not fussy about soil but, like clematis, enjoy a cool root run. They are prone to aphid attack and regular spraying may be necessary.
L. × *americana* is a superb deciduous hybrid honeysuckle with a powerful clove scent. Its

flowers are yellow, suffused with reddish purple, and make an impressive display in summer.
Sun or part shade. 6m/20ft. Z6
L. caprifolium, early cream honeysuckle, flowers at mid-summer but its blooms are a blend of white and yellow, with little or no red present, and have the typical fruity honeysuckle fragrance. This splendid plant is deciduous.
Shade. 6m/20ft. Z6
L. etrusca is an unusual and beautiful semi-evergreen honeysuckle for a wall that receives full sun, though it is not hardy in cold areas; it makes a good conservatory plant. The flowers begin cream, suffused with red, and mature to a rich yellow colour; they appear throughout late summer and have a fruity scent.
3.5m/12ft. Z8
L. × *heckrottii* ('Gold Flame') is a weak-stemmed shrub rather than a climber and

Lonicera periclymenum

Schisandra rubriflora

needs the support of a wall. It bears rich orange-yellow flowers, suffused with reddish purple, during late summer, and these have a spicy sweet scent. It is slow-growing. Shade. Z5

L. japonica **'Halliana'** is the finest form of the Japanese honeysuckle and a desirable plant for all but very cold gardens. In warmer climates, it is an invasive weed. It is more or less evergreen, and it is in bloom from early summer; the flowers open white and mature to yellow, and have a powerful fruity fragrance. It is very vigorous and may need hard pruning in spring.
Sun or light shade. 9m/30ft. Z5

L. periclymenum, common honeysuckle, is a familiar hedgerow and cottage garden plant, but has really been superseded by its two famous cultivars: 'Belgica', the early Dutch honeysuckle, produces its pale yellow and reddish purple flowers mainly at mid-summer; 'Serotina', even better, produces its darker flowers through the summer and autumn. Both are deciduous and have a rich fruit scent.
6m/20ft. Z5

L. splendida is an evergreen worth trying in all but very cold areas. It has lovely bluish green foliage and bears its scented flowers, yellowish inside and reddish outside, throughout the summer. It needs shelter from cold winds.
Full sun. Z9

Passiflora

P. caerulea, passion flower, bears the most intricate and intriguing of garden flowers; each displays a circular pattern of purple, blue and greenish white filaments surmounted by a central column bearing stamens, stigmas and ovary of chunky proportions, and is more like a product of the Industrial Revolution than of Mother Nature. The flowers appear throughout the summer and have a delicate, sweet scent; they are followed by orange, egg-shaped fruits. It will thrive on a sunny wall in all but the coldest regions, but needs protection for its first couple of winters. It is evergreen and relatively pest-free.
4.5m/15ft. Z7–8

Schisandra

S. chinensis is an unusual deciduous climber with scented flowers and aromatic leaves. The flowers, borne in spring, are pale rose-pink, and hang on long stalks; they are followed by attractive scarlet fruits. It is a novelty for a wall or pergola.
Shade. 6m/20ft. Z5

S. rubriflora is a more common species, bearing pendulous dark red bells in spring; it also has attractive fruits. Again, the flowers are fragrant and the leaves aromatic. It is an eyecatching plant in flower and fruit for walls or pergolas.
Shade. 6m/20ft. Z8

Stauntonia

S. hexaphylla succeeds on a sheltered, sunny wall in all but very cold areas. It is a leathery-leaved evergreen which bears small racemes of white, violet-tinged flowers in spring; these have a sweet scent. Edible, purple fruits follow after a hot summer. It is a handsome foliage plant, worth a place in the conservatory if it cannot be grown outside.
12m/40ft. Z8

Trachelospermum

T. asiaticum is reliable on a sunny wall in all but the coldest areas. Its creamy yellow, jasmine-like flowers breathe a bubblegum scent that is irresistible; they appear in high summer. It is evergreen, with small, dark leaves and a dense, compact habit.
5.5m/18ft. Z8

T. jasminoides, star or confederate jasmine, is more powerfully scented, with larger flowers and leaves. It is in the very first league of fragrant plants. Once established, this evergreen can be trusted outside on a sunny wall but it is less hardy than *T. asiaticum*; in cold areas, it should head the list of conservatory plants. The flowers are pure white and borne in high summer. Trachelospermums flower on old wood, so little pruning should be done; they like good soil. 'Variegatum' is a white and pink-splashed, evergreen version.
9m/30ft. Z9

Wisteria

The long violet racemes of wisterias drip down many a house front in early summer, but familiarity has not bred contempt. We all plant one if our property is not already endowed. They are sensational trained over pergolas and across bridges, and can also be grown as standards. They are vigorous growers but generally take a few years to start flowering. Pruning established plants consists of shortening the new, long, lateral growths to 15cm/6in after flowering, and shortening them again to two or three buds in winter. They are deciduous.
Sun. Deep soil.

W. floribunda, Japanese wisteria, produces its long racemes in early summer after its young foliage has expanded. In my view, this gives it the edge over the Chinese species. The flowers have a delicate pea scent. The species has been superseded in commerce by the form with immensely long racemes called 'Multijuga' ('Macrobotrys') and by the superb white 'Alba'.
7.5m/25ft. Z4

W. sinensis, Chinese wisteria, has a much better scent than *W. floribunda* and it carries in the air. It flowers in spring on bare stems, and the flowers show up very well on a pale wall. But it is also worth trying up trees; it is partnered, rather daringly but excitingly, with a red-flowered hawthorn in a garden near mine (wisterias up trees need not be pruned). 'Alba' is a good white.
15m/50ft or more, if unpruned. Z5

Trachelospermum asiaticum

Trachelospermum jasminoides

Wisteria sinensis

Rock and Water Gardens

When you meet a rose, the first thing you do (at least, I do) is to draw it to your nose. We may also try our luck with a large flowering shrub or tree. But when presented with a lowly alpine, few of us think to smell it. It is true that scented plants are not abundant among alpine flora, and that the great majority of the most commonly grown rock garden plants – aubrietas, campanulas, saxifrages, veronicas, sedums, lewisias, gentians, geraniums, sempervivums and so on – lack fragrance. But there is enough scent among alpines to warrant keeping your sense of smell alert, and certainly the creation of a magnificently fragrant rock garden is quite within our grasp.

If we are to enjoy a flower's scent, it usually needs to be within reach of the nose. The smaller the plant, the higher it needs to be raised off the ground. So these fragrant alpines should be at a comfortable level in the rock garden for sniffing, not in the lower shelves or in the limestone pavement. Troughs will be ideal homes for many, and some may be grown vertically, nearer nose level, in retaining walls. Sunken paths through the rock garden are another option.

You can open the year with dwarf bulbs like violet-scented *Iris reticulata* (whose purple flowers look so good against a tiny blue conifer like *Juniperus squamata* 'Blue Star') and crocuses like *C. versicolor* and *C. chrysanthus*. The latter comes in many colour forms and each has its own degree and quality of honey scent. I was once given, as a Christmas present, a box containing an assortment of different honeys from around the world and had an entertaining time matching their scents to those of the crocuses opening in pots in the house. Some of the matches were close, but the real lessons learned were that the flavours breathed even within one species of plant can be very diverse, and that labels such as 'honey-scented' cover endless nuances.

Scilla mischtschenkoana is another excellent bulb for the rock garden. It colonizes freely and its pale flowers, which appear over a long period from early spring, have a very sweet scent and make an attractive foreground for yellow, fruitily fragrant, small-flowered narcissi. Grape hyacinths and dwarf tulips should also be offered a home here.

As spring advances the rock garden becomes flooded with flowers. The most sophisticated scents are provided by the daphnes. The prostrate garland flower, *D. cneorum*, will cover a large area if its stems are encouraged to root as they creep overground; this is done by placing stones over them. An established plant, mounding itself over rocks and trailing down walls, is quite a spectacle when in flower as well as a feast for the nose, and this species – in its best form, 'Eximia' – would be on my short list for any rock garden. Other daphnes are equally rich in perfume. *D. collina* is neat and easy to accommodate, and *D. retusa* is small enough for a trough; both of these are good in pots in the cold greenhouse or alpine house. In larger rock gardens, room should also be found for *D. tangutica*, and even *D. × burkwoodii* 'Somerset'.

Another important group of scented plants for the rock garden are the pinks. The warm fragrance is breathed by a number of species and hybrids, and since it will hang on the air on still days, plants can happily be used at ground level, edging paths and sprouting from paving cracks. My favourite hybrids are those with intricate maroon, plum and crimson lacing, which look especially good in partnership with striped and splashed roses like Rosa Mundi and 'Ferdinand Pichard'. A similar heady scent, though not as strong, is evident in many of the alpine phloxes, and in perennial wallflowers (varieties of cheiranthus and erysimum) where it is blended to a greater or lesser degree with aniseed. The scent of *Onosma alboroseum* also has an aniseed flavour. The onosmas make striking occupants of rock garden crevices and walls; their clusters of drooping flowers contrast with all around them and are a substantial size. The scent of *Primula reidii williamsii* is also too good to miss. And for long-lasting colour, the more scented varieties of viola, such as 'Mrs Lancaster' and 'Little David', ought to be found a place in the garden.

Right *Rock gardens do not need to be mountainous constructions – low beds, mounded gently with a few large stones, fit more happily into the average garden, with sinks and troughs for the choicer alpines. Here, an assortment of pinks drench the garden in summer scent, while creeping thyme in the paving cracks awaits brushing by feet. Erodiums, campanulas, diascias and white lychnis add further colour.*

To supplement the flower scents, a range of plants with aromatic leaves can be added. Micromerias and lemon-scented edelweiss provide the fruit, origanums and thymes the spice while *Stachys citrina* supplies a dash of mint chocolate. Various dwarf rhododendrons will add further hot aromas.

Scent is not commonly found among the high alpines. These are the plants which are kept dry through the winter months by a heavy covering of snow and in cultivation must usually be grown under glass to protect them from rain. But enter an alpine house at any time during spring and early summer and you will soon find the exceptions. *Dionysia aretioides* has flowers with a rich cowslip scent and those of *Androsace cylindrica* have a strong almond scent; while the connoisseur's favourites *Petrocallis lagasca* (*P. pyrenaica*) and *Thlaspi rotundifolium* are also delicious. The scent from these is often so powerful that it wafts through the vents and you can savour it even in the garden outside.

An alpine house is nothing more than an unheated greenhouse with additional ventilation. The purist will have strict views on what should and should not be offered its hospitality, but for the scent-lover it provides a splendid opportunity to enjoy a range of early-blooming plants, their flowers protected from the elements and seen to perfection, and to accommodate a range of plants that are not quite hardy and that can be kept on the dry side during the winter and protected under insulating material (such as polypropylene fibre sheeting) during very cold spells. In the first category come winter and spring bulbs like crocuses and narcissi, irises and even florist's hyacinths. The smaller daphnes are usually well suited to pots and make excellent companions. In the second category come Mediterranean lavenders and rosemaries and honey-scented *Euphorbia mellifera* (successful and a manageable size when pot grown). You might consider training lemon-scented *Clematis forsteri*, or some of the other New Zealand clematis coming into circulation, over a narrow strip of roof. And if the greenhouse is big enough, and the climate not too hostile, a scented camellia such as 'Scentsation' or rhododendron such as 'Lady Alice Fitzwilliam' might also be tried; these would be plunged outside in a shady place for the summer, in their pots. Of all the plants you can grow in an alpine house, I think the show auriculas would be my first choice. They are such bizarre characters, especially those with green, white and grey-edged leaves, and I can spend ages marvelling at their intricate patterning and their unfolding buds, heavily dusted in meal. Add to this a piercing scent – primrose-lemony with an undertone of chocolate – and you have a nonpareil.

Sun and good drainage are basic requirements of most alpines: equal parts, by volume, of loam, moss peat and coarse grit is the standard medium. But the rock garden will inevitably have shady parts, and you may also have paved shady corners behind the house just begging for a trough. Here you can make special beds for those shade-loving species of gentian, primula, lily and ericaceous shrub. These need a moist, humus-rich soil – equal parts loam and moss peat – though drainage should be good and the ground free from waterlogging. They are largely lime-hating plants so the soil used must be neutral or acid and the rocks surrounding it granite or sandstone – peat blocks or railway sleepers are excellent alternatives. In limy areas, the beds must be raised about a metre or a couple of feet above the ground to prevent leaching from the surrounding land, and they should be watered with rainwater, not from the tap. Shade may be from walls, buildings or trees, but there should be no overhanging branches or eaves likely to cause dripping. The scented plants for peat beds include shrubs such as *Daphne blagayana* and *Mitchella repens*; bulbs such as *Arisaema candidissimum, Lilium cernuum, L. duchartrei* and snowdrops; and perennials such as *Anemone sylvestris, Linnaea borealis* and *Trillium luteum*.

A pond at the base of the rock garden, with perhaps a stream cascading into it, provides additional entertainment, and the two features sit very comfortably together. Everyone is attracted to water, and its plant and animal life are a source of interest throughout the year. Surrounding the pond with an area of boggy ground enables you to grow moisture-loving perennials that will furnish colour after the rock garden's main season has passed. The ground is made boggy by having the soil slope down over the edge of the pond into a mud shelf and allowing the water to rise by capillary action; a second ledge underwater prevents the soil from spilling into the pond's depths. The mud shelf should be thickly planted with marginal plants to prevent erosion. Of course, ponds and streams need not be attached to rock gardens. Ponds may be formal affairs, of geometrical shape, and used as centrepieces for neatly mown lawns or paved terraces. Streams may course naturally through your garden, and your ponds may be swathed in rushes and shaded by willows.

There is not an abundance of scented candidates for waterside planting. But, as with the rock garden, it is by no means impossible to pursue a fragrant theme. Firstly, floating on the water itself, there can be scented waterlilies. There are numerous hybrids available, in colours ranging from rose-pink to sulphur yellow, which exhale a fruity fragrance. The water hawthorn, *Aponogeton distachyos*, strikes a contrasting

note of vanilla and its white spikes and slender leaves empha-size the waterlilies' buxom, rounded form.

Among marginal plants, which will stand in a moderate depth of water, are plants with fragrant leaves such as the sweet flag, whose valuable strap-like foliage is scented of cin-namon; brass buttons (*Cotula coronopifolia*); and galingale (*Cyperus longus*). For the damp ground near the water there are a host of plants with scented flowers. The white version of bog arum (*Lysichiton camtschatcensis*) can kick the season off in early spring with its huge spathes, but you need to be able to reach them with your nose to catch the sweet scent. Larger gardens with natural ponds may also be able to accommodate some of the willows with scented catkins such as *Salix aegyptiaca* and *S. triandra*; and the scented-leaved bay willow, *S. pentandra*.

My favourite pondside fragrances come from the primulas. In early summer *P. alpicola*, *P. sikkimensis* and *P. prolifera* (better known by its former name, *P. helodoxa*) waft their

Above *Water and walls are the perfect combination for bringing about those still, warm, moist conditions in which flower scents are at their richest. Here, sweet flag* and lemon-scented Primula florindae *grow around the pool, with roses and honeysuckles on the walls. In the foreground is the Gallica rose 'Tuscany Superb'.*

lemon scent, perfectly complemented by the aniseed of *P. anisodora*, if you can grow it within the reach of your fingers. But the richest fragrance comes from the later-blooming giant Himalayan cowslip, *P. florindae*. A self-sown colony of these sulphur beauties looks stunning and the scent is intoxicating.

Of the shrubs you can grow at the waterside, the sweet pepper bush, *Clethra alnifolia*, would always be high on my list. The spikes of white flowers, which appear in high summer, are as heavily and sweetly scented as viburnum. And for aromatic foliage, the sweet fern, *Comptonia peregrina*, and the bog myrtle, *Myrica gale* are indispensable. Rhododen-drons such as *RR. viscosum* and *atlanticum* can also be relied upon for strong fruity flower scents.

Rock Plants

Alyssum

A. montanum. This ground-hugging alyssum bears loose heads of soft yellow, very fragrant flowers in early summer. It has small grey evergreen leaves.
Sun. Well-drained soil. Up to 15cm/6in.

Androsace

A. ciliata forms a tiny mound of leaves, arranged in rosettes, and in early summer produces rose-pink flowers that are strongly scented of almonds.
Gritty soil in the alpine house.
A. cylindrica has rosettes of downy, grey-green leaves and white flowers, with a strong almond scent.
Gritty soil in the alpine house.
A. pubescens makes a small hummock of tightly packed, grey rosettes. The short-stemmed, white flowers are scented of honey. It resents wet weather and will need the protection of a sheet of glass through the winter. It is suited to tufa cultivation and does well in the alpine house.
Sun. Gritty soil.
A. villosa is easier to grow than *A. pubescens*, and makes mats of hairy, grey-green leaves which, in spring, are surmounted by white or pink honey-scented flowers, each with a reddish eye.
Sun. Gritty soil.

Anemone

A. sylvestris, snowdrop windflower, is a beautiful anemone that has white drooping flowers in spring that are lit by golden stamens and breathe a delicate scent. It has deeply cut leaves and a running rootstock, and thrives in cool corners of the rock garden or in woodland borders.
Light shade. Humus-rich soil. 30cm/1ft.

Aquilegia

A. fragrans. Although this lovely plant is a little taller than others in this section, I include it here for convenience. It has bluish green leaves and long-spurred, white flowers which have an apple-like scent.
Sun and shelter. 60cm/2ft.
A. viridiflora is a fascinating columbine with dainty foliage and small flowers coloured green and maroon that have a sweet, delicate scent. It is a plant that is lost in the border, and I grow mine in a raised bed.
30cm/1ft.

Campanula

C. thyrsoides is a most unusual and impressive campanula with flowers that are not only sweetly scented but also yellow. They are carried on a flower spike 30cm/1ft high. The leaves are narrow and hairy. It dies after flowering but is otherwise easy to grow and readily raised from seed.
Sun. Well-drained soil.

Cheiranthus

C. cheiri 'Harpur Crewe'. This bushy perennial wallflower has double, golden yellow flowers with a strong aniseed scent. It is an old favourite for the rock garden and makes a good splash of colour in early summer. The double, red and yellow wallflower 'Bloody Warrior' makes a curious companion for it, and is also scented. Both are readily propagated by summer cuttings and plants are best renewed every couple of years, as old plants are inclined to die suddenly.
Sun. Poor, well-drained soil. 30cm/1ft.

Daphne

The low-growing daphnes are essential in the scented rock garden. Their refined, clove-shaded fragrance is quite delicious. The flowers are often followed by shiny, highly poisonous fruits. Daphnes are woody plants, and the taller species are described under 'Shrubs'.
D. blagayana is an evergreen, rather straggly, species for a raised bed which bears deliciously scented, cream flowers in spring and has broad leaves. It is not difficult to grow, provided it has a cool, moist root run. Leaf-mould and peat should be incorporated into the soil, and each spring, the previous year's stems should be pegged down and covered with stones. This encourages the plant to layer, and it will gradually cover a wide area.

Light or medium shade. Well-drained, acid or alkaline soil. Up to 60cm/2ft. Z6
D. cneorum, garland flower, is perhaps the best known and best loved of the rock garden daphnes. The richly scented, rose-pink flowers emerge from red buds and a large plant in bloom in late spring is an exceptionally beautiful sight. It can make a dense mound of foliage, if its shoots are clipped back during its youth and it is layered as it advances. Its roots should be kept cool with peat and leaf-mould. 'Eximia' is a superior, vigorous form; 'Variegata' has cream-edged leaves and is more compact.
Sun or light shade. Well-drained soil. 30cm/1ft. Z5
D. collina is a pretty dwarf shrub with evergreen leaves which produces clusters of highly scented, rosy flowers in spring. Its roots should be allowed to reach cool, peaty conditions below the soil.
Sun or light shade. Well-drained, acid or alkaline soil. 60cm/2ft. Z7
D. retusa is a short version of *D. tangutica* and is one of the easier – although painfully slow

Aquilegia fragrans

– species to grow. It makes a neat mound of evergreen leaves and in late spring bears white flowers suffused with rose.
Sun or light shade. Humus-rich, acid or alkaline soil. 60cm/2ft. Z7
D. tangutica is similar to *D. retusa* but it is more vigorous. Like *D. retusa*, its fragrance is particularly good at night.
Sun or light shade. Humus-rich, acid or alkaline soil. 1.2–1.5m/4–5ft. Z7

Dianthus

The clove scent of pinks and carnations is one of the most evocative of fragrances and on warm, early summer days and evenings it will infuse the air. The alpine pinks are at home nestling among stones in the rock garden, while the larger pinks and carnations are just as happy lining cottage-garden paths or fronting rose borders. All benefit from a mulch of pea gravel.
Sun. Well-drained, limy soil.
D. arenarius is a very fragrant pink for the rock garden. Similar to *D. squarrosus*, it forms mats of green foliage above which white, cut-petalled flowers appear all summer.
46cm/18in.
D. gratianopolitanus, Cheddar pink, is a British native that varies in colour from deep rose to flesh pink and even white. The flowers are fringed and strongly scented, appearing in early summer. It forms mats of narrow, blue-green leaves and revels in cracks between rocks.
10–20cm/4–8in.
D. monspessulanus sternbergii is an unusual, fragrant pink that has large, fringed, rose-red flowers over a glaucous mat of foliage.
30cm/12in.
D. petraeus has narrow leaves and tiny white flowers which are very sweetly scented. The form with double white flowers and its subspecies *D.p. noeanus*, also white, are equally desirable.
25cm/10in.
D. squarrosus is a popular and easy alpine with narrow green leaves and white flowers. It is very sweetly scented.
30cm/12in.
D. superbus makes a lax plant with broad green leaves and lilac-pink flowers all summer; these are green eyed, deeply cut and very fragrant.
30–60cm/1–2ft.

Daphne cneorum 'Variegata'

Daphne tangutica

Dianthus squarrosus

Dianthus 'Brympton Red'

Dianthus 'Doris'

Hybrid Dianthus

A huge number of named varieties are available. They come in a range of heights and colours and can be double or single, blotched, laced and fringed; most are highly scented. They can produce far too many flowers and the buds may have to be thinned. Pinks root easily from cuttings and it is sensible to keep renewing your stock.

Among the smaller pinks, I recommend 'Little Jock', a semi-double rose-pink with a darker eye; 'Nyewood's Cream', a compact, cream white; and 'Waithman Beauty', a single crimson, marked in white. 15cm/6in or less.

The larger pinks can be divided into two groups. The old-fashioned and laced pinks generally bloom only at mid-summer but include some wonderful old world characters. Among these I recommend 'Bridal Veil', a double fringed white with a crimson centre; 'Brympton Red', a crimson with deeper marbling; 'Musgrave's Pink' ('Charles Musgrave'), a single white with a green eye; 'Dad's Favourite', a semi-double white, laced and centred with crimson; 'Hope', a pink with maroon lacing; 'Inchmery', a pale pink; 'Laced Romeo', a rose pink with crimson lacing; 'London Delight', a mauve-laced pink; and 'White Ladies', a double, fringed white and an improvement on the popular 'Mrs Sinkins'. 23–30cm/9–12in.

Among the modern hybrids, which flower on and off all summer, I recommend: 'Doris', a double shrimp pink; 'Gran's Favourite', a white, laced with mauve; and 'Haytor', a double white. 23–30cm/9–12in.

Spicy-scented border or clove carnations have become scarce. This is a pity because they are a handy size and flower in late summer, when pinks are over or are tiring. 'Old Crimson Clove' and 'Fenbow Nutmeg Clove' are the most likely to be offered by nurseries.

Dionysia

D. aretioides is one of the easier dionysias but needs to be grown in the alpine house; it succeeds well in tufa. It forms tight cushions of hairy rosettes which are studded in spring with almost stemless, yellow flowers; they breathe the scent of cowslips. It should be watered sparingly and with great care. Sun. Well-drained soil.

Erysimum

E. alpinum is a perennial wallflower whose sulphur yellow flowers have a sweet clove scent. It makes a low mound of foliage and blooms in spring. There is a more beautiful hybrid called 'Moonlight' whose pale yellow flowers come from red buds. Other scented hybrid erysimums are available. They are useful plants for the front of the border, as well as the rock garden, since they provide cheerful colour in the gap between spring and summer.
Sun. 15–30cm/6–12in.
E. helveticum (*E. pumilum*). This tiny, semi-evergreen wallflower has heads of fragrant, bright yellow flowers in early summer.
Sun. Well-drained soil. 10cm/4in.

Leontopodium

L. haplophylloides (L. aloysiodorum) is well worth having for it is strongly lemon-scented in leaf and flower. It is a Himalayan relative of edelweiss and has white hairy leaves and heads of grey-white flowers in early summer. It dislikes winter damp.
Sun. Well-drained soil. 23cm/9in.

Linnaea

L. borealis, twin-flower, is an attractive prostrate, creeping, evergreen sub-shrub found in the colder parts of the Northern hemisphere. The flesh-coloured bells appear in pairs during early summer and are almond-scented. The American variety, *L.b. americana*, has larger, crimson-pink flowers.
Shade. Peaty, lime-free soil.

Micromeria

M. chamissonis (Satureja douglasii) is a prostrate sub-shrub whose oval leaves have an aromatic scent of lemon; they can be used to flavour gin-based drinks. It carries purple flowers in summer.
Sun. Well-drained soil.
M. varia has aromatic yellow-green leaves and pale purple flowers.

Mitchella

M. repens, partridge berry, is a woody evergreen which hugs the ground, rooting as it goes. It carries pairs of small white, fragrant flowers through mid-summer and they are followed by scarlet fruits. The glossy leaves are scented of hay when dry.
Shade. Acid, peaty soil.

Onosma

These are distinctive and very desirable alpines with narrow hairy leaves and branching, pendant heads of fragrant, tubular flowers in summer. They are intolerant of winter wetness but prove reliable in rock garden crevices and walls.
Sun. Well-drained soil.
O. alboroseum bears white, pink-flushed flowers in early summer that are scented of aniseed.
15cm/6in.
O. tauricum has golden yellow, honey-scented flowers in summer.
23cm/9in.

Origanum

There are a number of good marjorams for the rock garden, and all have leaves with a degree of marjoram-like scent. They are especially valuable for their long-lasting flowers, which appear in high summer. Coming mainly from the Mediterranean region, they like heat and shelter and are not reliably hardy in very cold areas.
Sun. Well-drained soil.
O. dictamnus, dittany, has rounded, grey woolly leaves and drooping heads of green bracts from which appear pink flowers. It performs best in the alpine house.
23cm/9in.
O. laevigatum makes quite a feature when grown in a generous drift, and is a perfect underplanting for *Verbena bonariensis* in the summer border. It produces a haze of small mauve flowers on wiry stems above a mat of bluish leaves. 'Hopleys' is a distinct form with more substantial flowerheads.
23cm/9in.
O. rotundifolium has rounded, bluish leaves and drooping heads of bracts and pink flowers. 'Kent Beauty' is a fine hybrid that has semi-prostrate stems clad in glaucous leaves and topped with rounded bracts and purplish flowers.
23cm/9in.

Oxalis

O. enneaphylla is a miniature alpine with fans of rounded, grey-green leaves and comparatively large white or pink-flushed flowers in spring; surprisingly (since scent is not commonly encountered in oxalis) these have an almond fragrance. There is a fine pink form called *rosea*. It thrives in sheltered corners of the rock garden.
Shade. 7.5cm/3in.

Papaver

P. alpinum, alpine poppy. It is a surprise to find scent in any poppy, but this species has a fair degree of musky fragrance. The flowers, which appear all summer, can be orange, yellow, pink or white and cross-fertilize freely. It pops up all over the rock garden and in paving cracks, but never becomes a weed.
Sun. Poor, well-drained soil. 10cm/4in.

Paradisea

P. liliastrum (Anthericum liliastrum), St Bruno's lily, is a beautiful European alpine that has slender leaves and translucent, white, lily-like, fragrant flowers in early summer. It is easily grown in the rock garden or border.
Sun. 50cm/20in.

Linnaea borealis americana

Origanum rotundifolium 'Kent Beauty'

Patrinia

P. triloba palmata is a short, erect perennial, easily grown and hardy, which produces heads of golden yellow, scented flowers. These appear late, in high summer. It has deeply lobed leaves and reddish stems.
Sun. Well-drained, fertile soil. 20cm/8in.

Petrocallis

P. pyrenaica. This is a beautiful alpine that bears a mass of white, lilac-tinged flowers in spring; these are deliciously scented of vanilla and honey. It is suitable for the alpine house or scree.
Sun. Gritty soil.

Phlox

P. caespitosa is one of the more common scented alpine phloxes. It makes low mounds of long, pointed leaves and is studded, in spring and summer, with white or pale lilac flowers. These have a heady sweet fragrance. An easy plant to grow, Alpine phlox dislikes hot, dry conditions.
Sun or light shade. Well-drained, fertile soil.
P. 'Charles Ricardo' is one of many hybrid phloxes with a degree of scent; it has

lavender blue flowers with a purple centre. 20cm/8in.
P. hoodii makes prostrate mats of foliage and, in summer, bears almost stemless, scented flowers in white or lilac.
Sun. Well-drained, fertile soil.

Polygonatum

P. hookeri is a tiny Solomon's seal with almost stemless, sweetly scented pink flowers, borne in early summer.
Shade and coolness.
P. odoratum is a dwarf version of the common white Solomon's seal, *P. × hybridum*, which is not really worth growing except in its variegated forms. 'Variegatum' is a little gem, with broad white edges to its leaves. The flowers have a slight scent.
Shade.

Primula

P. auricula. This heading covers an enormous band of garden and alpine house plants. All are hardy and form rosettes of fleshy leaves, topped in spring with tubular flowers, which often have gorgeous and eccentric combinations of colours. The scent

it sweet, compared by many to honeysuckle, but to my nose usually a delicious blend of lemon and chocolate. To discuss cultivation I shall divide them into three groups.

The first group consists of the alpine auriculas. Unlike the other auriculas, these have no floury covering on their leaves and flowers, and they may be planted outside. Among the most popular varieties are 'Argus', with dark plum, white-centred flowers; 'Bookham Firefly', with crimson, gold-centred flowers; 'Gordon Douglas', with cream-centred, violet-blue flowers; 'Joy', with velvety crimson, white-centred flowers; and 'Mrs L. Hearn', with cream-centred, bluish purple flowers.
Shade from midday sun. Well-drained, fertile soil.

The second group consists of the border auriculas. These do not conform to the florist's standards for the alpine and show classes, though many are of great antiquity. They usually have a floury covering on their leaves and flowers but because of their hardiness and vigour are invariably grown outside. Among the most popular varieties are 'Blue Velvet', a bluish purple with a small white centre; 'Old Irish Blue', a frilled, rich violet-blue with a white centre; 'Old Red Dusty Miller', a rich red with a heavy covering of flour; and 'Old Yellow Dusty Miller', a heavily floured golden yellow.
Shade from midday sun. Well-drained, fertile soil.

The third group consists of the show auriculas. These are among the wonders of the plant world; the flowers are perfectly shaped, often of extraordinary colouring, and heavily coated in meal. They are grown in clay pots (long toms are the favoured type) in cold, well-ventilated greenhouses and must be shaded from strong sunshine. Among the most popular varieties are 'C. G. Haysom', a white-edged variety; 'Chloe', a green-edged variety; 'Chorister', a yellow self; 'Fanny Meerbeck', a crimson self; 'Lovebird', a grey-edged variety; 'Neat and Tidy', a deep red dark self; and 'Rajah', a bright scarlet fancy with a green edge. The scent from a collection under glass is intoxicating.
Shade from midday sun.
P. latifolia **(P. viscosa)** is a variable species with long, often rather sticky leaves. Its heads

Polygonatum hookeri

Primula × pubescens and P. marginata

of flowers are borne on short stems in late spring. They are usually a shade of rosy-purple and sweetly scented, but there are good cream and crimson forms.
Well-drained, peaty soil. 15cm/6in.
P. palinuri is a handsome plant for a sheltered spot in the rock garden or the alpine house. It has broad, serrated-edged, green leaves and powdery stems, topped in early spring with pure yellow, bell-shaped flowers which have a cowslip scent.
Sun. Well-drained, fertile soil. 20cm/8in.
P. × *pubescens* is the name given to a range of hybrid primulas, many sweetly scented, for crevices in the rock garden. One of the earliest and easiest to grow is 'Mrs J. H. Wilson', which has heads of lilac, white-centred flowers; 'Faldonside' is crimson; 'Freedom' is a rich purple; 'Rufus' is terracotta with a biscuit eye; and 'The General' is a velvet orange-red.
Sun. 7.5–15cm/3–6in.
P. reidii williamsii is a beautiful Himalayan primula with green, toothed leaves and pendant, blue or white, bell-shaped flowers that are wonderfully fragrant. This form is more robust than the species itself and may be grown outside in a shady border: it also succeeds in a pot in the alpine house. It is short-lived but comes readily from seed.
Light shade. Moist soil. 15cm/6in.

Rhodiola
R. rosea (Sedum rosea, S. rhodiola) is a curious plant that always attracts attention. It forms a woody base which is studded in pink buds early in the year. These gradually expand into fleshy stems bearing glaucous blue leaves, and in early summer they are topped with yellow stars. Curiously, the scent is in the roots, which, when broken, smell of roses. This is a lovely plant at the front of the border as well as in the rock garden.
Sun. Well-drained soil. 30cm/1ft.

Rhododendron
Dwarf rhododendrons are not suitable for alkaline soils, but are among the finest early flowering shrubs for rock gardens and raised beds. They will tolerate more sunshine than their larger relatives, but dislike hot, dry conditions. Scent usually comes from the foliage rather than the flowers. I continue

to discover ever more aromatic varieties – *R. kongboense*, scented of balsam; *R. campylogynum* Myrtilloides group, scented of coconut – so this list is provided only in order to whet the appetite.
Light shade. Well-drained, peaty soil, neutral or acid in reaction.
R. atlanticum is a vigorous, deciduous azalea from the eastern United States; it spreads by stolons and makes mounds of bright green leaves. The tubular flowers, borne in late spring, are a pink-flushed white and have a spicy sweet scent.
90cm/3ft. Z6
R. cephalanthum is a bushy evergreen with aromatic glossy foliage. It is attractive in spring when it produces its heads of white or pink-flushed flowers.
30cm–1.2m/1–4ft. Z7
R. flavidum is a dwarf rhododendron with aromatic, evergreen leaves and clusters of primrose yellow flowers in spring that forms an erect bushy shrub. 'Album' is a taller version with larger leaves and white flowers.
90cm/3ft. Z6
R. sargentianum has aromatic, evergreen leaves and clusters of pale yellow or cream flowers in spring. It is an attractive, compact shrub but is often reluctant to bloom.
60cm/2ft. Z8

Sedum
S. populifolium is an erect, woody sedum with slightly fleshy leaves shaped like those of a poplar. It is an interesting plant, and its greenish pink flowers, produced in late summer, have a scent reminiscent of hawthorn but without the fishy undertones.
Sun. Well-drained soil. 46cm/18in.

Sisyrinchium
S. filifolium comes from the Falkland Islands and produces pendant bell-shaped flowers above its tuft of rushy leaves in late spring. These are white, veined in reddish purple, and are sweetly scented.
Sun. Well-drained soil. 15cm/6in.

Stachys
S. citrina is a diminutive relative of lamb's ears. Its felted grey-green leaves are fragrant of chocolate mints when rubbed. Pale yellow flowers are produced in early summer.
Sun. Well-drained soil. 15cm/6in.

Sisyrinchium filifolium

Thlaspi
T. rotundifolium. This is a connoisseur's alpine that bears numerous heads of rosy-lilac, sometimes white, highly fragrant flowers in early summer. The stems spread underground from a fleshy rootstock and appear as rosettes of dark, round leaves. It is suitable for the alpine house or scree.
Sun. Gritty soil. 5–10cm/2–4in.

Trillium
T. luteum has lemon yellow flowers which are pleasantly scented, unlike those of the common *T. erectum* which are rather fetid. They appear in spring, each standing upright above the characteristic three large leaves, that are attractively patterned in green and brown. It is easily grown and is an obvious candidate for a peat bed.
Cool, humus-rich, retentive soil. Shade. 30cm/12in.

Water and Bog Plants

Acorus

A. calamus, sweet flag, was used for strewing floors in the Middle Ages. The strap-like leaves are scented of cinnamon when bruised; the roots are even more fragrant. Cones of sober greenish yellow flowers appear in summer. It is not especially ornamental, but its cream-striped version 'Variegatus' would be no disgrace to a pond. Shallow water or damp ground.
90cm/3ft.

Aponogeton

A. distachyos, water hawthorn, is a shade-tolerant aquatic, whose tuberous roots grow in the mud while the leaves float on the surface of the water. All through the summer and autumn, spikes of white flowers emerge, and in the evening they release a scent of vanilla. It is one of the stalwarts of the garden pond, though sometimes over-generous with its seedlings.

Cotula

C. coronopifolia, brass buttons, is a short annual which self-sows freely at the pond edge and in shallow water. It is most often grown for its small, golden, button-like flowers, but its foliage releases an aromatic lemon fragrance when crushed. There is a rare cream-flowered version called 'Cream Buttons'.
15–30cm/6–12in.

Cyperus

C. longus, galingale, is an attractive though invasive British native for the pond margin. It has shining green, grassy leaves and branching, chestnut-brown flowerheads in the summer. The stems release a sweet, mossy scent when broken; and the fragrance is also present in the roots.
60cm–1.2m/2–4ft.

Filipendula

F. ulmaria, meadowsweet. This familiar inhabitant of European river banks makes a splendid garden plant. It is most ornamental

Aponogeton distachyos

Lysichiton camtschatcensis

Lysichiton americanus

in its golden-leaved, and, to a lesser extent, golden-variegated, forms, 'Aurea' and 'Variegata'. Their plumes of creamy white flowers, borne in summer, have a heavy scent, reminiscent of hawthorn but without the fishy undertones.
Light shade. Moist soil. 60cm/2ft.

Hottonia
H. palustris, water violet, is a European aquatic plant which bears whorls of scented lilac flowers, 23cm/9in above the water, in early summer. It grows underwater and is a good oxygenator.

Houttuynia
H. cordata has recently become very popular in its variegated form 'Chameleon', whose heart-shaped leaves are streaked with green, yellow and red. The species itself has dark metallic green leaves, that colour well in the autumn. The foliage of both is sharply scented when bruised; British gardeners tend to think it smells of orange peel, American gardeners of rotten fish! Spikes of white flowers are produced in summer, and they are particularly ornamental in the double-flowered, green-leaved 'Flore Pleno'. It can

become invasive and is easier to control when grown in a tub in very shallow water. Sun or shade. Damp soil or shallow water. 15–46cm/6–18in.

Lysichiton
L. camtschatcensis is the white counterpart to the familiar and evil-smelling yellow bog arum, *L. americanus*. It is slightly smaller in all its parts, but is still a large, architectural plant. The pure white spathes appear in early spring and have none of the fetid undertones of the yellow bog arum; the scent is clean and sweet. The huge, banana-like leaves soon follow.
Sun or light shade. Damp soil or ditches. 90cm/3ft.

Mentha
Mints are often invasive and must be treated cautiously. They will attempt to weaken your resolve with their refreshing scents, but try to remember that containers and secure beds are their proper homes! Many gardeners plant them in buckets that are then inserted into the border; drainage holes have to be pierced through the bottom.
M. aquatica, water mint, is a British native

and has whorls of mauve flowers and serrated, oval leaves. It is extremely vigorous in wet ground.
Up to 1.2m/4ft.
M. longifolia, horse mint, has woolly grey leaves and heads of lavender-blue flowers and excels in the bog garden.
Up to 1.2m/4ft.
M. pulegium, pennyroyal, makes attractive prostrate mats of small, shining green leaves, and is very much at home in damp soil. It is a haze of mauve when in flower in late summer and has a pungent mint scent.
15cm/6in.

Nymphaea
Waterlilies are the aristocrats of the garden pond. Their floating islands of round leaves are a symbol of tranquillity and the flower buds, which appear all summer, are fascinating to watch as they rise to the surface and unfurl their pointed petals. Many, such as *N. odorata*, have an exotic, sweet scent. They are planted in spring either directly into the soil bottom of the pond, or in baskets of soil enriched with well-rotted manure. When grown in baskets, they may need to be lifted, divided and re-planted

Nymphaea 'Firecrest'

Nymphaea odorata

every few years. They like still water and although they will thrive at shallower and deeper depths, most enjoy being 30–46cm/ 12–18in below the surface.

Among the best scented hybrids are: 'Firecrest', a deep pink; 'Laydekeri Lilacea', a soft lilac-rose; 'Marliacea Albida', a superb white, suitable for larger ponds; 'Masaniello', a deep rose colour with a good, sweet scent; 'Odorata Sulphurea Grandiflora', a large sulphur yellow; 'Odorata W.B. Shaw', a pale pink; 'Rose Arey', a bright rose pink; 'Sunrise', a scented golden yellow; and *tuberosa* 'Rosea', a very fragrant soft pink for larger ponds.

Primula

P. alpicola produces white, yellow, violet and purple flowers with the scent of cowslips, particularly evident in the evening. The colour forms are fairly stable and you can produce monocolour groups from selected seed. It flowers in spring and early summer, and plants usually produce just one umbel of flowers on each stem.
Light shade. Moist soil. 46cm/18in.

P. anisodora, a perennial, has leaves and roots that are strongly scented of aniseed. It is one of the candelabra primulas, producing tall, slender stems hung with umbels of very dark crimson, green-eyed funnels in early summer.
Light shade. Moist soil. 46cm/18in.
P. chionantha. This lovely, easily grown primula carries whorls of sweetly scented white, yellow-eyed flowers in late spring.
Sun or shade. Moist soil. 60cm/2ft or more.
P. florindae, giant Himalayan cowslip, is a magnificent and robust primula which is ideal for damp borders and the pond edge. It blooms late, towards high summer, and produces large powdery heads of sulphur yellow flowers which are powerfully lemon-scented; the fragrance of a generous group will fill the evening air. Orange and red forms are available but in my view the yellow stands supreme. The foliage is rounded and a shining green. It is very happy on lime.
Sun or light shade. 90cm/3ft.
P. ioessa produces stems topped with comparatively few flowers, but they are a good size and very fragrant. It varies in

Primula alpicola violacea

Primula florindae

Saururus cernuus

colour from mauve-pink to deep violet.
Light shade. Damp soil. 10–30cm/4in–1ft.
P. prolifera (P. helodoxa) is a lovely
candelabra primula that produces whorls of
large bright yellow, lemon-scented flowers in
early summer. It is easily grown but often
short-lived. It thrives on lime.
Light shade. 90cm/3ft.
P. reidii williamsii is a lovely but short-lived
primula that produces white or pale blue,
highly fragrant flowers in late spring.
Light shade. Damp soil. 15cm/6in.
P. sikkimensis comes in various shades of
yellow and has a fine lemon scent. The
flowers appear in early summer, in one or
two superimposed umbels at the end of the
stems. Attractive but perhaps not in the first
flight of primulas.
Light shade. Moist soil. 46cm/18in.

Saururus
S. cernuus, American swamp lily or lizard's
tail, is an aquatic plant that has lush green,
heart-shaped leaves and in summer produces
dense, nodding spikes of scented white
flowers.
Shallow water or pond edge. 60cm/2ft.

Rose Gardens

Roses are the undisputed sovereigns of the scented garden. Their fragrances are sophisticated and diverse, sometimes delicate, sometimes heady but nearly always delicious. They bloom profusely, contribute important splashes of colour to the garden and often keep flowering for weeks on end. There is a wealth of varieties of different character, size and habit of growth and they tolerate a range of soils and climates. Indeed, they present the gardener with so rich a choice that it is often difficult to know how to exercise restraint and set about making a selection.

I think the best starting point is to consider the setting into which they will be put and the effect you wish to create. Different categories of rose require different treatments and evoke different moods. They are all, however, sun-lovers, and this should be borne in mind at the outset. Some roses, it is true, will accept a degree of shade – such as the Albas and climbers like 'Madame Alfred Carrière', 'Zéphirine Drouhin' and 'Albéric Barbier' – but most need several hours, at least, of full sunlight each day in order to perform well. Furthermore, they require shelter from cold winds and do not thrive in very exposed or draughty spots. Hedged and walled enclosures are ideal, and here their fragrances will be held captive.

Where the setting is very formal, such as a rectangular bed in front of a house or a geometrical pattern of beds around a sundial, Hybrid Teas, with their uniformity of growth and perfection of flower shape, may be the perfect candidates. Indeed, manicured compositions of velvet, sharp-edged lawns, weed-free paving and immaculate paintwork seem to cry out for them. I prefer to see them in mono-colour groups – guardsman's scarlet against emerald grass, white against cool, grey stone, yellow reflected in pools of waterlilies – but a mixture of varieties does bring life to a small front garden or a drab city street. Some Hybrid Teas are scentless or give only a faint whiff of tea. But when a rich 'rose' fragrance overlays the tea scent, some truly sumptuous concoctions result, as in 'Alec's Red', 'Fragrant Cloud', 'Prima Ballerina', 'Whisky Mac' and the old Hybrid Teas, 'Ophelia', 'Lady Sylvia' and 'Madame Butterfly'.

The Floribundas are even better bedding roses. They have never been famed for their scent and they are still likely to disappoint. I took a stroll along the rows in a nursery field recently and more than half the roses I nosed were either without scent or, even worse, downright nasty; yellow roses seem most likely to offend. But rich scent is present in a number of varieties and rose breeders are pursuing it further. 'Arthur Bell', 'Chinatown' and 'Margaret Merril' (probably the best scented white bedding rose) are outstanding. Their lavish display is particularly welcome in paved and patio gardens, where they can be combined with small-flowered Polyanthas, Miniature and Patio Roses and pompon-flowered Shrub roses like 'Cécile Brunner' and myrrh-scented 'Little White Pet' (excellent as a standard). Like Hybrid Teas, they bloom all summer and autumn, entering the stage when the surge of early flowering roses is dying away.

The idea of having bedding roses in isolation on bare soil mounded up like a grave unfortunately still persists. Apart from looking ugly, this is a great waste of good earth. For spring, you could underplant with hyacinths, honey-scented muscari and, if you can turn a blind eye to their dying foliage later, sweet-scented daffodils. For summer, you could have snapdragons or, even better, nostalgically perfumed heliotropes. Or you could make a permanent edging of camomile, catmint, thymes, cottage pinks or *Geranium macrorrhizum*.

In the more relaxed setting of the cottage garden, which many of us possess in some form or other, stiff formal roses can easily look out of place. Here roses may have to participate in the rough-and-tumble of the border and share ground with other shrubs and wispy perennials; they may be lapped by rough grass or a stream; and they may have a backdrop of

Right *The old shrub roses plunge the mid-summer garden into a sumptuous crimson, pink and white colour scheme. At Mottisfont Abbey in Hampshire, the rose scents are held captive by walls and are supplemented by the warm clove fragrances of dianthus, seen here in the foreground. Spires of white foxgloves rise above* Rosa gallica officinalis, *and in the distance* 'Constance Spry', *with its peculiar cold-cream scent, climbs over a painted wooden seat.*

fields, trees and higgledy-piggledy housing. Groups of Floribundas and Polyanthas often fit comfortably into such surroundings but it is the shrub roses that are most at home.

Shrub roses are simply flowering shrubs; they are not pruned to stumps each year, but instead are encouraged to form a natural structure that, depending on variety, can be anything from 1–3m/3–10ft in height and spread. The earliest shrub roses, which start to open in spring, include many species and hybrids with single flowers and small leaves, and

Above *Shrub roses ask to be allowed to grow generously and not to be pruned to stumps each winter. They can either be left to form a natural shape or their stems can be arched onto supports. Here 'Fritz Nobis', a modern shrub rose of outstanding quality, showers its clove-scented blooms over a path. A gentle contrast in scent is provided by the fruitily fragrant variegated applemint beneath.*

these are especially suited to the wilder parts of the garden or to woodland clearings. Most only bloom once – the little gem 'Stanwell Perpetual', with double pink flowers, is an exception – but afterwards they do not necessarily cease to contribute. Some, such as *R. eglanteria* (*R. rubiginosa*) and *R. primula*, waft scent from their leaves, while others produce a bountiful display of hips. The more striking single-flowered varieties and the early doubles (mainly forms or descendants of *R. rugosa*, *R. pimpinellifolia*, *R. foetida* and *R. eglanteria*) will hold their own against the most flamboyant of companions in the summer border. The great spicy-scented saucers of 'Frühlingsgold' and 'Nevada' are, for example, stunning with fiery oriental poppies.

A scented garden should not be without the Rugosas. Their powerful scents, well-flavoured with clove, infuse the air around them; the single white *R. rugosa* 'Alba' and the double white 'Blanc Double de Coubert' are arguably the most scented of all roses, and the sulphur yellow 'Agnes' has a lemon fragrance all of its own. There are no other roses that give a longer display of flowers than the double Rugosas, and few roses give as impressive a crop of hips. On top of all this, they are luxuriant in foliage, pest and disease free, and depart in the autumn in a burst of golden yellow.

The arrival, at mid-summer, of the old shrub roses, the old-fashioned, blowsy beauties that have come to us largely from the nurseries of nineteenth-century France, marks the high point of the scent-gardener's year. If borders are strewn with their petal-packed flowers, which come in every conceivable shade and combination of white, pink, magenta and crimson, there will be a truly intoxicating sweetness wafting across the garden for almost a month. 'Old rose perfume', rich, complex and intense, is the norm among these roses, though it varies greatly in composition and flavour. Old shrub roses fall into several classes. The Gallicas are short and bushy with a refined, full scent, strongly coloured flowers, dark leaves and almost thornless stems. Because of their suckering habit they make very good low hedges, but they are easily accommodated near the front of any sunny bed. They are very happy in the dry conditions of the 'Mediterranean' border where the perfume will blend with the gummy aromas of cistuses and the scents of lavender and rosemary. 'Charles de Mills', 'Président de Sèze' and *R. gallica* 'Versicolor' (Rosa Mundi) are superb varieties that float their perfume on the air.

The Damasks and Albas, with softer-coloured flowers and grey-green leaves, are taller, as are the rather coarser Provence/Centifolia and Moss roses. Some of them, especially the Albas, will make attractive free-standing shrubs but most benefit from having their long growths wrapped around a framework of metal or wooden posts.

The Damasks are spicily scented and include one variety in their ranks, 'Ispahan', which blooms for longer than any other old shrub rose. 'Celsiana', 'La Ville de Bruxelles' and the incomparable 'Madame Hardy' are also in the first flight. Among the delicately perfumed Albas, I would single out the White Rose of York, 'Alba Semiplena', which follows up its show of gloriously scented white flowers with a display of orange hips; 'Madame Legras de Saint Germain', 'Céleste' and 'Great Maiden's Blush' are also irresistible.

The scent of the Provence/Centifolia roses and the moss roses is usually strong and heady and carries well. Among the former I rate 'Fantin-Latour' and 'Petite de Hollande' (a short rose for the front of the border) very highly; and among the latter, 'William Lobb' and 'Nuits de Young'.

These tall roses have only one drawback. After their sumptuous mid-summer display of flowers, they slip into an uneventful retirement. You can turn a blind eye if you are only growing a few but a collection of them can present a problem. For the devotees, there are really two solutions. The first is to grow them in their own enclosure where they cannot become an eyesore later. The second is to interplant generously with late-flowering shrubs like buddlejas and hebes and to make use of other, repeat-flowering roses. In this category come the Hybrid Perpetuals and fabulously scented Bourbons, roses with old-fashioned flowers but usually with some of the stiffer habit and coarser growth of the modern bush rose. They bloom intermittently after mid-summer and in my view a scented garden is not complete without them. Many have strong fruity scents, raspberry often being the dominant flavour; the Bourbons 'Honorine de Brabant' and 'Adam Messerich' possess it, as does the Hybrid Perpetual 'Ferdinand Pichard'. Few roses can rival the Bourbon 'Madame Isaac Pereire' for strength of fragrance.

These roses are rarely as reliable and showy in their later crops as China roses – 'Old Blush China' has such a long season that it is called the monthly rose – or the Portland and Damask Perpetual roses, which are like small Damasks but with richer colouring; 'Comte de Chambord' and 'Jacques Cartier' are excellent varieties. These roses sit well at the front of the border and are also successful in tubs on the patio. We can also draw on the Hybrid Musks to prolong the season. Like the Rugosas, these roses have an intense and far-reaching perfume, but with distinctive fruity and spicy flavours of their own. They are also distinctive in appearance and carry Floribunda-like trusses of flowers in a range of creamy,

Above *Box edging and weed-free gravel make an ordered setting for a carefree display of flowers. The combination of a rather formal ground plan and a quantity of shrub roses is invariably a happy one, for the design is interesting even when the roses cease blooming. The soft pink Alba rose in the foreground, the 'Königin von Dänemark' ('Queen of Denmark'), is underplanted with sweet Williams.*

yellowy and salmony shades, colours that are absent from all the classes of old shrub roses. They are important for the scented garden and can be used as free-standing shrubs, as climbers or as hedges.

Another breed of repeat-flowering shrub rose has emerged in recent years. From David Austin Roses of Albrighton, Wolverhampton, England, come the 'English Roses' that combine the colours, shapes and scents of the old shrub rose with an ability to bloom intermittently all summer. Like the Bourbons and Hybrid Perpetuals, English roses tend to inherit the stiffer habit and coarser growth of the China roses but they are first-rate plants that are becoming extremely popular; they seem to succeed even in hot climates. Other modern shrub roses that repeat well include 'Golden Wings', 'Nymphenburg' and 'Cerise Bouquet'; these do not have old rose flowers.

I have mentioned rose hedges several times. Informal flowering hedges can be a wonderful feature in the garden, especially where the setting is predominantly green. Rugosas are commonly used, being vigorous, bushy, floriferous and disease free; 'Sarah van Fleet', 'Scabrosa' and 'Fru Dagmar Hastrup' are particularly good choices. Hybrid Musks, especially silver-pink 'Felicia', are also well suited for hedging. For a low hedge, upright Floribundas like 'Chinatown' and 'Everest Double Fragrance', Portlands, Dwarf Polyanthas and 'Old Blush China' rose are suitable, as well as the suckering Gallicas (there is a superb double hedge of striped Rosa Mundi at Kiftsgate Court in Gloucestershire, England). In more natural settings, use *R. eglanteria* and its Penzance hybrids, with their apple-scented leaves, and *R. canina*, and interplant with honeysuckles.

Shrub roses are so generous and varied in their production of scent that you may feel they do not need fragrant companions to enhance their flavours. But I can never resist introducing fruity philadelphus, peonies, irises, dictamnus, *Lilium regale* and *L. candidum*, spicy cottage pinks and clove carnations to supplement the scents of the mid-summer roses; and buddlejas, escallonias, olearias, hybrid lilies, salvias, herbaceous clematis, lavenders and bergamot to complement the late performers.

There is never enough ground space for all the roses you want to grow and it is fortunate that the family can also be grown vertically. Scented climbing roses can be trained against any sunny wall, along pergolas and fences, or up wooden tripods erected at the back of borders. On walls they can join company with wisteria and ceanothus, myrtles, passion flower, *Buddleja crispa* and carpenteria; on pergolas with akebia, jasmines and honeysuckles. Many richly scented varieties of bush and shrub rose have climbing counterparts ('Ena Harkness', 'Etoile de Hollande', 'Madame Abel Chatenay', 'Souvenir de la Malmaison', for example) and many can be turned into climbers simply by training them upwards ('Aloha', 'Madame Isaac Pereire', 'Madame Plantier'). But climbing roses vary greatly in character. Some, such as 'Aimée Vibert' and 'Blush Noisette', have clusters of tiny, double or semi-double, button flowers; some, such as 'Guinée' and 'Paul's Lemon Pillar', have fine tea rose flowers; others, such as 'Lawrence Johnston' and 'Cupid', have large, open, single or semi-double flowers; and some, such as 'Gloire de Dijon' and 'Madame Alfred Carrière', have large flowers congested with petals. Some bloom continuously all summer and some give one show, with perhaps a short encore in the autumn.

The range of scents is also great. The Noisette climbers, with their clusters of small flowers, have a pervasive fragrance well-flavoured with fruit and spice. 'Lady Hillingdon' is tea-scented, as is 'Gloire de Dijon', though the tea is blended with sweeter flavours. 'Constance Spry' has a scent of cold cream or calamine lotion, said to resemble myrrh; the scent of the rambler 'Félicité Perpétue' is similar. There are many others with an exceedingly rich fragrance, among them 'Madame Abel Chatenay', 'Etoile de Hollande', 'Crimson Glory', 'Madame Butterfly' and 'Madame Grégoire Staechelin'.

The once-flowering Rambler roses can be used in the same way but usually dislike being lashed back to a wall. The smaller varieties, like apple-scented *R. wichuraiana* and its hybrids, are at home on pergolas, ropes and wire mesh fences or wandering through fruit trees; 'Rambling Rector' is outstanding in this role. But the big ramblers like 'Bobbie James', 'Seagull' and the monstrous 'Kiftsgate', with their pervasive fruity scent flavoured with incense, need very large trees or a large expanse of shed roof, very solidly supported. Recently a friend of mine saw a small summerhouse with a 'Kiftsgate' rose planted on each corner and we were wondering how long it would be before the structure collapsed; the original 'Kiftsgate' rose is over 15m/50ft high and 24m/80ft across.

Right *Among the finest of pink-flowered climbing roses, 'New Dawn' succeeds well on a wall and has a gentle and subtle fruity scent. It gives its main performance after mid-summer but produces odd blooms more or less continually thereafter. Less generous climbing roses can be partnered with honeysuckles or fragrant clematis to maintain a succession of scented flowers.*

Roses

Gallica Roses

The Gallicas are the oldest garden roses. They bloom only once, at mid-summer, but give a sumptuous display of crimsons, magentas and bright pinks; the fragrance is invariably the rich, true 'old rose' perfume. They make short, compact, bushy shrubs that are prone to suckering and are useful as low hedges. Being tolerant of poorer and drier soils than other roses, they are excellent in the borders of grey-leaved shrubs and perennials. They need little pruning but respond to some thinning of shoots and the removal of weak wood, which may be carried out after flowering.
Z6

'Assemblage des Beautés' has shocking magenta-crimson, fully double flowers that age to purple.
1.2m/4ft.

'Belle de Crécy' has richly scented double flowers that begin cerise but soon assume grey and mauve tints. It forms an arching shrub and has grey-green foliage.
1.2m/4ft.

'Belle Isis' is a parent of 'Constance Spry' and has the same myrrh/calamine lotion scent. The double flowers are flesh pink and are set off well by the grey-green leaves.
1.2m/4ft.

'Camaieux' is one of the curious striped roses, its double white flowers being splashed first with crimson-pink and then, as they age, with purple and grey.
1.2m/4ft.

'Cardinal de Richelieu' bears perfect, almost ball-shaped, double flowers of rich crimson-purple and has a delicious scent. The foliage is dark green.
1.2m/4ft.

'Charles de Mills' is one of the best Gallicas. The bright crimson-pink flowers are extremely flat when half open but expand to reveal beautifully quartered, double blooms that turn to violet and purple. The scent is powerful and delicious. It is a vigorous and generous rose.
1.5m/5ft.

'Duc de Guiche' is similar to 'Assemblage des Beautés', with perfect, cup-shaped flowers in bright magenta-crimson; they have a green eye and reflex almost into a ball-shape as they age. It is less compact in growth than other Gallicas. The scent is magnificent.
1.2m/4ft.

'Duchesse de Montebello' is a splendid Gallica with blush pink double flowers that make an arching shrub clad in light green foliage.
1.2m/4ft.

'Président de Sèze' is another outstanding Gallica with beautifully shaped double flowers in a blend of crimson, magenta and lilac. The scent is powerful and delicious. It makes a neat shrub and has grey-green leaves.
1.2m/4ft.

R. gallica officinalis, the apothecary's rose, is a fine bushy rose with highly scented, semi-double, light crimson flowers illuminated by bright yellow stamens. It is an ancient rose and still one of the best.
1.2m/4ft.

'Charles de Mills'

'Tuscany Superb'

'Céleste'

R. gallica **'Versicolor' (Rosa Mundi)** is the most popular of the striped roses. It resembles the apothecary's rose, of which it is a sport, except that the flowers are heavily streaked with white. Like its parent, it is an outstanding Gallica.
1.2m/4ft.

'Tricolore de Flandre' has well-scented, semi-double blush white flowers heavily striped in magenta-purple. It is untypical of Gallicas in its profusion of thorns.
1m/3ft.

'Tuscany Superb' is one of my favourite Gallicas, with sumptuous deep maroon-crimson flowers that are tightly bunched around golden yellow stamens. The perfume is not as rich or strong as in some other roses.
1.2m/4ft.

Alba Roses

The Albas are romantic shrub roses with grey-green leaves and an abundance of pink or white flowers at mid-summer. Their perfume is light and sophisticated. They make fairly large upright plants that take their place well at the back of the border. They are also useful in shadier spots where other roses would not be expected to thrive. They need only periodic thinning after flowering, though they respond well to a more severe winter pruning when their long growths may be shortened by about 1m/3ft.

'Alba Maxima' (Great Double White, Jacobite Rose) is a tough old rose, not as elegant as some but possessing a very rich scent. The untidy double flowers are creamy white.
2m/6ft.

'Alba Semiplena' (White Rose of York) is one of the roses grown for the distillation of attar of roses. Its semi-double pure white flowers, lit by golden stamens, have a powerful scent and are followed in the autumn by striking clusters of red hips.
2m/6ft.

'Céleste' ('Celestial') is a beautiful Alba with semi-double, shell pink flowers set against especially good grey foliage. The scent is rich and sweet and it has a sturdy upright habit.
2m/6ft.

'Félicité Parmentier' is a short Alba with flat, petal-packed flowers of flesh pink that reflex almost into a ball shape.

R. gallica officinalis and *R.g.* 'Versicolor'

'Great Maiden's Blush' ('Cuisse de Nymphe') is my favourite Alba and one of the loveliest old shrub roses. It makes a fine branching shrub and the blush pink double flowers have a delicious fragrance.
1.5m/5ft.

'Königin von Dänemark' ('Queen of Denmark') is a beautiful rose with rich pink, double, highly scented flowers. It is excellent when trained to grow up posts or into an apple tree.
2m/6ft.

'Madame Legras de Saint Germain' has unusual yellow-flushed double white flowers and splendid grey foliage. It is one of the best in this group and has the added advantage of possessing very few thorns.
2m/6ft.

'Madame Plantier' bears large clusters of creamy petal-packed flowers and is a very good tall rose for training up posts and apple trees.
3.5m/12ft.

Damask Roses

The Damasks are mid-summer roses with greyish foliage and fine scents. The flowers are carried in generous bunches. They require only a light thinning of weak and overcrowded shoots after flowering.
Z5

'Celsiana' makes a very pleasant grey-green shrub and its semi-double, clear pink petals are folded around prominent golden anthers. The scent is rich and strong.
1.5m/5ft.

'Ispahan' has a long flowering season and lives up to its evocative name. The scent is sumptuous and the double flowers are a romantic pink.
1.5m/5ft.

'La Ville de Bruxelles' is a splendid and vigorous Damask, luxuriant in foliage and bearing clusters of very large flowers. These are pure pink and the petals are packed around a button eye. The scent is excellent.
1.5m/5ft.

'Madame Hardy'

'Madame Hardy' is the first shrub rose I ever grew and remains a firm favourite. The flat, double, pure white petals incurve around a green eye and are set off perfectly by fresh green foliage. The scent is deliciously fruity. It should be in every collection of old roses.
1.5m/5ft.

Portland and Damask Perpetual Roses
These roses are closely related to the Damasks but are a little smaller and bloom throughout the summer and autumn. These are the roses for the front of the border and for small gardens. Unfortunately, there are very few varieties available; the following are particularly outstanding and deserve to be in every collection:
'Comte de Chambord' ('Madame Knorr') is one of the best shrub roses. Its large flowers are bright pink and intensely fragrant and are borne on and off for many months. It makes a bushy, erect shrub.
1.2m/4ft.
'De Rescht' has small shocking pink flowers that are extremely fragrant and carried over a long period. It makes a small, compact shrub, well clad in green leaves.
1m/3ft.

'Jacques Cartier' ('Marquise Boccella') is similar to 'Comte de Chambord' but the pink flowers are less cupped. It also flowers repeatedly.
1.2m/4ft.

Provence Roses
The Provence or Centifolia roses are rather thorny, coarse in leaf and lax in habit but their flowers are large and the profusion of nodding heads at mid-summer is a lovely sight. The fragrance is also intense and far-reaching. They should be pruned in the same way as Alba roses and benefit from a reduction of their long stems in winter.
Z6
R. × centifolia is the cabbage rose featured in Dutch paintings. The double, pink flowers are powerfully scented and nod in clusters against the grey-green leaves. It is a shrub of lax habit but a charmer.
1.5m/5ft.
'De Meaux' is a miniature Centifolia bearing a profusion of pink flowers that are fully double.
60cm/2ft.
'Fantin-Latour' is one of the loveliest of all the pink shrub roses. The cupped, petal-packed flowers are softly coloured and clear, and the fragrance is exquisite. The foliage is dark green and smooth.
1.5m/5ft.
'Petite de Hollande' is a splendid and compact small Centifolia for the front of the border. The small double flowers are bright pink and the scent is superb.
1.2m/4ft.
'Robert le Diable' has flowers coloured with an extraordinary suffusion of greys and purples splashed with pink and red. It is a small bushy shrub that is very lax in habit and succeeds well when spilling down a sunny retaining wall.
1m/3ft.
'Tour de Malakoff' is a large lanky plant best lashed around wooden posts or trained against a wall. But it is a show stopper in bloom for the flowers are big and blowsy, coloured a dazzling magenta at first but later taking on violet and grey tints. The fragrance does not disappoint.
2.3m/7ft.

Moss Roses
The Moss roses are either direct mutations or have been developed from mutations of the Centifolias or the Damasks. They are characterized by the presence of bristles or soft mossy growth around their flower stalks and buds. With some notable exceptions, they are not outstanding roses and their value is principally as curiosities. They are usually coarse in growth and many are prone to mildew. Their flower scent, however, has the same sophisticated and refreshing quality as the Centifolias; the mossy covering also has its own fragrance that is often powerfully balsamic. They should be pruned in the same way as Centifolias.
'Capitaine John Ingram' is a dark crimson velvet rose, fully double and with an especially strong scent. The colouring varies according to the weather and age of the flower and the blooms take on attractive purple tints. The buds have a light covering of reddish moss. It makes a dense shrub.
1.5m/5ft.
× centifolia 'Muscosa' (Old Pink Moss, Common Moss) is the original Moss rose. It has extremely fragrant double flowers in clear pink and plenty of green moss.
1.2m/4ft.

'Fantin-Latour'

compact but scantily clad shrub and has little moss. It is a sensation at its best.
1.2m/4ft.
'Shailer's White Moss' ('White Bath') releases a very rich scent from its double white flowers and has good dark foliage and plenty of moss.
1.2m/4ft.
'William Lobb' (Old Velvet Moss) has large semi-double flowers that fade from dark crimson to magenta, violet and grey. The scent is superb. It is a tall, vigorous, well-mossed rose that needs support.
2.5m/8ft.

Bourbon Roses

The Bourbons straddle the boundary line between the old and new roses. They combine petal-packed, old-fashioned flowers with the ability to produce further flushes of blooms after mid-summer. Their perfume is often very strong and fruity. They are vigorous roses, sometimes with lush and dark 'modern' foliage, and require regular pruning: a light pruning of flowered shoots after the first mid-summer flush and a reduction of the long stems by a third or more in late winter.
Z6–8
'Adam Messerich' has semi-double, rich pink flowers that possess a powerful raspberry fragrance. It makes a bushy, upright shrub and blooms throughout the season.
1.5m/5ft.
'Boule de Neige' bears small clusters of pure white globular flowers throughout the summer and autumn. They have a rich scent and show up well against the dark foliage. It makes a slender, erect shrub.
1.2m/4ft.
'Commandant Beaurepaire' blooms only at mid-summer but makes a sumptuous show of large, double, pink flowers striped and flecked with carmine, purple and scarlet that have a good scent. It makes a dense shrub clad in rather pale, pointed leaves.
1.5m/5ft.
'Louise Odier' is one of the best Bourbons. The bright lilac-pink flowers resemble camellias in their rounded shape and the perfume is very strong. It blooms throughout the season and makes an attractive shrub, well clad in fresh green leaves.
1.5m/5ft.

'Comtesse de Murinais' has superb blush-white double flowers and the fragrance from the bright green moss is remarkable. A tall, vigorous rose, it needs some support.
2m/6ft.
'Général Kléber' has bright satin pink flowers that open double and flat. It makes a bushy plant and has good lush foliage and green moss.
1.2m/4ft.
'Gloire des Mousseuses' has exceptionally large double blooms of clear pink with a fine scent. It has plenty of green moss.
1.2m/4ft.

'Maréchal Davoust' has double flowers in a blend of carmine and purple colours. It makes a neat shrub with grey-green leaves and dark moss.
1.2m/4ft.
'Mousseline' is an excellent compact and healthy shrub rose that blooms continuously through the summer and autumn. The flowers are semi-double and blush pink with a good scent.
1.2m/4ft.
'Nuits de Young' is an especially dark rose with double, maroon-purple flowers illuminated by golden stamens. It makes a

'Madame Isaac Pereire' is described by Graham Stuart Thomas, the great rosarian, as 'possibly the most powerfully fragrant of all roses'. The magenta-pink flowers are huge, rather untidy and even a little vulgar but its perfume more than compensates for any faults. It makes a vigorous, leafy bush and blooms in bursts through the season.
2.3m/7ft.

'Madame Lauriol de Barny' breathes an exceptionally good fruity scent. It produces its large, double, silvery pink flowers on and off through the season but its main burst is at mid-summer. It is attractive when trained against a pillar.
2m/6ft.

'Madame Pierre Oger' has globular flowers in translucent creamy pink touched with rose and a strong sweet scent. It blooms throughout the season.
1.5m/5ft.

'Reine Victoria' bears lilac-pink, silky flowers that are beautifully cupped and have an especially rich scent. It blooms throughout the season.
2m/6ft.

'Souvenir de la Malmaison' is invariably the most bewitching rose on the stands at the Chelsea Flower Show in London, with its beautifully quartered, pale pink flowers, well endowed with perfume. It blooms continuously and gives an especially fine autumn display.
60cm–2m/2–6ft.

'Variegata di Bologna' has blush white flowers striped with crimson and is the most effective of the paler striped roses. The blooms are beautifully cupped and fully double. Its mid-summer performance is followed by sporadic flushes later in the season.
1.5m/5ft.

Hybrid Perpetual Roses

The Hybrid Perpetuals are very similar to the Bourbons and are often grouped together. They have old-fashioned flowers that are produced at mid-summer and then usually in bursts thereafter. Pruning is as for Bourbons.
Z6–8

'Baron Girod de l'Ain' has bright crimson double flowers, pencilled at the edges with white. It has a superb scent and blooms throughout the summer.
1.5m/5ft.

'Empereur du Maroc' is a deep maroon-crimson and very richly scented. It is rather a weak grower and prone to disease but at its best is magnificent.
1.2m/4ft.

'Ferdinand Pichard' is my favourite striped rose. It has a strong scent of raspberry and the double pink flowers are heavily streaked in crimson and purple. It makes an attractive bushy plant and flowers repeatedly.
1.5m/5ft.

'Gloire de Ducher' bears huge reddish purple flowers and is particularly notable for its extravagant autumn display. It is very fragrant. It produces tall arching branches and needs support.
2.3m/7ft.

'Mrs John Laing' is one of the best Hybrid Perpetuals, flowering repeatedly and possessing an excellent scent. The cupped lilac-pink flowers are shown off well against the grey-green foliage.
1.2m/4ft.

'Reine des Violettes' is also in the first flight of Hybrid Perpetuals. The flowers open purple and fade to soft violet and are beautifully quartered and well scented. It makes a most attractive shrub with greyish leaves and almost thornless stems.
2m/6ft.

'Souvenir d'Alphonse Lavallée' is not commonly offered but is a rose to hunt for. The double flowers are a sumptuous dark maroon-crimson and captivate all who see them. The scent is appropriately rich. It makes a tall, open shrub and is best pegged down or trained on to a support.
2.3m/7ft.

'Souvenir du Docteur Jamain' is my favourite dark rose. The flowers are an intense damson-purple and deliciously scented. Its main season is at mid-summer but it produces a second flush in the autumn. It should be planted out of strong midday sun.
2m/6ft.

Hybrid Musks

These roses, most of which were bred by the Revd Joseph Pemberton in Essex, England, in the early part of this century, are powerfully fragrant, free-blooming and vigorous shrubs

'Madame Isaac Pereire'

'Souvenir de la Malmaison'

that deserve to be in every scented garden. They have little to do with the musk rose *R. moschata* – their strong fruity scents suggest a different parentage, especially *R. multiflora*. Their main display is at mid-summer, just as the old shrub roses are tiring, and they continue intermittently through the summer, with a triumphant final flush in the autumn. They carry their blooms in trusses, in the manner of a Floribunda, and the scent is usually rich and pervasive. They may be pruned back by a third or more in early spring.

'Buff Beauty' is one of the loveliest Hybrid Musks. It bears fully double flowers in apricot yellow that have a rich tea rose scent. The foliage is excellent, beginning bronze and maturing to dark green.
1.5m/5ft.

'Cornelia' carries large clusters of small, rosette-shaped flowers that are a blend of apricot, cream and pink. Its autumn display is especially notable. It has a powerful fragrance.
1.5m/5ft.

'Felicia' makes a fine bushy shrub, smothered in double, silvery pink flowers at mid-summer and maintaining a good display through the summer and autumn. It has a rich fragrance.
1.5m/5ft.

'Francesca' has semi-double flowers that begin apricot and fade to a warm yellow. The scent is strong, with a tea rose flavour. It is a graceful shrub with good glossy foliage.
2m/6ft.

'Moonlight' bears trusses of almost single, creamy white flowers that are superb against the dark leaves and reddish-brown stems. It has a strong fragrance.
2m/6ft.

'Penelope' is a popular Hybrid Musk with salmon-pink buds opening to semi-double, creamy pink flowers that have a strong scent. It gives a fine autumn display and concludes the year with coral-pink hips.
2m/6ft.

'Vanity' carries large, almost single flowers in deep pink continually through the summer and autumn. The scent is strong and sweet.
2m/6ft.

Right 'Felicia'

'Mrs John Laing'

'Blanc Double de Coubert'

'Fru Dagmar Hastrup'

'Roseraie de l'Haÿ'

China Roses

These are small, dainty roses that flower repeatedly and are ideal for the front of the border. They are a little tender and perform best in warm, sheltered sites and against walls. Regular pruning is unnecessary, except for the removal of dead and weak wood. Sun. Z7–8

'Comtesse du Cayla' has almost single flowers in bright colours – a blend of salmon, orange and pink – and possesses an exceptionally rich tea rose scent.
1m/3ft.

Old Blush ('Pallida'), the monthly rose, is valued for its continuity of flowering. Its silvery pink flowers have an excellent sweet scent and it makes an upright, almost thornless, twiggy bush.
1–2m/3–6ft.

Rugosa Roses

Rugosa or Japanese roses and their hybrids are among the most potently scented of all garden shrubs, their spicy sweet perfume infusing the air on still, damp days. The double-flowered varieties usually continue blooming generously from early summer until autumn, while the single-flowered varieties produce crops of plump, tomato-shaped hips. The rough-textured foliage is distinctive and often luxuriant and assumes good yellow autumn colouring. Plants are quite resistant to pest and disease problems. They make excellent flowering hedges, and may be pruned over lightly in early spring. Z2

'Agnes', a hybrid between *R. rugosa* and *R. foetida* 'Persiana', is one of my favourite roses. The double flowers are an unusual amber yellow and the scent is a potent blend of lemon and spice. It is sometimes not generous with flowers after its first early summer flush.
2m/6ft.

'Blanc Double de Coubert' is arguably the most fragrant of all roses. The dazzling white flowers are semi-double and glow against the dark green leaves; they are borne continually throughout the summer and autumn.
1.5m/5ft.

'Conrad Ferdinand Meyer' is a vigorous Rugosa hybrid, whose long stems may need to be substantially reduced in early spring. The scent from the double, silvery pink flowers is especially rich. It is prone to rust.
2.5m/8ft.

'**Fru Dagmar Hastrup**' has single fragrant flowers in clear pink followed by crimson hips. It is bushy and compact and makes a fine flowering hedge.
1.2m/4ft.
'**Mrs Anthony Waterer**' has a good crop of richly scented, double crimson flowers in early summer but few thereafter. It is more spreading than upright.
1.2m/4ft.
'**Roseraie de l'Haÿ**' is a popular and vigorous Rugosa with semi-double, crimson-purple flowers and a rich scent. It has especially lush, fresh green foliage.
1.2–1.5m/4–5ft.
R. rugosa has single flowers, variable in colour between pink and carmine-purple, and these are well scented. The clash with the bright red hips is startling.
2.3m/7ft.
R. rugosa '**Alba**' is worthy of a place in any garden. It bears its pure white, pervasively scented flowers over a long period and they are joined in autumn by large orange hips.
2.3m/7ft.
'**Sarah van Fleet**' has semi-double, well-scented flowers in clear pink and blooms continuously. It is a vigorous, upright, bushy shrub and makes a good hedge.
2.5m/8ft.
'**Scabrosa**' is a luxuriant Rugosa, lush in foliage and bountiful with its large, single, crimson-purple flowers and its crop of orange hips. The scent is rich and sweet. It is another good hedging rose.
1.2m/4ft.

Species and Near-Species Shrub Roses
'**Dupontii**' has single white flowers with the delicious scent of banana. It is a beautiful rose – the crisp, pure blooms with a boss of golden stamens are offset by grey-green foliage. It flowers after mid-summer, giving one splendid show but providing some orange hips later.
2.3m/7ft. Z6
R. eglanteria (*R. rubiginosa*), the sweet briar or eglantine, is another indispensable species, cherished for the scent of green apples released by its foliage. The fragrance is strongest at the tips of the shoots. A fine hedging plant, it should be clipped in late winter. Single pink flowers, themselves sweetly scented, appear in early summer and

'Dupontii'

are followed by an impressive display of red hips. Strongly scented foliage is passed on to many of its forms and hybrids, among which 'Lady Penzance', with less appealingly scented single, coppery pink flowers, 'Lord Penzance', with sweetly scented, single, pinky buff-yellow flowers (both provide a show of hips later), and 'Manning's Blush', a more compact shrub with pleasantly scented, double, blush-white flowers, are outstanding.
2m/6ft or more. Z6
R. '**Headleyensis**' is a hybrid of the golden rose of China, *R. hugonis*, and like its parent blooms in early summer. The single, creamy yellow flowers are very fragrant and are displayed on arching brown branches well clad in ferny foliage.
2.3m/7ft. Z6

R. eglanteria

R. macrantha is a vigorous spreading rose that gives a good show of large single flowers, which fade from blush pink to white and have a rich fragrance. These are followed by a fine display of red hips. 'Daisy Hill' is a pinker version.
1.5m/5ft. Z6

R. pimpinellifolia (*R. spinosissima*), the burnet or Scottish rose, gives some highly scented and attractive varieties including 'Double White' and 'Double Pink', both with a deliciously sweet perfume and globular flowers. The double yellow, *R. × harisonii* 'Harison's Yellow', is a fine buttery tone, but the scent is not so appealing; there are, however, double yellow Scottish roses with pleasant scents – I grow one, but it came as a cutting from an unnamed shrub. 'Stanwell Perpetual' is a particularly fine hybrid that, unlike these others, continues to bloom all season after its main mid-summer display; the double flowers are blush pink and very fragrant and the foliage is grey-green. All these roses make thorny plants well furnished in small leaves.
1.5m/5ft. Z5

R. primula is an essential ingredient of the fragrant garden. The ferny leaves release the scent of incense after a shower of rain; this is especially marked early in the season when the foliage is young. Small, single, primrose yellow flowers, sweetly scented, appear in early summer and are effective against the mahogany stems.
1.5m/5ft. Z7

R. pulverulenta (*R. glutinosa*) is not commonly offered but is of interest to the scent lover for the fragrance of its foliage – a blend of orange and pine. It has small pink flowers followed by large, globular red hips. It makes a low prickly shrub and is suitable for a dry, sunny border.
1m/3ft.

R. serafinii is an unusual miniature rose whose foliage gives off a resinous scent. The single flowers are clear pink and are followed by red hips. It makes a dense thorny shrub.
1m/3ft. Z7

Modern Shrub Roses

Under this heading come a range of roses of diverse parentage and character. They are different in personality from the Old Shrub Roses and are of more recent origin. The majority need little pruning, other than the removal of dead and weak wood; but shrubs benefit from having several of their oldest stems cut to the ground periodically.

'Cerise Bouquet' is a graceful rose with small grey leaves and clusters of cerise rosette-shaped flowers borne throughout the summer. These are a vibrant cerise and have a strong raspberry scent. It may be grown as a rambler.
2.7m/9ft.

'Fritz Nobis' blooms only once, in early summer, but makes a superb display. It has Hybrid Tea flowers in clear pink that have a good clove scent; these are followed by an abundance of reddish hips.
2m/6ft.

'Frühlingsgold' is a magnificent rose for early summer with long, arching branches and large, single, pale yellow flowers that are powerfully fragrant. It is splendid with oriental poppies.
2.3m/7ft.

'Frühlingsmorgen' has large, single flowers that are rose-pink with pale yellow centres. The scent is rich and sweet. It occasionally provides later crops of flowers but its main display is in early summer.
2m/6ft.

'Golden Wings' is an excellent, compact rose that blooms continuously with large, single, warm yellow flowers. It has a rich and sweet scent.
2m/6ft.

'Graham Thomas' is a splendid English Rose from David Austin carrying apricot yellow,

'Fritz Nobis'

old-fashioned flowers intermittently all summer. Since yellow is absent from the old shrub rose palette, this is a very valuable introduction. It has a strong tea perfume. It is a vigorous, upright rose that will grow energetically if not hard pruned in winter. 2m/6ft or more.

'Nymphenburg' releases a powerful apple scent from its large, double flowers that are a blend of salmon pink, yellow and orange. It blooms continuously through the summer and makes a big, arching shrub. 2.5m/8ft.

'Pretty Jessica' is a small English Rose with rich pink flowers of old shrub rose fullness and a very powerful old rose fragrance. It repeats well. 1m/3ft.

'The Countryman' is an English Rose with large, deep pink, old rose flowers and a powerful rose scent. It has a good arching habit and Portland rose foliage, and gives at least two flushes of flower. 1m/3ft.

Hybrid Teas

The Hybrid Teas give poise and pointed perfection in the rose flower. As bushes, they are invariably coarse and gawky, self-conscious and stiff in the border and very unattractive in winter when they present only thorny, woody stumps. Their place is in a formal setting close to the house or in an enclosure that is visited at flowering time and can be avoided at other times of the year. In a vase or buttonhole they are displayed at their best. Scent has been forsaken by many breeders in pursuit of the ideal show bloom, but there are still richly fragrant varieties in abundance and in recent years there has been an increased awareness among breeders of the importance of satisfying the nose as well as the eye. Hybrid Teas should be cut down to 15–25cm/6–10in from the ground in early spring; trim lightly in late autumn to prevent cane breakage in winter winds. They also require regular spraying with insecticides and fungicides for best results.

Right 'Frühlingsgold'

R. primula

'Golden Wings'

'Fragrant Cloud'

'**Alec's Red**' has a superb, sophisticated perfume and is an excellent Hybrid Tea. The cherry red flowers are freely produced all summer and are well displayed against the dark, glossy leaves.
1m/3ft.

'**Anna Pavlova**' is a new Hybrid Tea with an exceptionally strong perfume. The flowers are pale pink.
1m/3ft.

'**Apricot Silk**' has large reddish apricot flowers with a good scent.
1m/3ft.

'**Blessings**' produces well-scented, salmon pink blooms all summer.
1m/3ft.

'**Blue Moon**' is the popular silvery lilac Hybrid Tea, and probably the best 'blue' rose; with the creamy browns, this shade also takes the prize for decadence. It has a strong fruity perfume.
1m/3ft.

'**Champion**' has large, creamy gold flowers flushed with pink that possess a good scent.
1m/3ft.

'**Crimson Glory**' is a strongly scented old Hybrid Tea with large velvet crimson flowers. The necks are weak but it is a lovely rose. There is a climbing version that is quite a sight in full summer dress.
60cm/2ft; 4.5m/15ft as a climber.

'**Dainty Bess**', a parent of 'White Wings', is a single-flowered Hybrid Tea with large silvery pink flowers. It makes a fine show and has a good sweet scent.
1m/3ft.

'**Dutch Gold**' is a fine scented Hybrid Tea with pure golden yellow flowers, freely produced all summer.
1m/3ft.

'**Eden Rose**' is a robust rose with large, scented flowers in deep pink.
1m/3ft.

'**Ernest H. Morse**' is a popular and reliable Hybrid Tea with very bright crimson-red flowers from shapely buds.
1m/3ft.

'**Fragrant Cloud**' is a much-loved rose with an exceptionally rich perfume. It makes a vigorous bush and produces its coral red flowers in abundance through the season; the blooms glow against the dark foliage. It is also available as a climber.
1m/3ft.

'Grace de Monaco' has large, deep silvery pink flowers for which the dark foliage is an excellent foil. The fragrance is delicious. 1m/3ft.

'Josephine Bruce' is one of those sumptuous dark velvet crimson roses for which I always fall. The scent is very good and it is more reliable than 'Papa Meilland'. 1m/2ft.

'Just Joey' has large, well-scented blooms in a blend of pinks and coppery orange. 60cm/2ft.

'Lady Belper' has richly scented, apricot yellow flowers, suffused with coppery orange, and is a lovely rose. 60cm/2ft.

'La France' is of interest as probably the first Hybrid Tea ever raised, in 1865. The pale pink flowers have an old rose character and a strong scent. 1.2m/4ft.

'Madame Louise Laperrière' is an excellent Hybrid Tea with deep crimson flowers and a strong perfume. 60cm/2ft.

'Mister Lincoln' is a popular dark red with a good fragrance. 1m/3ft.

'Mojave' is a very popular rose with well scented flowers in warm orange tinged with red. It has an attractive glossy foliage and makes a vigorous and reliable bush. 1m/3ft.

'Mullard Jubilee' is a vigorous and reliable Hybrid Tea with large rose-pink flowers and a good scent. 60cm/2ft.

'Ophelia' is an old variety, much loved and still worth a place in the garden. The blush pink flowers are strongly scented and it makes a vigorous, upright plant. There is a climbing version and two fine sports, 'Lady Sylvia' with pale pink flowers and 'Madame Butterfly' with soft pink flowers. 1m/3ft.

'Papa Meilland' is one of my favourite Hybrid Teas. The blooms are the darkest damson-red and the fragrance is strong and sophisticated. Unfortunately, it is a weak and unreliable rose outside and needs a warm, sheltered position; it is superb under glass. 60cm/2ft.

'Paul Shirville' is a powerfully scented, salmon pink rose. It is a vigorous hybrid that

'Alec's Red'

has become very popular. 1m/3ft.

'Pink Peace' has well-scented, bright silvery pink flowers. 1m/3ft.

'Prima Ballerina' is a very reliable Hybrid Tea with richly scented, rose-pink flowers. 1m/3ft.

'Silver Jubilee' is, according to the well-known British rose grower Peter Beales, 'one of the best roses ever raised'. It is very free-flowering with clusters of silvery pink flowers suffused with apricot and cream. It has especially dense, glossy foliage. 1m/3ft.

'Sutter's Gold' has rich golden yellow flowers flushed with pink and a strong perfume. 1m/3ft.

'Wendy Cussons' is a very popular rose with deep cerise blooms and a rich fragrance. 60cm/2ft.

'Whisky Mac' is a much-grown hybrid with powerfully scented, amber yellow flowers It needs good soil and suffers in hard winters. 1m/3ft.

'White Wings' is a very beautiful rose with single white flowers. The petals are arranged around a boss of crimson stamens. It makes a tall upright plant. 1.2m/4ft.

Floribunda Roses

Like Hybrid Teas, Floribundas are valued for their continuous summer display. They are also rather stiff and self-conscious bushes better suited to formal beds and to manicured areas around the house rather than to shrub and mixed borders. The flowers are not as perfect in shape but they appear in large clusters and make a very colourful display. They require regular spray applications of fungicides and insecticides. Pruning consists of reducing the strongest stems by half in late winter and removing the weaker stems altogether. Floribundas are not generally as well endowed with scent as the Hybrid Teas, but the following are good.

'Amberlight' has clusters of semi-double flowers in amber yellow and makes a bushy plant.
60cm/2ft.

'Amber Queen' is a popular new rose with fully double, well-scented amber flowers.
60cm/2ft.

'Apricot Nectar' has apricot yellow flowers with a superb fragrance.
60cm/2ft.

'Ards Beauty' has shapely yellow flowers.
60cm/2ft.

'Margaret Merril'

'Arthur Bell' is popular and has an excellent scent. The blooms are semi-double, opening rich yellow and fading to creamy lemon.
60cm/2ft.

'Chinatown' is a big, vigorous shrub with large, double flowers in clear yellow. It makes a good shrub and hedging rose and the scent is outstanding.
1.5m/5ft.

'Dearest' is a very popular Floribunda with impressive clusters of semi-double, rich salmon-pink flowers and a strong scent. The blooms do not tolerate wet weather.
60cm/2ft.

'Dusky Maiden' is a sumptuous old variety with single flowers in velvet crimson, lit by golden anthers.
60cm/2ft.

'Elizabeth of Glamis' is a popular rose, though it suffers in hard winters and is prone to disease. The salmon-pink flowers are beautiful and the scent is good.
60cm/2ft.

'English Miss' bears shapely, well-scented flowers in pale pink.
60cm/2ft.

'Escapade' has almost single flowers in rosy violet and makes an attractive shrub and hedging plant.
1.2m/4ft.

'Everest Double Fragrance' is a tall, upright Floribunda with very highly scented, soft pink flowers.
1.2m/4ft.

'Korresia' is a very popular Floribunda with large clear yellow flowers. It is an excellent rose with a rich perfume.
60cm/2ft.

'Margaret Merril' is one of the best Floribundas. The blush white flowers are borne in small clusters and have an outstanding fragrance.
60cm/2ft.

Polyantha-Pompon Roses

These are excellent roses for the front of the border. They are bushy, compact plants and the bunches of little flowers are borne all summer. Once popular as bedding roses, there are now few varieties in circulation, and fewer still with a good scent.

'Cécile Brunner', the sweetheart rose, is a miniature shrub with tiny Hybrid Tea rose flowers in pale pink. It blooms continuously and has a delicate, sweet scent. There is a climbing version that, unlike its parent, is vigorous and luxuriant in foliage.
As a shrub, 1m/3ft; as a climber, 7.5m/25ft.

'Katharina Zeimet' has clusters of double white flowers.
60cm/2ft.

'Little White Pet' is a dwarf sport of the rambler 'Félicité Perpétue' and has the same cold cream scent. It is a pretty rose which bears small creamy white rosettes from pink marked buds all summer and autumn.
60cm/2ft.

'Nathalie Nypels' has semi-double flowers in pink.
60cm/2ft.

'Perle d'Or' is like a yellow version of 'Cécile Brunner'; it begins buff-yellow and fades to a pinky cream and has a delicate, sweet scent.
1–2m/3–6ft.

'Yesterday' has lilac-pink flowers.
1m/3ft.

'Yvonne Rabier' has semi-double, white flowers.
60cm/2ft.

Miniature and Patio Roses

Miniature and Patio roses are for pot and window box gardeners. They look out of place in borders and since you would have to raise them somehow to discover their scent, you may as well grow the real thing, a decent-sized rose. Many varieties do not possess a scent worth commenting on; the following are good.

'Colibri '79' has double yellow flowers flushed pink.
30cm/1ft.

'Dresden Doll' is a miniature Moss rose. The flowers are semi-double and shell-pink.
30cm/1ft.

'Golden Angel' has double, deep yellow flowers and has a strong scent.
30cm/1ft.

'Orange Honey' is a very fragrant double orange-yellow.
30cm/1ft.

'Peachy White' has blush white flowers and good pointed buds.
30cm/1ft.

'Regensberg' has double light pink flowers with white edges and reverse. The scent is excellent.
30cm/1ft.

Ground-Cover Roses

These roses are for sprawling down banks, around the base of pillars, and down low walls. They come from all parts of the rose kingdom and have differing characters.

'Cardinal Hume' is a low rose of spreading habit with deliciously scented, old-fashioned, double flowers in plum purple. These are followed by hips.
1m/3ft.

'Daisy Hill' has large, single, pink flowers followed by a good show of hips.
1.5m/5ft.

'Lady Curzon' is a Rugosa hybrid with single pink flowers and very thorny stems.
1m/3ft.

'Max Graf', also a Rugosa hybrid, has single, silvery pink, apple-scented flowers and good glossy foliage.
60cm/2ft.

'Scintillation' produces its large clusters of semi-double blush pink flowers over a long period. The scent is excellent.
1.2m/4ft.

Climbing Roses

Climbing roses offer a variety of scents at nose height. They include plants with Tea, Hybrid Tea, Floribunda, Bourbon and China rose character, and the Noisettes. As a general rule, the Teas, Chinas and Noisettes enjoy the warmth and protection of a sunny wall; while the others may also be grown in the open on pillars, pergolas and fences or against walls with a less favoured aspect. Most of these roses flower repeatedly. Pruning consists of tying-in the strong, long shoots each winter, bending them along horizontal wires (you need cut their ends only when they are outgrowing their allotted space) and shortening the lateral growths from these stems by two-thirds.

'Aimée Vibert' (Noisette) produces sprays of small, white, double flowers, with yellow stamens, in summer and usually flowers repeatedly. It has good glossy foliage and few thorns.
4.5m/15ft.

'Alister Stella Gray' (Golden Rambler) (Noisette) bears deliciously sweet-scented flowers throughout the summer and autumn. They are both yolk yellow in bud and open into large, quartered, ivory white blooms.
4.5m/15ft.

'Constance Spry'

'Aloha' (Floribunda) is a first-rate climber and powerfully tea scented. The quartered, rose-pink flowers are borne continuously.
3m/10ft.

'Blush Noisette' is an extremely free-flowering rose that bears clusters of semi-double, lilac-pink flowers. It has a rich clove fragrance and grows well in the open, even as a free-standing bush.
4.5m/15ft.

'Cécile Brunner, Climbing' (Polyantha) is a climbing sport of the sweetheart rose. Its tiny pink flowers are softly but sweetly fragrant. It flowers once, in early summer and is a vigorous and hardy rose.
7.5m/25ft.

'Céline Forestier' (Noisette) is a fine climber with old rose character and a powerful tea scent. The large flat flowers are double, quartered and creamy yellow and are borne continuously.
2.5m/8ft.

'Château de Clos-Vougeot, Climbing' (Hybrid Tea) has sumptuous deep maroon-red flowers that have a rich perfume. It produces some later flowers after its main summer display.
4.5m/15ft.

'Constance Spry' (Modern Shrub) has exceptionally large flowers, clear pink and petal-packed, and a plant in bloom is a magnificent sight. The scent is of myrrh (like cold cream), strong but not sweet. This is a very lovely rose.
6m/20ft.

'Desprez à Fleur Jaune' (Noisette) is a very fine climber whose clusters of creamy quartered flowers, tinged pink and yellow, are borne ceaselessly all season. The fragrance is powerful and fruity. It requires a warm wall and is good under glass.
5.5m/18ft.

'Devoniensis, Climbing' (Tea) is a creamy apricot rose, strongly tea-scented, for a warm wall or glasshouse.
3.5m/12ft.

'Ena Harkness, Climbing' (Hybrid Tea) has weak-necked flowers that hang attractively downwards. They are deep velvet crimson and are strongly perfumed. It has one main summer flush and some flowers later.
4.5m/15ft.

'Etoile de Hollande, Climbing' (Hybrid Tea) is a superb and very popular climber with powerfully perfumed, crimson-red blooms.
4.5m/15ft.

'**Gloire de Dijon**' (Tea) is one of my favourite climbing roses. The old-fashioned, petal-packed blooms are buff-apricot and look splendid even against orange-red brickwork. It is hardy, flowers repeatedly, and has a rich tea scent.
4.5m/15ft.

'**Guinée**' (Hybrid Tea) is a stunning rose with sumptuous dark maroon-crimson flowers and a strong perfume. Its main display is in summer, after which it blooms sporadically. I would not want to be without it.
4.5m/15ft.

'**Kathleen Harrop**' (Bourbon) is completely thornless and bears its clear pink, strongly scented blooms all season. To my mind, it is lovelier than its parent, 'Zéphirine Drouhin'.
3m/10ft.

'**Lady Hillingdon, Climbing**' (Tea) is an outstanding rose whose apricot yellow tea flowers contrast very effectively with the purple-suffused stems and foliage. It is reliable against a warm wall, flowering repeatedly, and has a tea scent.
4.5m/15ft.

'**Lady Sylvia, Climbing**' (Hybrid Tea) is a fine pink rose with perfect buds and a strong scent. It flowers repeatedly. 'Climbing Ophelia' is similar but a paler pink.
3.5m/12ft.

'**Lawrence Johnston**' (*R. foetida* '**Persiana**' **hybrid**), named after the maker of Hidcote garden in Gloucestershire, is a popular

Above 'Leverkusen'

climber with semi-double, bright yellow flowers. It blooms early and produces subsequent flushes throughout the season. It is a fine, vigorous plant with a good fragrance.
7.5m/25ft.

'**Leverkusen**' (*R. kordesii* **hybrid**) has semi-double, lemon yellow flowers and a sweet lemon scent. It flowers repeatedly after its main summer display. It may be grown as a free-standing shrub.
3m/10ft.

'**Madame Abel Chatenay, Climbing**' (Hybrid Tea) is an old Hybrid Tea, popular in Britain as a bush and a climber. The blooms are soft pink and intensely fragrant and it flowers repeatedly.
3m/10ft.

Left 'Guinée'

'Madame Alfred Carrière' (Noisette) is one of the very best climbers, succeeding even on a shaded wall; it may also be grown as a shrub. The large, white, pink-tinged flowers are produced all season and are powerfully scented.
6m/20ft.

'Madame Grégoire Staechelin' (Hybrid Tea) blooms only once, in early summer, but makes a superb display. The large, semi-double flowers are flesh pink with a deeper reverse and are followed by good orange hips. It has a strong, sweet scent.
6m/20ft.

'Maigold' (R. pimpinellifolia hybrid) makes one impressive early summer display. The semi-double flowers are rich buff yellow and are powerfully scented. It may be grown as a lax shrub. It is not reliably winter hardy in very cold regions.
3.5m/12ft.

'Mrs Herbert Stevens, Climbing' (Tea) is a fine old variety with shapely cream flowers and a strong tea scent. It is a vigorous, hardy plant and flowers repeatedly.
6m/20ft.

'New Dawn' is a sport of 'Dr W. Van Fleet', a shrub rose and hybrid of R. wichuraiana. It is one of the finest pink climbers (a soft, clear pink) and in the first flight of all roses. The foliage is healthy and glossy and the shapely semi-double blooms, which are fruitily fragrant, are borne continuously. 'New Dawn' is disease-free and very hardy.
3m/10ft.

'Paul's Lemon Pillar' (Hybrid Tea) is another favourite of mine. The blooms, perfect in bud, are very large and creamy lemon and the fragrance is delicious.
6m/20ft.

'Sombreuil, Climbing' (Tea) is a superb white rose for a warm wall or glasshouse. The blooms are flat, fully double and tea-scented, and it flowers repeatedly.
2.5m/8ft.

'Souvenir de Claudius Denoyel' (Hybrid Tea) has bright crimson-red, old-fashioned flowers, deliciously scented, which are borne sporadically after the main early summer display.
5.5m/18ft.

'Zéphirine Drouhin' (Bourbon) is a very popular, thornless Climber, succeeding even on a shady wall. The semi-double flowers are bright cerise pink (not everyone's favourite colour) and well scented, and are borne ceaselessly all season. It may be grown as a shrub.
3.5m/12ft.

Rambler Roses

This is the name given to the species climbers, and to the hybrids derived from crossing the species climbers with garden roses. They bloom only once, usually just after the main shrub rose season, but can be relied upon for a magnificent show. The flowers, though generally small, are borne in great bunches. Many then produce a display of hips. The scents are often very fruity: R. wichuraiana gives its green apple scent to many hybrids. Ramblers are generally better in open positions than against walls, where they often succumb to mildew. They are at their best scrambling into trees or trained over buildings and along fences. The species need little, if any, pruning; but the hybrids benefit from having some of their older canes removed, and their lateral growths shortened, as for climbing roses; but with once-blooming Ramblers, this should be done immediately after flowering, not in winter.

'Albéric Barbier' (R. wichuraiana hybrid) is a fine Rambler with glossy, almost evergreen, foliage and clusters of double, quartered, creamy yellow flowers with a delicious apple scent. It blooms at mid-summer but produces many later flowers.
6m/20ft.

'Albertine' (R. wichuraiana hybrid) is a popular Rambler with distinctive coppery pink flowers. It makes a memorable mid-summer display and the fruity scent carries far.
4.5m/15ft.

'Alexandre Girault' (R. wichuraiana hybrid) has clusters of large, fully double, coppery rose-pink flowers. It is an excellent rose with a strong apple scent.
4.5m/15ft.

'Bobbie James' (R. multiflora hybrid) is one of the best Ramblers for training into a tree. It has good glossy foliage and the semi-double, white flowers, filled with yellow stamens and borne in large clusters, are powerfully and fruitily fragrant.
9m/30ft.

'Bobbie James' and Lonicera periclymenum 'Belgica'

R. banksiae banksiae (R.b. alba-plena), the double white Banksian rose, is much better endowed with scent than its double yellow cousin. It needs the warmth of a sunny wall and succeeds well in a Mediterranean climate. The blooms are small and fully double and are borne in summer. Pruning is tricky since the best blooms are on two- or three-year-old wood, and should be limited to the removal of very old wood.
4.5m/15ft. Z8

R. bracteata, the Macartney rose, performs best in warm climates, though, like its offspring 'Mermaid', it often succeeds against shaded walls. Its single white flowers, with a prominent boss of golden stamens, have a fine lemon scent and are produced intermittently throughout summer and autumn. It has attractive, dark, glossy, evergreen foliage and behaves more like a wall shrub than a climber.
4.5m/15ft. Z7

R. brunonii **'La Mortola'** has the simple charm of a wild rose and is well clad in downy, grey-green leaves. The white flowers are single, filled with yellow anthers, and richly perfumed, and are borne in clusters after mid-summer. It is not suitable for very cold gardens.
6m/20ft. Z8

'Easlea's Golden Rambler' (Hybrid Tea) has large, double, butter yellow flowers in Hybrid Tea style, but it blooms only once. The foliage is glossy and distinctive. It is a very fine Climber/Rambler with an intense fragrance.
4.5m/15ft.

'Emily Gray' (*R. wichuraiana* descendant) has well-scented, semi-double, buff-yellow flowers and good glossy foliage.
3.5m/12ft.

'Félicité Perpétue' (*R. sempervirens* descendant) bears a mass of small, pink-tinged white rosettes after mid-summer and is one of the loveliest Ramblers. It has a distinctive calamine lotion or cold cream scent.
6m/20ft. Hardy to Z7.

R. filipes **'Kiftsgate'** is a monster of a rose. The clusters of small, single, creamy flowers, filled with yellow anthers, are produced soon after mid-summer and waft a rich fragrance. They are followed by a mass of orange hips.
12m/40ft or more.

'Francis E. Lester' (Hybrid Musk parentage) bears its single, white flowers, tinged with pink, in large trusses at mid-summer and they waft a delicious fruity scent. A crop of orange hips follows. It may also be grown as a shrub.
4.5m/15ft.

'François Juranville' (*R. wichuraiana* hybrid) has double, quartered flowers in rose-pink and an apple scent. It is a fine sight when giving its summer display.
7.5m/25ft.

'Goldfinch' (*R. multiflora* descendant) is a small Rambler with single, yellow flowers, fading to white in sunshine (try it facing north-west), and a rich, fruity scent.
3m/10ft.

R. helenae follows up its mid-summer show of single, creamy white flowers – borne in dense, round clusters and intensely scented – with a bountiful display of small red hips.
6m/20ft.

'Paul's Himalayan Musk' and *Lonicera periclymenum*

'Kew Rambler' (*R. soulieana* **hybrid**) has greyish foliage and clusters of single flowers, light pink with white centres, after mid-summer. The scent is powerfully fruity. 5.5m/18ft.

R. laevigata is a Chinese species but has naturalized itself in parts of the United States where it is known as the Cherokee rose; it is also the State Flower of Georgia. The large, single, white flowers, filled with golden stamens, are powerfully and spicily scented. It is not hardy in cold climates. Its form, 'Cooperi' (Cooper's Burma Rose), is more frequently seen in Britain; it makes a fine early-summer show against a warm wall. 6m/20ft. Z7

R. longicuspis bears large heads of single creamy flowers that waft a banana fragrance. It is a vigorous rose. Z9

R. moschata, the true Musk rose, was rediscovered by the rosarian Graham Stuart Thomas in E. A. Bowles' garden at Enfield, Middlesex, England, in 1963 and is once again a popular Rambler. Its glory is its late flowering – throughout high summer and into early autumn – and the delicious, sweet musk scent that wafts from the large clusters of single white flowers. The filaments, rather than the petals, are the source of the perfume. It performs best against a wall. 3m/10ft. Z7

R. multiflora has been an important species in the development of modern roses. It is a small Rambler or arching shrub that produces large clusters of single, creamy white flowers just after mid-summer. These have a pervasive, fruity scent. 4.5m/15ft. Z5

'Paul's Himalayan Musk' (parentage unknown) is another outstanding giant for leading into large trees. The clusters of small double rosettes, in pale lilac-pink, are borne after mid-summer and waft a fruity scent. 9m/30ft.

'Paul Transon' (*R. wichuraiana* **hybrid**) is an interestingly coloured rose that looks particularly good against old brickwork (as at Sissinghurst Castle, Kent, England). The flat, double flowers are a sort of coppery salmon colour. They are produced in abundance after mid-summer and sporadically later and have a strong apple scent. 4.5m/15ft.

'Rambling Rector'

'Rambling Rector' (*R. multiflora* **descendant**) is a good white-flowered Rambler for leading into old fruit trees and over sheds. The blooms are semi-double, with yellow stamens, and have a strong fruity scent. Hips follow. 6m/20ft.

'Sanders' White Rambler' (*R. wichuraiana* **descendant**) is a fine rose bearing a mass of small, pure white, double rosettes, fruitily scented, after mid-summer. 5.5m/18ft.

'Seagull' (*R. multiflora* **hybrid**) is a spectacular and vigorous Rambler with large clusters of semi-double, white flowers that are intensely and fruitily fragrant. 7.5m/25ft.

'The Garland' (*R. moschata* × *R. multiflora*), a favourite of Gertrude Jekyll and still one of the loveliest Ramblers, is a wonderful sight at mid-summer, when it bears its clusters of small, semi-double, creamy flowers. The scent is of oranges. 4.5m/15ft.

'Veilchenblau' (*R. multiflora* **descendant**) is one of those extraordinary crimson roses with violet and grey shadings. It is less richly coloured than 'Bleu Magenta' but much better endowed with scent. The blooms are semi-double, with yellow stamens, and are borne soon after mid-summer. 4.5m/15ft.

'Wedding Day' (*R. sinowilsonii* **hybrid**) is an excellent and vigorous Rambler with single, creamy flowers, yellow in bud, and with orange-yellow stamens, carried in very large clusters after mid-summer. It is ideal for leading into trees and over buildings. The powerful fragrance is of oranges. 9m/30ft.

R. wichuraiana, the parent of so many good Ramblers, is itself worthy of cultivation especially as a ground-cover rose, when it makes a dense, almost evergreen, carpet. The single white flowers, powerfully apple-scented, are produced after mid-summer and are followed by orange hips. 4.5m/15ft.

Herb Gardens

Botanically, most non-woody, non-shrubby plants are herbs. But in horticulture, we take the term to mean those plants that are useful to us, whether for medicinal, culinary or cosmetic purposes. A large number of plants come into this category, including shrub roses, peonies, primroses and balsam poplar, but in this chapter I have listed only the more obvious herbal plants and allowed those that nowadays fit more squarely into other categories to drift into other chapters. The scents of the herbs described in this chapter come mainly from leaves, roots and seeds, not flowers, and the flavours are mostly spicy and camphorous, sometimes sweetened with rose and fruit, and sometimes heightened with mint and eucalyptus.

There are many ways of growing herbs in the garden. They may be given their own corner and either arranged in a formal pattern or allowed to mingle casually with each other. They may be grown in pots and windowboxes. They can be used to make lawns, paths, seats and hedges. And they may be treated exactly as other garden plants and placed in mixed borders according to their height, bearing, colour and scent.

The earliest gardens were herb gardens, and herbs have a long and close association with garden history, literature and folklore. A collection of herbs always seems to have an air of the past about it and looks effective in traditional settings of symmetrical beds and straight paths. The other reason why this treatment works well is that many herbs are naturally wispy (even weedy), and an emphatic groundplan imposes structure and draws attention away from the worst offenders.

Low box hedging can be a useful part of the formal groundplan, enclosing the beds and even, as in Rosemary Verey's famous herb bed at Barnsley House, Gloucestershire, England, criss-crossing through the centre. Box does not mind supporting and being shaded by the foliage and flowerheads of floppy plants, providing it does not have to shoulder the burden for too long. If the herbs are herbaceous and are cut back once or twice in the season, they will give the box plenty of breathing time.

Like box, wall germander (*Teucrium fruticans*) and green and grey santolina are amenable to clipping and may also serve as edging material; they are sun-lovers, however, and do not tolerate the foliage of other plants resting on them. The most ambitious use of these three shrubby plants is to weave them into interlacing and labyrinthine patterns or 'knots'. As centrepieces for herb gardens, miniature knots are of absorbing interest, though, of course, labour-intensive. The gaps may be filled with small bulbs and short perennials or with gravel.

You can take your herb garden in quite a different direction. Non-shrubby herbs are often inveterate colonizers and if you are not of a neat-and-tidy mind, you can let them get on with it. The result will be an aromatic wild garden, with self-seeding misty fennels in bronze and green, balms in green and gold, blue-flowered borage and architectural angelica. I should avoid herbs which run underground furiously, like the mints, which are very difficult to control. With the rest, selective removal of flowerheads, cutting down and poisoning will give the garden some semblance of order.

Cooks like their herbs in one place, somewhere easily accessible from the house. But in my garden the herbs are everywhere, in the company of flowering shrubs and perennials, rock plants and bulbs. Here and there they are in little groups but often there is just a solitary herb wedged between more flamboyant neighbours.

If you are happy to scatter your herbs, you can use their colours, scents and characters to help create a range of effects. Herbs from the Mediterranean hillsides and scrubland can be united with other plants from the same or similar habitats to create a scheme of muted colours and spicy, camphorous aromas, evocative of the maquis. Sun and well-drained soil is the recipe for success, and gently sloping banks are ideal. It is in the heat of the day that the scents will be at their richest.

Right *This formal herb garden is on an intimate scale and the narrow paths mean that you cannot avoid brushing against aromatic foliage. Adopting a broad definition of the term 'herb' to include all garden plants which are in some way useful allows you to introduce extra colour and flower scents. Here mint, rosemary, lavender, curry plant, sweet Cicely and marjoram combine with the wholesome smell of box and the sophisticated perfume of shrub roses.*

There is no shortage of shrubby candidates with grey, grey-green and grey-blue leaves for a 'Mediterranean' scheme. Lavenders, sages, santolinas, rue, Jerusalem sage (*Phlomis fruticosa*) with soap-scented flowerheads, blue-flowered caryopteris, teucriums and artemisias can all be included. Rosemaries are essential to give some sprawling height and inject further sweetness into the bouquet garni. Cistuses, for their gummy fragrances and papery flowers, must be here in abundance, and so must thymes, rippling along the front of the bed. Hyssop, with its rich blue flowers in summer, is also indispensable. Calaminthas, and even dianthus, may be added to provide some complementary flavours – respectively, the scent of mint and fruit, and the scent of clove. Asphodels, verbascums and brooms will provide plumes of bright yellow, and marjoram some pools of gold. If the bed is backed by a wall, a myrtle could be planted to lift the scheme to nose height. And what about perovskia for late-summer drama, and Gallica roses for a touch of romance? All you need now are olives and pencil-slim cypress trees in the background; sea buckthorn (*Hippophaë rhamnoides*) and weeping silver pear (*Pyrus salicifolia* 'Pendula') are good substitutes for olives in cold climates, and pencil-slim forms of juniper and chamaecyparis hardy substitutes for cypresses.

Many of the Mediterranean herbs are in the first flight of traditional garden ornamentals, and look quite at home when used singly, tucked into the corners of buildings and the paving cracks of paths and patios, and when associating with the garden's lusher flora. Rosemary is one of the best medium-sized evergreen shrubs for a sunny wall, to my mind especially attractive in narrow beds where it spills forward on to the path. Forms with rich blue flowers I prize the most. In association with creamy brooms and blue ceanothus they look stunning. The unique scent of rosemary can be enjoyed all year and is an appetizing contrast to the pineapple of Moroccan broom and the bitter lemon of lemon verbena.

Lavenders bulge over paths at a lower level. As your legs brush past them they will release their fragrances, and when they are in bloom, you can draw your fingers over their flowerheads; this is one aromatic herb whose flowers do not disappoint. A drift of hardy lavenders in mixed colours – the range runs from purple through several shades of violet-blue to pink and white – is a pastel delight that one encounters far too rarely. And, of course, lavenders are much-loved companions for a host of cottage-garden favourites like roses and mock orange, Madonna lilies and peonies.

There are a number of desirable rosemaries and lavenders on the borderlines of hardiness, and in cold climates these

Above *The most convenient spot for culinary herbs is often by the back door, providing it receives enough sun. These herbs are mixed with ornamental plants such as sedum, sisyrinchium and sempervivum. Chives, lavender, wormwood and sage grow in the ground, with invasive mints and tender, scented-leaved pelargoniums in pots.*

may be grown in pots and housed under glass for the winter. In summer they can be assembled beside garden seats and up flights of steps. Trailing rosemary and woolly and toothed lavenders come into this category and each has its own distinctive fragrance. These will provide the complementary aromas to other fragrant pot plants such as pineapple sage (*Salvia rutilans*), blackcurrant-scented sages (*SS. discolor, microphylla* and *grahamii*) and peppermint, rose and fruit-scented pelargoniums.

Bay, when trained, can be the most architectural of herbal pot plants. Clipped into pyramids and lollipops, it adorns the portals of many a grand mansion and fashionable restaurant. In the garden such self-conscious shapes may also have a place, flanking a doorway or a painted seat. Outside very cold regions it can also be grown in the ground, but if it is likely to encounter much frost, you should not expose its trunk through clipping. Honey-scented flowers are a bonus to the aromatic leaves.

Low-growing herbs like thymes and marjoram can be used to make fragrant walkways. Popping out of paving cracks down the length of a sunny path, the bushy forms of *Thymus vulgaris*, *T. × citriodorus* and *Origanum vulgare* will create a welcome obstacle course for the feet and soften the hard surface with a haze of green, silver and golden foliage. You can actually walk on the more prostrate thymes – the forms of *T. serpyllum* – and as long as the pathway does not see very heavy wear, the proportion of paving to vegetation may be reversed; stepping stones are needed over the green and grey patterned carpet only for wet weather crossings and as platforms for weeding. These creeping thymes can also be woven into square, rectangular and circular Chinese rugs, to spread at intervals down wide terraces, or to be centrepieces for herb and rose gardens. Many patterns can be attempted, using patches of pale pink, mauve, crimson and white-flowered plants, and when in bloom, the rugs shimmer with bees. The most famous thyme lawns are at Sissinghurst Castle in Kent, England, and they are as lovely a feature as that garden can boast – a photographer's dream in all seasons.

Two other herbs are flat enough to make lawns: camomile and Corsican mint (*Mentha requienii*). Mossy, fruit-scented camomile is always a pleasure to walk and sit on, and is a useful alternative to grass on hot, dry ground. But it has to be weeded by hand, so I would not plant a large expanse of it. One of the best ways to use camomile and Corsican mint is as fragrant seats, which can be created by cutting a section out of a bank or giving a raised bed arms and a backrest. Corsican mint likes different conditions from camomile – a little moisture and shade – so choose accordingly. Camomile – preferably the non-flowering form 'Treneague' – may also be tried woven into a grass lawn, as indeed may creeping thymes and pennyroyal (*Mentha pulegium*). Their scents give an additional dimension to a game of croquet.

Mention of mints leads me to the second great category of herbs. Not all herbs demand sun and good drainage; there is a merry band of them that can cope with colder, damper and shadier sites and heavier soils. As well as the mints, this includes angelica, borage, feverfew, meadowsweet, fennel, lovage, lemon balm, bergamot, sweet cicely, chives and parsley. These plants are mainly green and herbaceous rather than grey and shrubby, and the scents, still predominantly from leaves, are mainly fresh, wholesome vegetable fragrances, enhanced by fruit and spice (and occasionally spoiled with onion), rather than camphorous, medicinal and resinous aromas. They are also less inclined to infuse the air, the fragrances usually having to be coaxed by hand. They are easily accommodated in the border. Aniseed-scented fennel is outstanding in the spring, its green and bronze foliage providing a feathery companion to early shrub roses, smilacina, tulips and wallflowers. It can be cut down at mid-summer and a second crop of leaves will appear. A similar treatment can be meted out to sweet cicely (*Myrrhis odorata*). This is another beautifully airy perennial, which gives a double dose of scent; its white flowers are fragrant as well as its leaves.

One would grow bergamot for its unique scent whatever it looked like, but it happens to be one of summer's most valuable border plants. It blooms for a long time, comes in a number of good colour forms, and has an interesting mophead shape. 'Cambridge Scarlet' is especially striking; there are very few hardy perennials with proper red flowers. This form looks well in the herbaceous border with purple salvias, and in the herb garden with the glaucous blue of 'Jackman's Blue' rue; the latter's tangy orange-peel scent also complements the bergamot's sweet blend of lemon and aniseed.

Angelica is a statuesque plant when in flower and beautiful when silhouetted against stone, grass or water. Most of the heads need to be removed before they drop seeds to avoid a profusion of seedlings; but some have to be left since plants die after flowering. Mints can also be a problem, but by running underground not by seeding. They cannot be trusted in mixed beds and are best confined by paving or grown in a bucket that has had its bottom knocked out before being sunk into the soil. The two most beautiful mints are variegated applemint, *Mentha suaveolens* 'Variegata', many of whose leaves emerge almost pure white; and buddleja mint, *M. longifolia*, with soft grey leaves and good mauve flowers in summer. The former has a fine fruity scent.

One of the richest and warmest of spicy fragrances is provided by sweet basil, but being a tender, tropical plant it has to be given special treatment. Seed sown indoors in spring must not be planted out until all danger of frost is past. Then it can be slotted into the front row of the herbaceous border or grown in a pot by the back door to waft its scent into the air. The purple-leaved form, 'Dark Opal', is particularly ornamental and aromatic. To prolong the season, you can make a second sowing outside in mid-summer and pot up some of these plants in early autumn to bring on to a sunny windowsill indoors; pinching out the growing tips ensures bushy growth.

Herbs

Allium

A. cepa proliferum, tree onion, bears clusters of small onions on top of its tubular stems, which may be used for flavouring stews and salads. The leaves have a typical pungent scent and may be chopped up and used like chives. Plant 20cm/8in apart.
Sun. 60cm/2ft.

A. fistulosum, Welsh onion, has evergreen leaves and makes a good substitute for chives in the winter.
60–90cm/2–3ft.

A. sativum, garlic, has pungent flat leaves and whitish flowers in summer. It is a popular culinary herb. Cloves planted in autumn or spring will increase and be ripe for lifting in high summer or autumn respectively. Plant 15cm/6in apart and 2.5cm/1in deep.
Sun. Light, well-drained soil. 30–60cm/1–2ft.

A. schoenoprasum, chives, is a very ornamental herb, especially in its giant form, *sibiricum*. The clumps of hollow, onion-scented, grassy leaves are neat and lush and are topped with domed flowers, usually in a shade of rose-pink. Plants may be shaved to the ground in early summer and a second flush of foliage and flowers appears. It makes an attractive edging for a herb garden.
Sun. Good, fertile soil. 10–38cm/4–15in. Z3

Anethum

A. graveolens, dill, is a hardy annual with feathery foliage and flat heads of yellowish flowers in high summer. The leaves have a spicy scent and are used for flavouring vegetables and fish, while the aromatic seeds are used in vinegars and in water to ease stomach upsets. Sow *in situ* in the spring and thin to 23cm/9in apart.
Sun. Well-drained soil. 60cm/2ft.

Angelica

A. archangelica has large, hollow, juicy stems that have a distinctive cool scent when bruised. It is the herb garden's most architectural subject, with its stout branching growth and its globular, green flowerheads. Its young leaf stalks give their muscat flavour to stewed fruits; the sliced stems are candied to use as decorations for cakes; the fragrant roots are used as an aid to digestion; and the leaves may be chopped and used in salads. It seeds itself furiously unless the heads are removed in time.
Light shade. Retentive soil. 1.5m/5ft.

Anthriscus

A. cerefolium, chervil, is a hardy annual with attractive ferny leaves and umbels of white flowers in summer. The foliage has a sweet aniseed scent and is used in soups, sauces and salads; it can be shaved to the ground to produce a further crop. Sow thinly *in situ*, in spring, and it will self-sow thereafter.
Light shade. Cool, moist soil. 46cm/18in.

Artemisia

A. abrotanum, southernwood, is a shrubby plant with filigree, grey-green leaves: the foliage is enjoyed by some for having a 'sweet and lemony' scent but to others (myself included) its pungency is rather offensive; its alternative common name is 'old man'! If it is hard pruned every spring, it makes a handsome cushion of foliage. It was used as a strewing herb, as an antiseptic and as a tonic.
Sun. Poor, well-drained soil. 60–90cm/ 2–3ft. Z6

A. absinthium, wormwood, has an even more pungent smell and can be used to repel moths and flies. But the form 'Lambrook Silver' is a fine silvery shrub with deeply cut, silky leaves and is worth a place among

Allium schoenoprasum

Anethum graveolens

Angelica archangelica

Artemisia abrotanum

Calamintha nepeta nepeta

white, pink and blue flowers in spite of its smell. Medicinally, wormwood is used against worms and for easing indigestion. It is hardy and evergreen.
Sun. Well-drained soil. 60–90cm/2–3ft. Z5
A. dracunculus, French tarragon, has a warm spicy scent and is a popular herb for seasoning. It has dark green, lance-shaped leaves and drooping white flowers in high summer. Grow from cuttings and plant 30cm/1ft apart. It needs a sheltered position and it is sensible to give it some protection through the winter. Russian tarragon, *A. dracunculoides*, is hardier but an inferior plant.
Sun. Well-drained soil. 60cm/2ft. Z5
A. pontica, old warrior, is a small version of southernwood, and makes a lovely haze of misty grey-green foliage. It is an energetic colonizer.
Sun. 60cm/2ft. Z6

Borago
B. officinalis, borage, is a hardy annual that seeds itself freely in most soils. Its leaves and peeled stems have a delicate, cucumber scent and can be used in salads or to flavour drinks; the sky blue, starry flowers, borne in drooping panicles all summer, were once candied and can also be added to salads.
Sun or light shade. 30–60cm/1–2ft.

Calamintha
C. grandiflora is a neat bushy perennial that is useful for edging the herb garden or for the rock garden. It has small, sweetly aromatic leaves, which are used to make herbal teas, and lilac-pink, sage-like flowers that are produced over a long period in summer.
Sun. Well-drained soil. 46cm/18in.
C. nepeta nepeta (*C. nepetoides*) is another excellent, long-flowering, edging plant with mint-scented leaves that blooms later, during the autumn; its lavender flowers are loved by bees.
Sun. Well-drained soil. 30cm/1ft.

Carum
C. carvi, caraway, is usually treated as a hardy biennial, the seed being sown at the end of the summer to be harvested the following year. The entire plant is aromatic, from the lacy, evergreen leaves to the parsnip like roots. The camphor-scented seeds are used in bread and cakes and, when crushed into boiling water, provide relief from flatulence. The umbels of white flowers appear in early summer.
Sun. Well-drained soil. 60–90cm/2–3ft.

Chamaemelum
C. nobile, camomile, is a low, creeping perennial with mossy, fruitily scented foliage and daisy-like flowers in summer; the flowers are infused into boiling water to make camomile tea. An entire camomile lawn is difficult to manage, though it does provide a cool green carpet for areas too dry for grass. The non-flowering form, 'Treneague', is the best for lawns; otherwise choose the double-flowered form 'Flore Pleno'.
Sun. Well-drained soil. 15cm/6in.

Coriandrum
C. sativum, coriander, has seeds that have a spicy orange scent when ripe; they are used to flavour soups and curries. It is an annual, and seeds are best sown outside in spring. Mauve flowers appear in summer and as the seedheads ripen they should be cut and hung over newspaper to dry, somewhere warm and airy. The leaves have a fetid smell, as do the seeds before they are properly ripe.
Sun. 46cm/18in.

Foeniculum
F. vulgare, fennel, is one of my favourite foliage plants. The mounds of fresh green, feathery leaves are a fine, hazy complement to brightly coloured flowers and chunky

leaves, and are particularly appealing when shimmering with raindrops. Shave the plants to the ground as the flowerheads are forming in early summer for a second crop of juvenile growth. There is a bronze version, *purpureum*, which is wonderful in hot colour groups; it comes true from seed and, like green fennel, self-sows furiously if allowed. The scent from the foliage is of aniseed, and the leaves are used to flavour fish.
Sun. 1.8m/6ft, if allowed to flower.

Galium

G. odoratum, woodruff, has the scent of new-mown hay, or coumarin, when dry, and used to be hung in bunches to scent the air or placed in the linen cupboard to scent the sheets. It is a prostrate perennial with whorls of slender leaves and branching heads of white flowers in early summer. It is an attractive plant for growing around shrubs or in the woodland garden.
Shade. 15cm/6in.

Geum

G. urbanum, herb bennet, has clove-scented roots that are used to flavour drinks. There is a faint clove fragrance in the leaves too, but the golden yellow flowers, borne in high summer, are scentless.
Light shade. 30cm/1ft.

Helichrysum

H. italicum (*H. angustifolium*), curry plant, is one of those neat, dumpy little shrubs that help to counter the wispy untidiness of their companions. Its evergreen mounds of silver foliage make excellent cornerposts or edging for the herb garden, though they are likely to be killed in severe winters in colder regions. In high summer it is topped with puffs of golden flowers. Its only drawback is its scent. Some people find the hot curry fragrance ambrosial, but I am afraid I don't. Plant santolina instead, if you prefer subtler scents.
Sun. Well-drained soil. 60cm/2ft. Z8

Hyssopus

H. officinalis, hyssop, is an attractive evergreen perennial, especially valuable for its flush of rich blue flowers in late summer

Helichrysum italicum and *Borago officinalis*

Laurus nobilis

Lavandula angustifolia 'Hidcote'

Lavandula dentata

and autumn; bees love them. The slender foliage is pleasantly aromatic. Plants should be hard pruned in spring to keep them compact and they then make neat edging plants. There is a splendid dwarf blue called *aristatus*, and less good white- and pink-flowered forms. Hyssop tea is made from the 'tops' (flowers and leaves).
Sun. 30–60cm/1–2ft.

Laurus

L. nobilis, bay laurel, in clipped pyramid or lollipop shapes, has become the symbol of the gardener with good taste. Unfortunately, its evergreen leaves are scorched by cold winds and plants are cut to the ground by hard frosts. Cautious gardeners, and gardeners in inhospitable areas, will grow it in a tub and bring it indoors for the winter. Others will grow it in the border and rely on its powers of rejuvenation after winter setbacks. Its leaves have a familiar aromatic fragrance, but the yellow tufts of flower, produced in spring, are also scented, of honey. There is a pale green, willow-leaved form called *angustifolia* and a less hardy yellow-leaved form called 'Aurea'. Shelter from wind is important.
Sun or shade. Most soils. 4.5m/15ft. Z7

Lavandula

There is a wealth of lavenders available with which to line paths and place on strategic corners. They have one of the most pleasant and nostalgic of herb scents, and on a hot summer's day it can infuse the air and transport you to dry hillsides of southern Europe. The hardier sorts associate well with rosemary and cistus in an informal shrubby mix, as well as providing the material for low hedges. The less hardy sorts are best grown in pots and taken into a cold greenhouse for the winter. They should be pruned in spring. Full sun. Well-drained soil.

L. angustifolia (*L. officinalis*, *L. spica*), common lavender, the source of the true oil of lavender. It is a variable plant, found wild in the western Mediterranean region and naturalized in parts of central Europe. The grey-green foliage is exceptionally fragrant, as are the spikes of lavender-purple flowers borne in summer. The compact forms commonly grown in gardens include 'Munstead', in lavender-blue'; 'Hidcote', in deep violet and with very silvery foliage; and 'Twickel Purple', in violet and with broader, richly scented leaves. 'Loddon Pink', in mauve-pink, and 'Nana Alba', a dwarf white, are interesting and worthwhile as colour

variants but are less scented.
Sun. Well-drained soil. 30–43cm/12–17in. Z6
L. dentata has toothed green leaves and stout stems bearing lavender-blue flowers. It has a distinctive medicinal fragrance when rubbed but is not one of the more scented varieties. It is not reliably hardy.
60cm/2ft. Z9
L. lanata is a very different species, with broad, woolly, silver leaves and violet flowers. It makes a very dense plant and is excellent in a pot; but it is not hardy and has little fragrance.
60cm/2ft. Z9
L. stoechas, French lavender, is my favourite. It has curious flowerheads, like inflated seed pods, which are crowned with a tuft of purple bracts; they are always a talking point. In a mild year it is in flower more or less continually; a hard frost kills it but invariably a host of seedlings appear in the spring. There is a white form, *alba*, and a stunning mauve form, *pedunculata*, with an even more impressive topknot; these I grow in pots and carry under glass for the winter. They all have a strong medicinal scent.
60cm/2ft. Z8–9

Hybrid Lavenders

There are many hybrid lavenders in circulation. The 'Dutch' clones are generally late-flowering. 'Grappenhall' is a large, vigorous late-flowering hybrid with broad, grey-green leaves and lavender-purple flowers.

Levisticum

L. officinale, lovage, is a tall herb of little beauty but it has a refreshing vegetable scent; used in stews, the dark, segmented leaves impart a strong celery taste. With its umbels of yellow flowers, borne at high summer, it resembles a slender angelica. Sun or light shade. 1.5m/5ft.

Melissa

M. officinalis, lemon balm, is not high on my list of desirable plants. It is dull and nettle-like to look at, seeds itself everywhere, and its scent is that of cheap lemon soap, not sharp and tangy like lemon verbena. The golden and golden-variegated forms, 'All Gold' and 'Aurea', are worthier of attention. Sun or light shade. 90cm/3ft.

Mentha

The scents of mint leaves are cool and refreshing. But most varieties are rampant colonizers and are best planted in confined beds or in bottomless buckets sunk into the soil.
Sun or light shade.
M. × gentilis, ginger mint, is usually seen in its yellow-variegated form, 'Variegata'. It has a warm, spicy mint scent and can be used in salads.
46cm/1½ft.
M. longifolia, buddleja mint, is an attractive mint with woolly, grey leaves and mauve flowers.
75cm/2½ft.
M. × piperita, peppermint, is usually seen in its black form, *M. × p. piperita*, which has dark purplish green leaves and a delicious peppermint scent. White peppermint, *M. × p. officinalis*, is greener.
30–60cm/1–2ft.
M. × p. citrata, Eau-de-Cologne or bergamot mint, is bronze-flushed and has the most refined of mint scents.
30cm/1ft.

M. requienii, Corsican mint, is minute and is excellent for troughs and paving cracks. It likes moisture and warmth.
M. × rotundifolia **'Bowles'**, Bowles' mint, is tall with downy leaves. It has a fruity mint scent and many consider it the best culinary variety.
90cm–1.8m/3–6ft.
M. spicata, spearmint, is a green and sharply toothed herb. It has a fine spearmint scent and is a good culinary variety.
60cm/2ft.
M. suaveolens **'Variegata'** (formerly *M. rotundifolia* 'Variegata'), variegated applemint, is the most ornamental of mints, with soft green leaves heavily splashed with white. The scent is of russet apples. It is good in salads and sauces.
60cm/2ft.

Monarda

M. didyma, bergamot or bee balm, is a herb that can take its place with pride in the herbaceous border, while in the herb garden it contributes a welcome splash of strong colour. The mopheads of hooded flowers, produced in high summer, are scarlet and are striking alongside Jackman's blue rue. The pointed leaves have a delicious scent, a blend of lemon and mint, and can be infused into boiling water to make Oswego tea. The hybrid 'Cambridge Scarlet' is similar but superior.
Sun, but it resents dry soil. 90cm/3ft. Z4
M. fistulosa is comparable but with smaller heads of lilac-purple flowers and less scent. A range of pink, purple and white hybrids is also available, including 'Croftway Pink', 'Prairie Night' and 'Snow White'. All are first-rate plants for the summer border.
Sun. Tolerates dry soil better than *M. didyma*. 90cm–1.2m/3–4ft. Z3

Myrrhis

M. odorata, sweet cicely, is a graceful perennial that is related to cow parsley. The large, lacy leaves are scented of liquorice and aniseed and can be used in salads; the roots used to be boiled as a vegetable. Umbels of cream flowers appear in spring and are followed by black seeds. It is lovely in the wild garden.
Light shade. Retentive soil. 60–90cm/2–3ft.

Mentha × rotundifolia 'Bowles'

Monarda 'Cambridge Scarlet'

Ocimum

O. basilicum, sweet basil, a tropical plant, is grown as a half-hardy annual and is best sown under glass in spring and planted out in summer; it also makes a good pot herb on the windowsill. Its triangular leaves are scented of clove, and are used to flavour tomatoes, soups and sauces. 'Dark Opal', a form with bronze leaves, is especially rich in scent and taste and is a sombre foil for pale flowers and silver foliage in the herb garden. Basil needs a warm, sheltered position. Lemon-scented basil, *O.b. citriodorum*, does not have a notable lemon scent. Bush basil, *O.b. minimum*, has smaller leaves and is less aromatic but because of its compact growth makes a good pot plant.
Sun. Light, fertile soil. 46cm/18in.

Origanum

O. majorana, oregano or knotted marjoram, is usually grown as a half-hardy annual outdoors, or as a pot perennial on the kitchen windowsill. Its small grey leaves have a warm, spicy scent.
Sun. Well-drained soil. 30cm/1ft.
O. onites, French marjoram, is a hardy perennial with fresh green, highly aromatic leaves. It has more flavour than English marjoram.
Sun. 30cm/1ft.

O. vulgare, common or English marjoram is the most commonly grown species and makes a fine sprawler for the front of the border. The golden-leaved form, *aureum*, is especially striking and is an indispensable foliage plant for the herb garden; the mauve-pink flowers provide rather a disastrous colour combination, though, and plants are best cut back when they appear. The balsam scent is strong.
Sun. 23cm/9in.

Petroselinum

P. crispum, parsley, is a hardy biennial that needs warmth and moisture to germinate well. Soak the seed in warm water for 24 hours before sowing; sow outdoors in spring for a summer crop, and in high summer for a crop the following spring. Plants can be cut back for a new flush of foliage. There are curly and plain-leaved varieties, all of which have a refreshing vegetable scent.
Sun. Fertile, retentive, preferably alkaline soil. 30cm/1ft.

Rosmarinus

Rosemary is a mainstay of the scented garden and its fragrance is deliciously suggestive of Mediterranean holidays and Sunday lunches of roast lamb. It makes an evergreen shrub of relaxed shape, that sits comfortably on house

Ocimum basilicum

Rosmarinus officinalis

Myrrhis odorata

Ruta graveolens

Salvia officinalis

corners, bulging over paths; common rosemary may also be used as a hedge – prune after flowering. No variety will tolerate excessive frost, but some are hardier than others. All need shelter from cold winds. Full sun. Well-drained soil.

R. × *lavandulaceus* is a prostrate rosemary for trailing down retaining walls. It has violet-blue flowers in spring and is not at all hardy. Z9

R. officinalis, common rosemary, has long been a favourite garden plant. It has grey-green leaves and in spring smothers itself in pale violet-blue flowers. 'Miss Jessopp's Upright' is a robust, erect-growing form. 1.2m/4ft.

The other variants tend to be less hardy, but they are all worth trying. It is prudent to take cuttings in the summer. *Albus* has white flowers; *aureus* has gold-splashed foliage: 'Benenden Blue' is short with narrow, dark leaves and blue flowers; and 'Severn Sea' is a dwarf with even brighter blue flowers. 46–90cm/18in–3ft. Z8

Ruta
R. graveolens, rue, is, in its metallic blue form 'Jackman's Blue', one of the very best small evergreen shrubs. The ferny leaves have a pungent scent, reminiscent to some of orange; but they should not be touched on sunny days by gardeners with sensitive skin, or blistering may occur. 'Jackman's Blue' being so popular, the ordinary blue-green form is now interesting as a curiosity! The variegated form is miffy. Clip back in early spring.
Sun. Well-drained soil. 90cm/3ft. Z5

Salvia
S. officinalis, sage, is another small evergreen shrub that is as valuable in the flower border as in the herb garden. It is particularly attractive sprawling over paving. I would grow the coloured-leaved forms in preference to the dusty green; the sage scent is just as marked. 'Icterina' has yellow variegation' 'Purpurascens' is purplish; and the less vigorous and more tender 'Tricolor' is splashed white, green and purple. Violet-blue hooded flowers appear in early summer. Clip in spring. It needs a sheltered position.
Sun. Well-drained soil. 90cm/3ft.

Sanguisorba
S. minor, salad burnet, has serrated leaves that give off a refreshing scent. It is used in salads and drinks, and has a flavour reminiscent of cucumber. Purple and green flowerheads appear in summer.
Sun. Well-drained soil. 60cm/2ft.

Santolina
S. chamaecyparissus, cotton lavender, has a pungent scent that appeals to some and not others. But as a foliage plant it is always admired. It makes a mound of silver-grey coral, topped in summer with golden yellow button flowers. It responds well to clipping and can be used as a low hedge or for knot gardens. There is a dwarf, compact form called *nana* for more intricate work.
Sun. Well-drained soil. 46cm/18in. Z7

S. pinnata neapolitana is a more upright species with lemon yellow buttons.
30cm/1ft. Z6

S. rosmarinifolia rosmarinifolia (*S. virens*, *S. viridis*). The green-leaved santolina has its attractions too.
45cm/18in.

Satureja
S. hortensis, summer savory, is a half-hardy annual whose small linear leaves have a pungent thyme-like scent. They are used to flavour beans. Whorls of lilac or white flowers are borne in summer. Sow outdoors

in spring or grow in pots on the windowsill. Sun. Well-drained soil. 20cm/8in.

S. montana, winter savory, is a perennial, semi-evergreen shrub and is more commonly grown than *S. hortensis*. It is equally strongly scented and is a useful culinary herb. Lilac flowers appear in summer. Plant with thyme at the front of the border.
Sun. Well-drained soil. 38cm/15in.

Tanacetum

T. parthenium (*Chrysanthemum parthenium*), feverfew, is one of the prettiest weeds when bearing its heads of white daisies, but it seeds itself everywhere. The foliage has a pungent scent and used to be used, infused in boiling water, to treat fevers; it is still popular as a treatment for migraine. The golden-leaved form, *aureum*, and several double-flowered forms, are commonly cultivated.
Sun or light shade. 46cm/18in.

T. vulgare, tansy, has a similar camphor-like scent and is used to make tansy tea. It has elegant leaves but must be sited carefully since it is an errant colonizer. Yellow button flowers are carried in summer. The variety *crispum* has attractive curled leaves.
Sun or light shade. 90cm/3ft.

Teucrium

T. chamaedrys, wall germander, is a low-growing shrub whose small oval leaves have a pungent, aromatic scent. Reddish purple, lipped flowers are borne in late summer. It is often used in knot gardens as an accompaniment to box or as an edging to a formal bed.
Sun. 15–30cm/6–12in.

Thymus

Thymes are an essential part of the scented garden. The prostrate forms can be grown in paving cracks and thyme lawns, where they can be trodden upon; the bushy forms spilling over the edges of paths, where they can be brushed against. All have a familiar thyme aroma but each is subtly different and shaded with other flavours. They can be short-lived, and a summer shearing to encourage youthful vigour and periodic renewal from cuttings may be necessary, especially with upright varieties. All need a sheltered position.
Sun. Well-drained soil.

T. azoricus (*cilicicus*) makes a cushion of slender foliage resembling tufts of pine needles. The scent is also of pine, shaded with orange. Pale lilac flowers appear in high summer; *T. caespitosus* (*T. micans*) is a white-flowered form.
2.5–7.5cm/1–3in.

T. × citriodorus, lemon thyme, is a bushy thyme with an aromatic lemon scent. It has green leaves and lilac flowers. There are many popular varieties including 'Aureus', with gold-variegated leaves, and 'Silver Queen', with silver-variegated leaves. They are very desirable plants but shelter is important; they are unreliable in very cold, wet areas.
23–30cm/9–12in. Z4

T. herba-barona is a semi-prostrate thyme that is scented of caraway. It has shiny green leaves and rosy purple flowers at high summer.
5–13cm/2–5in.

T. serpyllum, wild or English thyme, provides us with a range of mat-forming thymes for lawns and paving cracks. It has green hairy leaves, with a true thyme scent, and lilac-pink flowers at high summer. Other attractive and desirable forms include *albus*, that has white flowers; *coccineus* with crimson flowers; *lanuginosus* (*T. pseudolanuginosus*), with woolly grey leaves and mauve flowers; and 'Pink Chintz' with grey-green leaves that are offset by delicately coloured pale pink flowers.
2.5–7.5cm/1–3in.

T. vulgaris, common thyme, has dark green leaves and varies in colour from lilac to rosy purple.
15–20cm/6–8in.

Tanacetum parthenium

Thymus × citriodorus and *T. × c.* 'Silver Queen'

Plants for Conservatories and Mild Climates

Flower scents are especially potent in warm, moist conditions, so we should expect that the flora of warm temperate and tropical climates should be richly endowed. Heavy, exotic scents, fruity or spicy, sometimes cloying and heady, are to be found here in abundance, together with powerful leaf aromas. Equally memorable are the scents of the drier climates of the Mediterranean, parts of Australia, southern Africa and California. The most typical fragrances are perhaps those of the resinous leaves of conifers and eucalyptus, of the shrubs of the scrubby hillsides and maquis, the dusty heaths, rocky terrains and garigue. But, as in the tropics, there is also an abundance of flower scents. The fragrances are typically lighter or more purely fruity or aromatic than those of warm, humid climates – acacia, carpenteria, coronilla and broom are some of the natural flavours. But gardeners in these regions usually draw on a number of plants with heavy, exotic scents from warmer, humid parts of Asia, Africa and South America – jasmines, hoya, gardenia and citrus, for example – to enrich the bouquet.

In Britain and much of North America, most of the scented plants of milder regions have to be protected from the elements. Some plants from the cooler temperate regions may be tried outside in sheltered spots. In Britain, a sunny wall may suit *Buddleja auriculata*, coronilla, *Euphorbia mellifera*, lemon verbena, pittosporums and prostantheras, and maybe even acacias, callistemon, leptospermum, michelia and pancratiums. An open-sided glass verandah or an unheated greenhouse will offer an even more favourable microclimate for such plants, while an unheated porch or loggia, with a solid roof, may provide enough protection for half-hardy rhododendrons and camellias, which can cope with lack of overhead light. Other plants can be grown as tender bedding plants, spending the summer in an outdoor border but being lifted and stored in boxes of moist peat for the winter, in a frost-free garage or cellar – examples are pelargoniums, hedychiums and peppery-scented dahlias.

The remaining plants require winter heat. Many of the more compact varieties are very successful inside the house. A sunny windowsill suits pelargoniums, boronias, *Epiphyllum anguliger*, bouvardia, heliotropes, *Primula × kewensis*, *Cytisus × spachianus* and, when small, pittosporums. If the house is kept warm at all times, stephanotis, acokanthera, hoya, citrus and some orchids can also be expected to thrive. Large plants are likely to be less happy here, mainly because of lack of sunlight. Windows greatly reduce light intensity and filter out ultraviolet rays, and there is rarely much overhead light.

The ideal environment is provided by a greenhouse or conservatory, where lighting, temperature and humidity are all managed for the welfare of the plants. The plants you can grow here are largely determined by the temperature you maintain. Few of us can afford to support a tropical environment throughout the year; and in a conservatory that is also used as a living-room, such heat and high humidity are very unpleasant. It may be possible to construct a small tropical tank or compartment for a few special orchids and other exotics, but this will only be contemplated by the real enthusiast.

What most people want to know is how low a temperature they can get away with and still be able to grow a wide range of plants. The majority of plants described in this list of tender plants will be happy if the temperature is kept above freezing. A minimum winter temperature of 40°F/5°C will just about keep them in growth. But these levels are rather chilly for

Right *Many tender plants are tolerant of a nomadic life, wintering under glass and spending the summer in a sheltered spot outdoors. This seat is enveloped in scents. White* Datura × candida *breathes tropical sweetness at nose height, while lemon verbena is within reach of the fingers. Opposite is a collection of scented-leaved pelargoniums and* Datura versicolor *'Grand Marnier'.*

them, and for us; many winter-flowering plants will be discouraged from blooming, you will have to watch your watering very carefully because plants that fall dormant will need to be kept almost dry, and there will be little incentive for you to linger on cold days. A minimum temperature of around 50°F/10°C is much more comfortable and gives much better results, and since this is the season when you will most appreciate an indoor garden, I would plump for this higher level, if feasible. The temperatures given in the plant portraits are the lowest optimum growing temperatures.

Many plants can be overwintered in low temperatures under glass and taken outside in pots for the summer. Plants in flower, such as daturas, lilies, hedychiums and heliotropes, can be stood around the patio to waft their fragrances, while those with scented leaves, such as lippia, eucalyptus, prostantheras and salvias, can be put beside seats for you to tweak.

Winter is the most important season in the glasshouse. Most of the shrubs and climbers inside it will be evergreen so

you are assured a backdrop of greenery. Forced hyacinths and narcissi and an array of spring bulbs will provide good splashes of colour and layers of scent. But there are many other exciting flowering plants to entertain you. The various acacias provide a succession of fluffy yellow flowers through the season and will fill the air with their violet mimosa scent. This contrasts well with the exotic fragrances of jasmine and citrus blossom. I prefer the less heady and potent scent of *Jasminum sambac* to that of the common pot jasmine, *J. polyanthum*, which can be suffocating under glass. It is the species used for jasmine tea and it has a similar bubblegum flavour in its scent and taste to that in citrus blossom.

Of all the various citrus trees available, 'Meyer' lemon would always be my first choice. It is rarely without fragrant white flowers and it is a reliable and continual cropper. It is the height of sophistication to be able to reach out and pluck a lemon from your own tree. For strong flower scent, neither should you be without the Seville orange 'Bouquet'.

Fruity flower scents for winter come from all quarters. The slender white panicles of *Buddleja asiatica* possess a superb soft lemon perfume. The popular pot primula, *P. × kewensis*, is also sweet and lemony. And especially rich and strong is the orange fragrance exhaled by the reddish purple stars of *Daphne odora*. The soapy lemon scent that is released from the leaves of *Eucalyptus citriodora* is not in the same league, but the fruity scents of salvias and pelargoniums provide refreshingly sharp complementary flavours.

As spring gets under way, other fruity scents are released – lemon from *Boronia megastigma*, peach from freesias, and, later, banana from *Michelia figo* and more peach from yellow coronilla. Some of these overlap with the thick honey scent of *Euphorbia mellifera*. Only one warning: the euphorbia's flowers are very likely to be crawling with ants, so look before you inhale!

The white flowers of *Pittosporum tobira* are fragrant of orange blossom, not honey, and are among the blooms you can introduce to maintain a succession of exotic scents through the spring. Bulbous *Pamianthe peruviana* is very desirable and wafts its scent richly in the evening. Tender rhododendrons provide an array of fruity and spicy lily scents throughout the season. The *maddenii* series is exceptionally sweetly scented. And shrubby Natal plum, *Carissa grandiflora*, is well worth having, in spite of the hint of mothballs in its perfume.

Exotically scented climbers arrive in strength during the summer. Stephanotis opens early and continues throughout the season. It is a plant that enjoys more warmth and humidity

Right *Rhododendrons are obvious candidates for conservatories and porches in which the light is too poor for most other scented plants. Here one of the tender* maddenii *rhodos releases its powerful fruit fragrance, just before the jasmines spiralling up the white pillars begin to fill the room with their own potent perfume.*

Left Daphne odora *is not as hardy as its golden-edged form, 'Aureomarginata', and is best grown under glass. Here it will bloom in mid-winter and freely disperse its rich orange scent. The fragrance of all winter-flowering shrubs and climbers is fuller and more easily savoured indoors, and even hardier plants such as* D. bholua *and* Clematis cirrhosa *may be offered hospitality.*

than many glasshouses can provide, and it may be better on a windowsill in the house where it can be given individual attention. A winter temperature of 55°F/13°C is the bare minimum. Hoyas, wax plants, are more tolerant, and their fragrances are no less thrilling.

More jasmines open during the summer, together with other scented climbers that may be overlooked but should not be: beaumontia, mandevilla, dregea (formerly wattakaka), and trachelospermum. These are all excellent in cooler temperatures and with delicious, but not overpowering, fragrances.

Among summer-flowering scented shrubs, daturas are probably the most spectacular. Although red spider mites are a problem with daturas, a specimen in fine health and full flower is a memorable sight. The sweet scent is superb and especially strong at night. But the first prize for fragrance – whatever the competition, in my opinion – goes to gardenia. The clean, rounded bouquet of apricot and clove is one of the wonders of the floral world. Tuberose is also justly famed for its scent. It needs heat to be a reliable perennial, but gardeners with only cool conditions to offer it can grow imported bulbs as annuals and buy fresh stock each spring.

Beside these thick, heavy scents, you need some contrasts.

The leaf aromas of pelargoniums are a source of pleasure all year. Peppermint, apple, orange, lemon, spice and rose are all available. Acid lemon is also offered by *Aloysia triphylla* (*Lippia citriodora*) and pineapple and blackcurrant by salvias.

A favourite of mine for autumn is acidanthera, a bulbous plant now assigned to the genus *Gladiolus*. You can flower it outside in a sunny border but a potful on the patio or indoors is a treat for the nose. The blooms are very sweet and waft their fragrance in the evening. Acidantheras are produced in such quantity by the Dutch bulb firms each year that you can treat it as an annual with a clear conscience; it can be difficult to persuade to bloom after its first season.

A more unusual bulb is *Cyrtanthus mackenii*, worth growing for its banana-scented flowers. Its blooming usually coincides with the second crop of flowers on coronilla and the first crop from seed-sown freesias, and this makes a pleasant 'fruit salad' of fragrance. *Camellia sasanqua* varieties also bloom in the autumn and waft a light scent. Heliotropes brought back indoors will continue to exhale their vanilla-like perfume and it is also well worth bringing sweet basil inside, for culinary as well as hedonistic reasons. The scent of a variety like 'Dark Opal' will hang in the air, contributing an undercurrent of spice to complement the sharper flavours.

Conservatory and Tender Plants

Note: *The temperatures given in this chapter are the minimum required for keeping plants in growth; most will stand 10°F/5°C lower, and some will even tolerate a slight frost.*

Acacia

The acacias bloom in winter and spring, and their fluffy heads of round yellow flowers have a distinctive, often strong, violet scent. They succeed as pot plants, and sometimes in sheltered spots outside, but they are vigorous growers and can quickly outgrow their allotted space. They can be hard pruned after flowering. Pots may be plunged outside in a sunny border for the summer.
Sun or light shade. Min. temp. 40°F/5°C.
A. baileyana, Cootamunda wattle, is one of the most beautiful evergreen conservatory trees and has finely-cut, glaucous blue-grey leaves on pendulous branches and bright yellow flowers in spring.
Up to 9m/30ft.

A. dealbata, a florist's mimosa or silver wattle, is a popular species with pinnate leaves in silvery blue-green and very fragrant lemon yellow flowers in early spring. In mild areas it will succeed outside in a sheltered border or against a sunny wall.
Up to 15m/50ft or more.
A. podalyriifolia, Queensland silver wattle, is a lovely shrub with rounded leaves, in silvery blue-green, and long racemes of rich yellow, scented flowers in winter and spring. It is also successful in mild areas against a sunny wall.
3m/10ft.
A. rhetinodes, wirilda, has a fine sweet scent and often blooms for many months, beginning in late winter. The long, slender leaves are dark green and the flowers are pale yellow. It may also be tried outside in mild areas.
Up to 9m/30ft. Z9–10

Aloysia

A. triphylla **(Lippia citriodora)**, lemon verbena, has a sharp lemon fragrance that is released by its leaves and it is one of my favourite scents. I grow mine as a pot shrub to be stood outside beside a seat in summer and to be brought in under glass for its winter hibernation. But in mild areas, it can be trusted outside against a sunny wall. It is deciduous, with lance-shaped leaves and panicles of insignificant flowers in summer. Prune in spring. A scented garden should not be without it; it is very effective when grown as a standard.
Sun. Up to 3m/10ft. Min. temp. 40°F/5°C.

Babiana

B. stricta, baboon flower, looks rather like a freesia and has a similar sweet scent. The flowers are borne in short racemes and are accompanied by pleated, sword-shaped leaves. There are many colour forms and

Acacia baileyana

Aloysia triphylla

Babiana stricta

hybrids available in shades of violet, red and white. The corms, a popular food of baboons in southern Africa, should be potted up – and re-potted annually – in the autumn and kept fairly dry until shoots appear. Plants bloom in late spring.
Sun. 30cm/12in. Min. temp. 40°F/5°C.

Beaumontia

B. grandiflora, Herald vine, is a desirable Indian climber for a pot or border in the cool conservatory. The broad leaves have a glossy surface and a downy underside and the large white flowers, trumpet-shaped but prominently lobed, have an exotic scent. These appear in clusters during the summer. The plant needs to be pruned after flowering.
Sun or light shade. Up to 6m/20ft or more. Min. temp. 40°F/5°C.

Boronia

Boronias are Australian evergreen shrubs with fruitily aromatic foliage and often powerfully lemon-scented flowers which succeed on a sunny windowsill as well as in the conservatory. They may be hard pruned after flowering and their pots plunged outdoors for the summer.
Sun. Min. temp. 40°F/5°C.
B. megastigma is an indispensable ingredient for the scented conservatory. The small flowers, solitary and pendant, appear in profusion among the narrow leaflets in early spring. They are unusually coloured – brown-purple on the outside and mustard yellow within – and waft an irresistible lemon scent.
60cm/2ft.

Bouvardia

B. longiflora (*B. humboldtii*) is a small, semi-evergreen shrub from Mexico that bears a profusion of exotically scented, tubular white flowers from summer until winter. It needs a warm winter temperature but is otherwise easily grown in the house or conservatory. Plants should be cut back after flowering.
Sun or light shade. 1m/3ft. Min. temp. 50°F/10°C.

Brunfelsia

B. americana, lady of the night, is, as its name indicates, a night-scented beauty. The

Buddleja asiatica and *Narcissus* 'Hawera'

large, lobed flowers open pale yellow and fade to white and breathe a spicy-sweet fragrance. Hailing from South America, this leathery-leaved shrub enjoys warmth and humidity but grows happily in a pot and flowers well during the summer.
Up to 3m/10ft.
B. pauciflora (*B. calycina*) is the most common species in cultivation. Its flowers fade from deep violet to pale violet to white over a three-day period giving it the common name of yesterday, today and tomorrow.
60cm/2ft.

Buddleja

The two tender evergreen buddlejas included below are among the aristocrats of cool conservatory shrubs. They bloom in winter and early spring, just when indoor scent is most needed, and their perfume is fruity and sweet and more sophisticated than the honey of their hardy relatives. They succeed in the conservatory border or in pots which may be plunged outside for the summer, and can be pruned after flowering.
Sun. 3m/10ft or more. Min. temp. 40°F/5°C.
B. asiatica has long, tapering, grey-green leaves and slender drooping panicles of white flowers, intensely lemon-scented, in late winter and spring. No conservatory should be without it.
B. auriculata thrives against a sunny wall. It will succeed in many areas but its scent is best savoured under glass. Its panicles of creamy flowers are less than half as long as those of *B. asiatica*, but broader, and its leaves are also shorter and dark green in colour. This is another gem for the conservatory.

Camellia sasanqua 'Narumi-gata'

Cyclamen persicum

Camellia

Scent in camellias is usually light and it becomes noticeable only under glass. Most of the popular showy camellias including, I understand, all the cultivars of *C. reticulata*, are scentless. But in certain cultivars of *C. japonica* the scent is more pronounced; reddish pink 'Kramer's Supreme' and silvery pink 'Scentsation' are good examples. Among cultivars of *C.* × *williamsii*, single pink 'Mary Jobson' is notable. The most scented camellia species, *C. lutchuensis*, from the Ryukyu Islands between Japan and Taiwan, is currently being used by hybridists to breed more scent into camellias; a scented hybrid called 'Fragrant Pink' is now in commerce and we can look forward to many more.

C. sasanqua **'Narumi-gata'** is the best-known scented camellia with a refreshing fragrance. It has single, cup-shaped, white flowers, pink-tinged at the edges, in the autumn, and typically dark, glossy leaves. Outside, it can be trusted against a sunny wall – the sasanquas need more sun than other camellias – but it makes a very good

evergreen conservatory shrub and may be stood outside for the summer. It may be pruned in spring.
Sun. Acid or neutral soil. 3m/10ft. Min. temp. 40°F/5°C.

Carissa

C. grandiflora, Natal plum, is an attractive evergreen shrub with single, white, jasmine-like flowers. These are exotically sweet-scented but there is a definite hint of mothballs at close range. They are borne in late spring and are followed by edible red fruits. It has leathery, dark green, oval leaves. *C. g.* 'Nana' is a dwarf, compact form.
Light shade. 4.5m/15ft in the wild; 2m/6ft in a pot. Min. temp. 50°F/10°C.

Cedronella

C. canariensis (*C. triphylla*), the false balm of Gilead, has slender ternate leaves which, when bruised, have a pungent aroma of fruit and mint. It carries whorls of white or mauve flowers in summer.
Light shade. 1m/3ft. Min. temp. 40°F/5°C.

Citrus

Citruses give us a treble dose of scent. The fruit and leaves are sharply fruity when bruised, the former, of course, being softer and sweeter in flavour when nosed or savoured in the air and when cut open. The white flowers, star-shaped and fleshy, are exotically sweet, with a definite hint of bubblegum. They grow well in pots in the cool conservatory and will fruit if the temperature is sufficiently high; they benefit from being stood outside in a sunny position during the warmest summer months. Plants may be lightly pruned in spring, if necessary. Scale insects can be a problem.
Sun. Min. temp. 40°F/5°C (higher if possible).

C. aurantium, Seville orange, is one of the hardier and more reliable citruses and a handsome foliage plant. It is also exceedingly fragrant in fruit and flower. The rind from its small bitter fruits yields an essential oil, and its large flowers are the source of the perfume, Oil of Neroli. In addition, its oranges make the best marmalade. 'Bouquet' ('Bouquet de Fleurs') is a highly fragrant dwarf variety.
Up to 9m/30ft.

C. limon, lemon, has good-sized white flowers opening from purplish buds and makes a handsome shrub. The compact variety 'Meyer' is the most popular of all citruses for the house or conservatory, being fairly robust, flowering almost continually, and fruiting freely. 'Variegata', with cream-variegated leaves and green-streaked lemons and 'Villafranca', a reliable cropper with large fruits, are also desirable.
3m/10ft.

Clerodendrum

C. philippinum (*C. fragrans*) is a deciduous shrub from the Far East with heart-shaped leaves and rounded heads of creamy, clove-scented flowers through summer and autumn. It succeeds as a house plant or in the warm conservatory and should be cut back hard after flowering.
Sun. Up to 2m/6ft. Min. temp. 40°F/5°C.

Clethra

C. arborea, lily of the valley tree, is a small evergreen tree from Madeira that is exceptionally lovely when it is carrying its

panicles of dangling, bell-shaped flowers, white and piercingly fragrant, in late summer and autumn. The leaves are broadly lanceolate and deep green. It may be pruned after flowering but will need to be renewed occasionally from cuttings.
Light shade. 9m/30ft in the wild. Min. temp. 40°F/5°C.

Coronilla

C. glauca is a popular and first-rate conservatory shrub which blooms abundantly in spring and early summer and usually again in the autumn. The pea flowers are golden yellow, carried in rounded clusters, and possess a delicious fruity scent by day. The evergreen leaves consist of 5 to 7 glaucous blue-green leaflets and are a perfect foil for the flowers. It succeeds outside in milder areas, in sheltered borders or against sunny walls. The closely related *C. valentina* is smaller, with greener leaves. There is a lovely lemon-yellow form, *C. g.* 'Citrina', and a form with cream-variegated leaves, *C. g.* 'Variegata'.
Sun. 1.5m/5ft or more. Min. temp. 40°F/5°C.

Cyclamen

C. persicum is a welcome harbinger of spring in the house and cool conservatory. The small flowers of this species, with their erect, twisted petals, have an intensely sweet lily-of-the-valley fragrance. They are white, pink or rose-purple and are stained carmine at the mouth. Even more variation is evident in the patterned foliage. Plants should be dried off in late spring and the pots put in a sunny cold frame, which is airy but dry. Only when new growth is observed should they be watered again and, if necessary, re-potted. The large florist's hybrids are scentless.
Sun. 20cm/8in. Min. temp. 40°F/5°C; dislikes very warm conditions.

Cymbopogon

These tropical oil grasses are seldom encountered outside botanic gardens, but they are intensely aromatic and the basis of several perfumery oils. *C. citratus* provides lemon-grass oil; *C. nardus*, citronella oil; and *C. martinii* is scented of rose and is the source of palmarosa oil.
Sun. 30cm/1ft. Min. temp. 50°F/10°C.

Coronilla valentina

Cyrtanthus

C. mackenii is a bulbous plant from southern Africa whose tubular white flowers have a banana-like scent. These are borne in umbels, predominantly in spring or autumn, and are accompanied by strap-shaped leaves. A marsh plant, it needs plenty of water when growing but enjoys some shade and a drier spell during the summer. The creamy-yellow variety, *cooperi*, is especially lovely. Colourful hybrids are coming into circulation.
30cm/1 ft. Min. temp. 40°F/5°C.

Cytisus

C. × *spachianus* (*C. racemosus* of gardens) has sweetly scented yellow pea-flowers borne in slender racemes during winter and spring, and is a cheerful pot plant for the house or conservatory. It makes a large evergreen shrub but may be trimmed after flowering. It is susceptible to red spider mite.
Sun. Up to 3m/10ft. Min. temp. 40°F/5°C.

Left *Citrus limon* 'Villafranca'

Daphne

D. odora, winter daphne, is less hardy than its more common form 'Aureomarginata', with yellow-edged leaves and, in cold areas, needs the protection of a cool conservatory. Here it is an indispensable evergreen producing its heads of reddish purple starry flowers in late winter and early spring, and filling the room with its sophisticated orange perfume. It should be put outside for the summer, somewhere that is shaded for the hottest part of the day. There is a white form, *D. o. alba*. I should love to meet 'Mazelii', described by W. J. Bean, which blooms in early winter, and wonder whether it is still in cultivation.
Sun. 1.5m/5ft. Min. temp. 40°F/5°C. Z7

Datura

Daturas (angel's trumpet) are familiar conservatory shrubs which, in spite of their exotic appearance, do not need high temperatures. The huge pendant trumpets, strikingly lobed at the mouth, are often powerfully and sweetly scented, especially at night. They appear freely throughout summer and early autumn and are accompanied by large leaves. They need plenty of water and feed during the growing season and may be stood outside in the warmer months. They are best grown as standards and pollarded after flowering. In the conservatory border they can be cut back to within 15cm/6in of the ground in late winter. Red spider mites can be a problem. Light shade. 3m/10ft or more. Min. temp. 40°F/5°C.

D. arborea (**Brugmansia arborea**), *D. × candida* (*Brugmansia × candida*) – and its double form 'Knightii' – and *D. suaveolens* (*Brugmansia suaveolens*) have very fragrant white flowers. *D. versicolor* (*Brugmansia versicolor*) 'Grand Marnier' is less scented but has beautiful apricot flowers.

D. inoxia (**D. meteloides**) differs from these: it is a tuberous-rooted perennial and may be grown as a half-hardy annual. Its large white or violet trumpets are intensely fragrant.

Dianthus

D. caryophyllus, carnation. The florist's carnations are very popular specialist greenhouse plants. Many of the more colourful, streaked and striped varieties are deficient in scent but others, notably white 'Fragrant Ann', are well endowed with clove perfume and are worthy of any buttonhole. Flowering time is determined by the pinching out of the sub-lateral shoots; plants whose young growths are pinched out in summer will have their flowering delayed until winter. The summer-flowering border carnations, though hardy, also succeed in pots indoors; see 'Rock Plants'.
Sun. 1–1.5m/3–5ft. Min. temp. 45°F/7°C.

Diosma

D. ericoides, breath of Heaven, is an evergreen shrub from southern Africa whose needle-like foliage is pungently aromatic and whose small white flowers, borne in late winter, are scented.
Sun. Neutral or acid soil. 60cm/2ft. Min. temp. 40°F/5°C.

Dregea

D. sinensis (**Wattakaka sinensis**) is a desirable evergreen climber for the conservatory, bearing pendant umbels of white starry flowers during the summer. These are delicately streaked with pink and have a honey-sweet scent. Interesting seed-pods sometimes follow. In mild areas, it may be tried outdoors, against a sunny wall.
Sun. 3m/10ft. Min. temp. 40°F/5°C.

Epiphyllum

E. anguliger, fishbone cactus. This delicately scented bushy epiphytic cactus with slender, indented, leaf-like stems is a reliable bloomer and quite stunning when carrying its huge creamy flowers in summer. It must not be overwatered but is not as adapted to drought as other cacti. It will succeed in the house on a windowsill.
Sun. Up to 1m/3ft. Min. temp. 50°F/10°C.

Eucalyptus

E. citriodora, lemon-scented gum, is a very tender eucalyptus and, although it may be stood outside for the summer, it requires frost protection in winter. The long leaves, hairy in the juvenile stage and smooth in the

Datura versicolor 'Grand Marnier'

Dregea sinensis

adult, are scented of lemon; the fragrance is too soapy for me, but others love it. It makes a good evergreen conservatory shrub and may be pollarded in spring to keep it short. Sun. 2m/6ft or more; 45m/150ft in the wild. Min. temp. 40°F/5°C.

Eucharis
E. grandiflora, Amazon lily, is a bulbous plant that requires warmth and humidity to give of its best but makes a good pot subject for the house or warm conservatory. The white flowers, which are carried in umbels on stout stems and resemble nodding daffodils, are exotically scented and are accompanied by broad, strap-like, evergreen leaves. It likes humus-rich soil and plenty of water both during and after flowering. Light shade. 60cm/2ft. Min. temp. 60°F/15°C.

Euphorbia
E. mellifera. I have seen this splendid euphorbia growing luxuriantly in its native Madeira and in milder gardens in Britain, where it attains very impressive sizes, but I can only persuade it to bloom in a pot under glass. It produces almost spherical heads of tan flowers in early spring which look and smell like golden honey; they are even sticky to the touch. The leaves are long, slender and bright grass-green, with a central white vein. Sun. 2m/6ft. Min. temp. 40°F/5°C.

Freesia
F. refracta. Freesias are most familiar as cut flowers but because it is the modern hybrids, with their bright and varied colour range, that are usually offered, their fragrance is often disappointing. By growing your own corms in pots, you can choose your varieties and ensure that you give yourself a dose of that piercingly rich fruity scent, and the flowers last much longer than those on cut stems. *F. refracta* comes in white and yellow, and is powerfully fragrant, as are the hybrids 'White Swan', in creamy white, 'Yellow River', in canary yellow, and 'Romany', a mauve double. Corms should be planted in autumn and will bloom in winter or spring; they should be dried off after the leaves have faded. Sun. 30cm/12in. Min. temp. 50°F/10°C.

Gardenia jasminoides

Gardenia
G. jasminoides, Cape jasmine. Gardenia is one of the best-known greenhouse plants and has one of the best-loved fragrances – spicily sweet with the flavour of sun-ripened apricots. It sells on sight and on smell in garden centres, but needs ample warmth and humidity to perform well. It makes an attractive evergreen shrub which may be cut back after flowering. The double white blooms are borne in summer and autumn. Light shade. Peaty soil. Up to 1.5m/5ft. Min. temp. 50°F/10°C.

Gelsemium
G. sempervirens, Carolina jessamine, is a popular climber in Carolina, where I have seen it used to cover porches and telegraph poles, but I have never encountered it in Britain outside a conservatory. It is an attractive plant with clusters of golden yellow, funnel-shaped flowers in spring and early summer. These are sweetly scented but not as rich in fragrance as jasmine. There is a double form, 'Flore Pleno'. Sun or light shade. 4.5m/15ft. Min. temp. 40°F/5°C. Z8

175

Gladiolus

G. callianthus (Acidanthera bicolor, A. murielae). This gladiolus is produced by Dutch bulb growers by the thousand each year and is offered by nearly every garden centre. Corms should be planted in spring, 10cm/4in apart and 10cm/4in deep, in pots. These may be placed outside during the summer and as the flowers begin to open in the autumn, some may be brought back indoors. They may also succeed in sunny borders. The white blooms are striking with their pointed petals and maroon blotch and the scent from them is exotically sweet and especially powerful in the evening. Corms should be dried off after the foliage has faded; those growing in outside borders should be lifted. This is an indispensable plant for the scent-conscious gardener.
Sun. 1m/3ft. Min. temp. 40°F/5°C.

Hedychium

Ginger lilies are spectacular rhizomatous perennials that may be tried in sheltered, sunny borders outside in the mildest areas, but are usually grown in pots in the conservatory or for standing on patios in the summer. The scent from their flowerheads is appropriately exotic and heady, spiced with mothballs. The blooms are borne on stout stems and accompanied by paddle-shaped leaves. They enjoy rich, moist soil and their rhizomes should be only lightly covered with soil.

H. coronarium, white ginger lily, bears heads of large, powerfully fragrant, white flowers with yellow blotches during the summer. It requires warmer conditions than other species.
Sun. 2m/6ft. Min. temp. 50°F/10°C.

H. densiflorum has long spikes of coral-coloured flowers, with protruding red filaments, in late summer. 'Stephen' is a superior selection.
Sun. 2m/6ft or more. Min. temp. 40°F/5°C.

H. gardnerianum, Kahili ginger, is the most common and, in my view, loveliest ginger lily. The flowers, produced in late summer, are lemon yellow with protruding red filaments and are beautifully partnered with blue-green leaves.
Sun. 2m/6ft. Min. temp. 40°F/5°C.

Heliotropium

H. arborescens, heliotrope or cherry pie. The shrubby and standard heliotropes of the Victorian garden, which have to be propagated by cuttings and overwintered in warmth, have been largely replaced today by seed-raised annuals like 'Marine'. But for strength of perfume, you have to go back to the old cultivars, like 'Mrs Lowther' and 'Chatsworth' and the dark purple 'Princess Marina'. These waft their vanilla fragrances freely, and make fine conservatory pot plants which can be stood outside for the summer or planted in borders to be lifted and re-potted (or propagated) in the autumn. In warmth, they will bloom all year.
Sun. 1m/3ft or more. Min. temp. 40°F/5°C.

Hoya

Hoyas, wax flowers, give us a range of richly and sweetly scented evergreen climbers and shrubs for the warm conservatory. They have fleshy leaves and pendant umbels of thick-petalled, waxy flowers in summer. They may be cut back after flowering but since they are slow-growing this is not often necessary.

Gladiolus callianthus

Hedychium densiflorum 'Stephen'

Jasminum polyanthum

They like a humus-rich, acid soil and a moist atmosphere, and the climbers grow best in a conservatory border against a wall.
H. australis is a climber with exotically fragrant white or blush pink flowers with reddish markings.
Light shade. 4.5m/15ft. Min. temp. 60°F/15°C.
H. bella is an epiphytic shrub which succeeds best cascading from a hanging basket. The heavily scented flowers are white with purplish centres.
Light shade. 46cm/18in. Min. temp. 60°F/15°C.
H. carnosa, common wax plant, is an elegant climber with white, pink-centred flowers. It has a spicy sweet scent, particularly pronounced in the evening. There are a number of forms available.
Light shade. 6m/20ft. Min. temp. 50°F/10°C.

Hymenocallis
Spider lilies are bulbous South American plants, closely related to pancratiums, with flowers that resemble spidery daffodils or small tentacled jellyfish. These are exotically scented and appear in umbels above the strap-like leaves in summer. Keep the deciduous varieties on the dry side (but not completely dry) in winter.
Sun. 60cm/2ft. Min. temp. 50°F/10°C; 60°F/15°C for evergreen varieties.
H. × festalis (*Ismene × festalis*) is deciduous with fragrant white flowers.
H. × macrostephana is a fine white-flowered hybrid between two highly scented species, *H. narcissiflora* and *H. speciosa*. Being almost evergreen, it appreciates some extra warmth and moisture in the winter.
H. narcissiflora (*Ismene calathina*), the Peruvian daffodil, is a deciduous species with very fragrant white flowers.
H. speciosa is evergreen with greenish white flowers and needs extra warmth and moisture in winter.

Hymenosporum
H. flavum, Australian frangipani, is an evergreen shrub or tree with shiny oval leaves and panicles of powerfully and exotically scented tubular flowers in late spring. These open cream-coloured and turn a rich yellow.
Sun. 3m/10ft or more. Min. temp. 40°F/5°C.

Hoya bella

Jasminum
No conservatory should be without the scents of jasmines. If the heady fragrances of royal, common or pot jasmine are too much for you in an enclosed space, then you could try the sweeter, bubblegum-flavoured *J. azoricum* and *J. sambac*, or the finely perfumed *J. suavissimum*; these are all less vigorous than *J. officinale*, *J. o. affine* (*J. grandiflorum*) and *J. polyanthum*. The conservatory jasmines are mainly evergreen climbers, excellent for clothing pillars and rafters. By careful selection of varieties, you can have flowers in every season. They should be pruned and thinned lightly after flowering, as flowers are borne on new growths. They succeed best when their roots are slightly restricted, so transfer them into bigger sizes of pot only very gradually.
Sun or light shade.
J. angulare is a species from southern Africa with fairly large, fragrant white flowers.
3m/10ft. Min. temp. 40°F/5°C.
J. azoricum is a compact climber with purplish buds and sweetly scented white flowers. It is in bloom almost continually in summer and autumn.
3m/10ft. Min. temp. 40°F/5°C.
J. nitidum, windmill jasmine, has spidery white flowers from purplish buds and blooms mainly in summer.
3m/10ft. Min. temp. 40°F/5°C.
J. polyanthum, Chinese or pot jasmine, is the familiar garden centre jasmine with heavily scented white flowers, from reddish buds, in winter and spring.
3m/10ft. Min. temp. 50°F/10°C.
J. sambac, Arabian jasmine, is the species used for scenting tea. It bears its large white flowers almost continuously, even through the winter if the temperature is high enough.
3m/10ft. Min. temp. 50°F/10°C.

Lilium speciosum rubrum

Orchid *Vanda tricolor*

Leptospermum

L. scoparium, manuka or New Zealand tea tree, is a small evergreen shrub with slender, pointed leaves that are aromatic when bruised. It has recently become popular with gardeners – as have other New Zealand flora – especially in the milder areas where it may be grown outside. It gives an attractive show of white flowers in late spring; there are many colour variants in shades of pink and red. They make compact plants, and the dwarf form, *L. s. nanum*, will succeed on a sunny windowsill.

Sun. 2m/6ft or more. Min. temp. 40°F/5°C.

Lilium

Most lilies do well in pots and many of the scented hardy species, like *L. regale* and

L. auratum, are a pleasure to have indoors and will bloom earlier than those outside. But here I have listed only those lilies that grow particularly well in pot culture.

Sun or light shade. Well-drained, humus-rich soil. Min. temp. 40°F/5°C.

L. formosanum is an exquisite white lily. The large trumpet flowers, purple-flushed on the outside, have a sweet scent. It is short-lived and prone to virus but is easily raised from seed, flowering in its first year.
1.2m/4ft.

L. longiflorum is the florist's Easter lily. The long, pure white, fragrant trumpets open during the summer, but may be forced for spring. It is also easily raised from seed, usually flowering in its second year.
Lime-tolerant. 1m/3ft.

L. speciosum is an intoxicatingly scented lily with recurved flowers, almost like the turk's cap lily which is so popular with florists. The thick white flowers are usually shaded and spotted with carmine or crimson and there are numerous colour forms. *L. s. rubrum* is a rich carmine and exceptionally beautiful. It blooms in late summer but is easily forced.
1.2–2m/4–6ft.

Luculia

Luculias are evergreen shrubs with powerfully fragrant tubular flowers and are extremely attractive shrubs for the warm conservatory. They enjoy plenty of water when in growth and may be cut back after flowering.

Sun or light shade. Min. temp. 50°F/10°C.

L. grandifolia is a very handsome shrub or tree with oval, red-veined leaves and large clusters of white flowers in summer. 2m/6ft or more.

L. gratissima, also beautiful in foliage, carries its large clusters of wonderfully sweet, light rose pink flowers in late autumn and winter. 1–2m/3–6ft or more.

Mandevilla

M. laxa (M. suaveolens), Chilean jasmine, is a popular and highly desirable deciduous climber for the conservatory. The white flowers are jasmine-like but very large and possess a superb sweet scent. They are produced in clusters among the heart-shaped leaves during the summer. The plant prefers a border or large tub to a pot and may be lightly pruned in spring. The bright pink *Mandevilla* 'Alice du Pont' is unscented. Light shade. 3m/10ft or more. Min. temp. 40°F/5°C.

Michelia

M. figo is described in W. J. Bean's *Trees and Shrubs* as one of the most scented of all shrubs. The flowers breathe the fruity fragrance of bananas or pear-drops and a few flowers will scent an entire room. It is the most common michelia in cultivation and will succeed outside in the mildest areas, but makes a good pot plant in the conservatory. It is a slow-growing bushy evergreen with glossy leaves, and the creamy yellow flowers, flushed with purple, appear in succession during spring and early summer. *M. doltsopa*, a larger species with pale yellow flowers in spring, is also strongly scented. Sun. 3m/10ft or more. Min. temp. 40°F/5°C. Z8

Nymphaea

Many tropical waterlilies have rich fruity scents. They need warmth – a water temperature of 70°F/20°C – but are otherwise easy to grow in baskets in a conservatory pool or in water-filled tubs. In early autumn the baskets are lifted out of the water and the tubers stored in moist sand at a temperature of 55°F/12°C. Blue waterlily (*N. capensis*), pink-flowered 'General Pershing' and blue flowered *N. stellata* are scented day-blooming waterlilies; *N. caerulea* breathes its fragrance at night.

Orchids

A visit to an orchid house can be an intoxicating, evocative and memorable experience. Fruity, flowery, spicy and heady – all the exotic scents are here. But this is, in the main, a specialist's world, in which temperature, humidity and ventilation must be carefully controlled. There is no space here to go into the intricacies of cultivation or to sample more than a fraction of the many thousands of species and hybrids in existence but I am at least able to provide a glimpse through the misted glass; I should warn, however, that the scents seem to vary within species as much as flower colour, and my descriptions may not tally with plants you are sniffing.

The majority of cultivated orchids are epiphytic, that is to say, they grow naturally on branches and rocks, storing moisture in swollen stems known as pseudobulbs. Under glass they require special soil-free compost which is fibrous and free-draining. Pendant varieties are best grown in hanging baskets or suspended rafts or in mossy nests attached to cut tree and shrub branches (rhododendron and hawthorn wood is particularly good). Erect-growing epiphytic varieties and terrestrial orchids can be cultivated in clay pots. In summer they need shade from strong sunshine, plenty of water and a daily misting; in winter they need less water, unless still in growth, and some appreciate a fairly dry rest period. A minimum winter night temperature of 60°F/15°C and a maximum summer day temperature of 80°F/25°C suit most.

There are a great many powerfully and sweetly scented species and hybrids among the cattleyas – *C. velutina*, hyacinth-scented *C. labiata* and gardenia-scented *C. loddigesii* are notable – and among the coelogynes, including *C. cristata*, *C. nitida* and *C. pandurata*. Many of the cymbidiums smell deliciously fruity, often of apricots – *C. eburneum* and *C. tracyanum* are particularly good.

Spicy scents are often encountered among the lycastes, such as *L. aromatica* and *L. cruenta*, and among the epidendrum orchids, including *E. nocturnum*.

Sweet and spicy scents are found in the encyclias (*E. alata*, *E. citrina* and *E. fragrans*); dendrobium and bulbophyllum orchids are also likely to be either spicy or sweet –

D. heterocarpum, *D. nobile*, *D. moschatum* and *B. lobbii* are notable – but many are very nasty indeed. *B. caryanum*, for example, smells of rotting fish.

There are also a host of scented varieties among the angraecum (*A. eburneum*, *A. sesquipedale*), maxillaria (*M. picta*, *M. venusta*), Odontoglossum (*O. pulchellum*), Oncidium (*O. ornithorrhynchum*), vanda (*V. parishii* – now correctly *Vandopsis parishii* – *V. tricolor*) and stanhopea orchids (*S. tigrina* smells of vanilla).

Pamianthe

P. peruviana is an evergreen bulbous plant much prized for its large, exotically scented white flowers. These have spreading petals and green stripes and the fragrance is especially powerful in the evening. Although it requires less water in winter than in summer, bulbs should not be allowed to dry out completely. It blooms in late winter or early spring. Part shade. Rich, well-drained soil. 60cm/2ft. Min. temp. 55°F/12°C.

Pamianthe peruviana

Pancratium

The two Mediterranean bulbous plants described below, both powerfully sweet-scented and with fairly erect, slightly glaucous leaves, can be tried outside at the base of a sunny wall in the mildest areas. But they do well in pots under glass, appreciating a dry, summer baking; they should be fed and watered regularly through the winter. Plant 15cm/6in deep in well-drained soil.
Sun. Min. temp. 40°F/5°C.
P. illyricum is the more reliable species. It bears its umbels of starry white flowers in early summer.
46cm/18in.
P. maritimum, sea lily, bears its wispier white flowers in late summer and has narrow, evergreen leaves.
30cm/1ft.

Pelargonium

The familiar pot geraniums of windowsills, balconies, terraces and bedded summer borders all have some degree of scent. The distinctive 'rose-geranium' fragrance is, however, usually much more evident in soft-leaved zonal pelargoniums (*P.* × *hortorum*) than in the smooth and leathery-leaved regal and ivy-leaved hybrids. There are dozens of varieties available, far too many to list here, and selection has to be by the colour and pattern of flowers and leaves.

But there are pelargonium hybrids and species with strong scents and with scents that vary greatly from the rosy norm. Indeed,

the group provides a wider range of leaf scents than any other I know, including salvias. They are usually less showy in flower, but you cannot have everything.

All are easy to grow, if they are given well-drained soil and they are not over-watered, and they are usually very tolerant of neglect. Keep them fairly dry in winter.
Sun. 30cm–1m/1–3ft or more. Min. temp. 40°F/5°C.

Among the downy-leaved pelargoniums, *P. tomentosum* and the brown-blotched *P.* 'Chocolate Peppermint' smell of peppermint; the dwarf *P.* × *fragrans* smells of nutmeg or pine, and *P. odoratissimum* of apple. *P. abrotanifolium*, with finely-cut leaves, has a fragrance reminiscent of southernwood, *Artemisia abrotanum*.

P. crispum major (Prince Rupert geranium), *P.* 'Citronella', *P.* × *citrosum* (*P. citriodorum*) and *P.* 'Mabel Grey' have leaves scented of lemon; *P.* 'Prince of Orange', of orange.

P. graveolens and *P.* 'Attar of Roses' smell of roses; *P. denticulatum* of balsam and lilac; and *P. quercifolium* is pungently spice-scented.

P. triste and *P. gibbosum* have flowers that are sweetly scented in the evening; these tuberous and gouty species must be kept completely dry in winter.

Pittosporum

Pittosporums can be badly knocked in hard winters and most of us find it safer to grow them under glass. They are excellent tub plants, with attractive evergreen foliage, and the fragrance from their flowers is especially heavy under glass.
Sun. Min. temp. 40°F/5°C.
P. tobira, Japanese pittosporum, blooms in spring. The flowers are large and creamy white and carried in conspicuous umbels; and the scent is the sweet bubblegum scent of orange blossom. The foliage is quite broad and round and there is a lovely form with white margins to the leaves called 'Variegatum'.
Up to 3m/10ft or more. Z8

Plumeria

P. rubra, frangipani, is the tree which scents the evening breeze in the tropics. It is an exotic, fruity scent which comes from the clusters of funnel-shaped flowers. These can be any colour, from white and yellow to

orange and pink and are borne throughout the summer. They are accompanied by large, paddle-shaped leaves. The tree hails from Central America but has been widely planted wherever it will thrive. In cold climates it needs a warm conservatory and should be kept almost dry in winter when it is without leaves. *P. r. acutifolia* is a form with large white flowers that have a prominent yellow coloured eye.
Sun. 3m/10ft or more. Min. temp. 50°F/10°C.

Polianthes

P. tuberosa, tuberose, is a tender perennial with a legendary scent. The white funnel-shaped flowers are intensely and exotically fragrant – too intensely for some people – and are carried in erect racemes in summer and autumn. It needs plenty of water when in growth; it should be dried off and stored in sand, like a dahlia, in winter and started into growth again in late winter. The double-flowered form, 'The Pearl', is grown more often and is even more strongly scented.
Sun. Well-drained soil. 60cm/2ft. 60°F/15°C.

Pittosporum tobira

Polianthes tuberosa

Primula × kewensis

Primula

P. × kewensis is a popular golden yellow primula for brightening up the conservatory in winter and spring. The scent from the whorls of flowers is very sweet flavoured with lemon. There are two forms available, one with a heavy dusting of white powder (farina) on its foliage, the other without. It is easily grown and comes readily from seed sown in spring or summer.
Part shade. 30cm/1ft. 50°F/10°C.

Prostanthera

These evergreen shrubs, known as mint bush, have small, strongly aromatic leaves and showy flowers, also scented, in late spring or early summer. Their common name is deceptive since the foliage of some species does not smell of mint. They are worth trying outside in very mild areas, against a sunny wall, but they make good pot shrubs in the conservatory.
Sun. Min. temp. 40°F/5°C.
P. cuneata is a small spreading shrub whose dark leaves are powerfully scented of wintergreen or plasticine. The lipped flowers are mauve-white with purple markings. It is proving relatively hardy outside.
60cm/2ft.

Plumeria rubra

P. melissifolia is strongly mint-scented and the clusters of violet flowers are eyecatching. Up to 3m/10ft.

P. ovalifolia has leaves scented of wintergreen or plasticine and has short racemes of mauve-purple flowers. Up to 3m/10ft.

P. rotundifolia has mint-scented oval leaves and short racemes of violet-blue flowers. Up to 3m/10ft.

Quisqualis
Q. indica, Rangoon creeper, is a fast-growing creeper for the conservatory rafters. It bears small fragrant flowers all summer that are white when they open in the evening and turn to pink, red or orange.
Sun or part shade. 4.5m/15ft or more. Min. temp. 50°F/10°C.

Rhododendron
Many of the most powerfully scented rhododendrons are from warm temperate climates and, except in the mildest regions, need winter protection. They make excellent tub plants for the shadier parts of the cool conservatory and for porches that may have no overhead light and little heating. Many of these rhodos are epiphytic and of lax habit, and benefit from the support of walls or posts. The flowers are usually white and spicily or fruitily lily-scented. They are all very beautiful.
Part shade. Min. temp. 40°F/5°C.
RR. ciliicalyx, *maddenii*, *edgeworthii* (*bullatum*), *lindleyi* and *griffithianum* are exceedingly fragrant. 'Countess of Haddington', 'Lady Alice Fitzwilliam' and 'Fragrantissimum' are among the best-known scented tender rhodos, and are certainly some of the most desirable conservatory shrubs. *R. crassum* extends the season into mid-summer.
3m/10ft or more.

Salvia
The two tender salvias chosen below from a huge number of possible species, possess very fruity leaf scents and are in my top category of fragrant plants. They also have striking flowers. Both make sub-shrubby pot

Prostanthera melissifolia

Salvia discolor

Stauntonia hexaphylla

Stephanotis floribunda

plants of manageable size that can be stood outside, beside seats, for the summer or even planted in the border. Propagation is by cuttings, but *S. rutilans* is the more amenable and will even root in a glass of water.
Sun. Min. temp. 40°F/5°C.
S. discolor smells strongly of blackcurrant. The scent comes from the long sticky flower stems and from the green leaves, that have surprising grey-white undersides. The flowers, which appear all summer, are small, hooded and purple-black and protrude from grey-green calyces. It is a lax grower, sparsely clad in foliage but its fragrance excuses it these faults.
Up to 1m/3ft.
S. rutilans (*S. elegans*) has soft, fresh green leaves with a rich smell of pineapple. It makes a bushy shrub and is topped with scarlet flowers all summer.
Up to 1m/3ft.

Selenicereus
S. grandiflorus, queen of the night, is a slender climbing cactus from the West Indies. It opens its large white flowers, which

resemble those of epiphyllum, on summer nights and exhales a powerful and exotic perfume. An easy conservatory plant, it succeeds in pots or in the border.
Sun. Up to 4.5m/15ft. Min. temp. 50°F/10°C.

Solandra
S. maxima, capa de oro. This showy evergreen climber from Mexico has large, powerfully fragrant, trumpet flowers in golden yellow with maroon markings. It is a vigorous plant, clad in glossy leaves, and may be pruned after flowering. It should be kept fairly dry in winter and early spring until the flower buds appear. The display may last for several months.
Sun. 9m/30ft. Min. temp. 60°F/15°C.

Stauntonia
S. hexaphylla is a handsome evergreen climber that may be tried against a warm wall in mild areas. The fragrance comes from the white, violet-tinged flowers which are carried in small racemes in spring.
Sun or light shade. 9m/30ft. Min. temp. 40°F/5°C.

Stephanotis
S. floribunda, Madagascar jasmine. Stephanotis flowers have a well-known and well-loved perfume. It is exotically sweet, flavoured with bubblegum. The waxy white blooms are produced among the fleshy, glossy leaves in clusters from spring until autumn. The main stems and lateral growths may be pruned back in late winter. If your conservatory is not warm enough for it, it may be grown in a pot on a windowsill and trained over wire hoops. It enjoys a humid atmosphere and the compost should not be allowed to become too dry.
Light shade. 60cm–4.5m/2–15ft or more. Min. temp. 55°F/12°C.

Trichocereus
T. candicans, torch cactus, is one of several commonly grown species of trichocereus which have scented nocturnal flowers. These appear only on mature plants and the perfume is intense and exotic. The flowers are white and borne in summer. It is an easily grown plant, columnar in shape.
Sun. 1m/3ft. Min. temp. 50°F/10°C.

Index

Page numbers in **bold type** refer to illustrations

Bibliography and Selected Reading

Scent and Scented Plants

Brownlow, Margaret *Herbs and the Fragrant Garden* Darton, Longman and Todd, London, 1963

Genders, Roy *Scented Flora of the World* Robert Hale, London, 1977

Hampton, F. A. *The Scent of Flowers and Leaves* Dulau & Co., London, 1925

Proctor, Michael and Yeo, Peter *The Pollination of Flowers* Collins, 1973

Sanecki, Kay N. *The Fragrant Garden* Batsford, London, 1981

Thomas, Graham Stuart *The Art of Planting* Dent, London, 1984; Godine, Boston, 1984

Verey, Rosemary *The Scented Garden* Michael Joseph, London, 1982; Van Nostrand Reinhold, New York, 1981

Wilder, Louise Beebe *The Fragrant Garden* Dover, New York, 1974

General Plant Reference

Bean, W. J. *Trees and Shrubs Hardy in the British Isles* (4 vols) John Murray, London, (8th ed) 1980

Beckett, Kenneth A. (ed.) *The RHS Encyclopaedia of House Plants* Century, London, 1987

Beales, Peter *Classic Roses* Collins Harvill, London and Glasgow, 1985; Henry Holt & Co., New York, 1985

—— *Twentieth Century Roses* Collins Harvill, 1988; Harper & Row, New York, 1989

Chatto, Beth *The Damp Garden* Dent, London, 1982

Cox, Peter *The Smaller Rhododendrons* Batsford, London, 1985

—— *The Larger Species of Rhododendron* RHS/Batsford, London, 1979

Evans, Alfred *The Peat Garden and its Plants* Dent, London, 1974

Fox, Derek *Growing Lilies* Croom Helm, Kent, 1985

Grey-Wilson, Christopher and Matthews, Victoria *Gardening on Walls* Collins, London, 1983

Harper, Pamela and McGourty, Frederick *Perennials* HP Books, Los Angeles, 1985

Ingwersen, Will *Manual of Alpine Plants* Ingwersen & Dunnsprint, Sussex, 1978

Lloyd, Christopher and Bennett, Tom *Clematis* Viking, London, 1989; Capability's Books, Deer Park, Wisconsin, 1989

Mathew, Brian *Dwarf Bulbs* Batsford, London, 1973

—— *The Larger Bulbs* Batsford, London, 1978

Paterson, Allen *Herbs in the Garden* Dent, London, 1985

Perry, Frances *Water Gardening* Country Life, London, 1938

Rogers Clausan, Ruth and Ekstrom, Nicolas *Perennials for American Gardens* Random House, New York, 1989

Royal Horticultural Society *Dictionary of Gardening* Oxford University Press, 1951

Thomas, Graham Stuart *Climbing Roses* Dent, London, 1965

—— *Perennial Garden Plants* Dent, London, 1976; McKay, New York, 1977

—— *Shrub Roses of Today* Dent, London, 1974

—— *The Old Shrub Roses* Dent, London, 1979; Branford Newton Centre, MA, 1979

—— *The Rock Garden and its Plants* Dent, 1989; Timber, Portland, OR, 1989

Wyman, Donald *Wyman's Gardening Encyclopedia* Macmillan, New York, 1986

Zone Ratings

The hardiness zone ratings given for each plant – indicated in the text by the letter Z and the relevant number – suggest the approximate minimum temperature a plant will tolerate in winter. However, this can only be a rough guide. The hardiness of a plant depends on a great many factors, including the depth of its roots, its water content at the onset of frost, the duration of cold weather, the force of the wind, and the length and heat of the preceding summer.

Approximate range of average annual minimum temperatures zone

1 below −45°C/−50°F
2 −45°C/−50°F to −40°C/−40°F
3 −40°C/−40°F to −34°C/−30°F
4 −34°C/−30°F to −29°C/−20°F
5 −29°C/−20°F to −23°C/−10°F
6 −23°C/−10°F to −18°C/0°F
7 −18°C/0°F to −12°C/10°F
8 −12°C/10°F to −7°C/20°F
9 −7°C/20°F to −1°C/30°F
10 −1°C/30°F to 4°C/40°F

Acknowledgments

Author's Acknowledgments

My thanks go to the many fellow scent enthusiasts, in Britain and the United States, who have shared their knowledge with me, introduced me to new scented plants, and allowed me to sample the scents in their gardens. In particular, I must mention James Compton for escorting me on comprehensive nosings around the Chelsea Physic Garden; Holly Shimizu, of the United States Botanic Garden, for helping me with herbs; and Bert Klein, at the Royal Botanic Gardens, Kew, for enlightening me on the scents of orchids.

I am especially grateful to Dr Tony Lord, Leo Pemberton and Paul Meyer for checking the text; they have been most generous with their expertise and are responsible for numerous improvements. The mistakes, of course, are all mine.

Andrew Lawson's photographs lift this book into another orbit. Our views on scent rarely coincide, which has made garden visits together particularly entertaining.

Anne Kilborn and Diana Loxley, my editors, have shown patience beyond the call of duty, and Louise Tucker, my art editor, has worked tirelessly to reconcile Andrew's photographs and my descriptions. I thank them and the staff at Frances Lincoln Limited for their meticulous attention to detail and for allowing me to keep moving the goal posts. The only suggestion of mine which has fallen on deaf ears is that we should have scratch-and-sniff pages.

Photographer's Acknowledgments

Warmest thanks to the garden owners who so kindly gave me the freedom of their gardens. Those whose gardens appear in a recognizable chunk are:
7 The National Trust, Penelope Hobhouse and John Malins, Tintinhull House
8 Mr and Mrs Andrew Norton, East Lambrook Manor
11 John and Caryl Hubbard, Chilcombe House
12 The Savill Garden, Windsor
13 Exbury Gardens, Southampton
18, 101 Mr and Mrs Thomas Gibson, Westwell Manor
20, 155 Mr and The Hon. Mrs Guy Acloque, Alderley Grange
23, 36 Mrs Rosemary Verey, Barnsley House
27 Mr and Mrs P. Gunn, Ramster
31 Mrs Joyce Robinson and John Brookes, Denmans
37, 47, 103, 106 Mrs Gwen Beaumont, The Gables House, Stoke sub Hamdon
59, 71 Mrs Nancy Lancaster, The Coach House, Little Haseley
74 Mrs Margaret Ogilvie, House of Pitmuies
117 Mr and Mrs M. Farquar, Old Inn Cottage, Piddington
119, 153 Mrs Mirabel Osler, Lower Brook House
126 The National Trust, Wakehurst Place
137 Mr and Mrs A. H. Chambers, Kiftsgate Court
139 The National Trust, Knightshayes Court
145 *bottom* Mr and Mrs J. C. Turner, Berri Court, Yapton
150 *top* The late Humphrey Brooke, Lime Kiln Rosarium
151 Gothic House, Charlbury
156 Sevin Whitby, London
160 The National Trust for Scotland, Malleny House Gardens
167 Mr and Mrs Francis Sitwell, Weston Hall
171 Royal Botanic Gardens, Kew

I am no less grateful to other garden owners whose plants are illustrated by portraits:
Abbotswood; Batsford Arboretum; Mr and Mrs W. R. Benyon; Castle Ashby; Chelsea Physic Garden; Mr and Mrs Leo Clark; Caroline and Roger Eckersley; Joe Elliott; Miss Dolly Foster; Forde Abbey; Lucy Gent; Harry Hay; Haddon Hall; Hadspen Gardens; The Hillier Gardens and Arboretum; Kathleen and David Hodges; Kelways Nurseries; Len and Wendy Lauderdale; Briony Lawson; Logan Botanic Garden; Esther Merton; Penelope Mortimer; The National Trust (Acorn Bank, Barrington Court, Hidcote Manor and Nymans); The Northern Horticultural Society (Harlow Carr); Oxford Botanic Garden; Mr and Mrs R. Paice; Penny and Richard Purdon; Steve and Iris Pugh; Royal Horticultural Society (Wisley and Rosemoor); Royal Botanic Gardens, Kew; Royal Botanic Gardens, Edinburgh; Joan and Kurt Schoenenburger; Mrs B. Shuker and Mr and Mrs K. Pollitt; Dr James Smart; St John's College, Oxford; Threave Gardens; and Waterperry Gardens.

Publisher's Acknowledgments

The publishers would like to thank the following individuals for their help in the production of this book:

Hilary Dickinson and Serena Dilnot for editorial work; Ruth Carim for editorial assistance; Katy Foskew and Lucy Rix for clerical help.

Horticultural consultants	Tony Lord
	Leo Pemberton
	Paul Meyer
	Judith McKeon
Art editor	Louise Tucker
Designer	Kit Johnson
Editors	Anne Kilborn
	Diana Loxley
Picture editor	Anne Fraser
Production	Nicky Bowden
Art director	Tim Foster
Editorial director	Erica Hunningher